Inter-American Politics Series

CHILE
Experiment in Democracy

Sergio Bitar

Translated by Sam Sherman

A Publication of the
Institute for the Study of Human Issues
Philadelphia

Manufactured in the United States of America

1 2 3 4 5   90 89 88 87 86

Publication of this book was assisted by a grant from the Fundacion del Caribe para la
Ciencia y la Cultura, Caracas, Venezuela.

Library of Congress Cataloging in Publication Data

Bitar, Sergio.
    Chile: experiment in democracy.

    (Inter-American politics series; v. 6)
    Includes bibliographical references and index.
    1. Chile—Economic conditions—1970– . 2. Chile—Politics and government—
1970–   . I. Institute for the Study of Human Issues. II. Title. III. Series.

HC192.B56   1985   338.983   84-5618
ISBN 0-89727-062-2

For information, write:

Director of Publications
ISHI
210 South 13th Street
Philadelphia, PA 19107
U.S.A.

Foreword

Without a doubt this is the most important book written thus far on the attempted Chilean transition to socialism by democratic means. That this unusual experience was interrupted by a bloody military coup does not abrogate its historical significance as one of the first designs of a socially inspired reconstruction of the ideals of socialism and democracy. That this occurred in Latin America indicates that in this part of the world the political imagination attains prominence. Sergio Bitar lived that experience as an inclusive member in the government of Unidad Popular. His personal testimony alone is sufficient to lend value to the book. But there exists much more to it than this. Since the first moments of his imprisonment he contemplated in truthful passion the historical process which came to be brutally interrupted, conscious that its significance transcends the historical circumstances of his country. The picture he presents is one of extraordinary detail and rigor. All the factors of the political economy are herein described, and the interaction of the effects of that policy on society and the political system, are exhaustively observed.

The initial question that Bitar poses is the following: Can the experience of Unidad Popular be qualified as revolutionary, or would this only be a question of reformism? In his opinion the revolutionary character is evident, not so much through the nature of each one of the measures introduced but through the amplitude of the process and speed of execution. These measures would necessarily transform the means of participation of the popular classes in the structure of power. However, these reforms were within the institutional framework in which all fundamental liberties are respected. The space that exists for the transformation of structures in a pluralistic society with a long tradition of institutional stability is therefore much greater than is generally supposed. Hence the real problem elapses into that of the shape the transformation assumed. It was at this point that the principle of contradiction originated: obtaining rapid results legitimately by means of deepening and enlarging the support of certain social strata ended; determined reforms were executed in a rhythm that carried trepidation and disorder. Thus, to a certain extent, the operating efficiency of the economic system was rendered illegitimate. The

Translated from the Portuguese by Kathy Meyer.

v

result, therefore, was the inverse of that which was desired. The opposition was thus able to stage a counteroffensive in the political plan. An identical process occurred in the armed forces that had acquired growing influence among right-wing groups. Inefficiency emerged in the operating plan, now illegitimate, and this opened the door to attack from the reaction.

Sergio Bitar considers alternative hypotheses, concerned that the most possibly real picture of what occurred is related to the reader. Indeed the information that is transmitted to us removes the veil of mystery. For the most part the explanation of the takeover with what was executed in economic and social policies must be sought for in the disruption of Unidad Popular; its inability to produce a strategy over which there was certain agreement in the long term and in its coercive and scandalous action in the short and medium terms. This end was augmented with the characteristics of the type of leadership that was practiced by Allende, master of manipulation but reluctant to fully assume command. These two points can be observed in the priceless documents containing the minutes of the final cabinet meetings of Allende, of which Bitar relates to us his personal testimony. Even in the last weeks when the military coup was imminent, the leaders of Unidad Popular could not agree on two issues which Allende considered basic: the opening up of dialogue with the Christian Democrats and the call for a plebiscite. Meanwhile Allende knew that everything had already been put into play. "From here I go to the cemetery," he said to his friends amidst desperation and melancholy on the eve of the coup.

This book will have readers impassioned so long as there are those who believe that something can be learned from history.

CELSO FURTADO

Preface

It is very difficult to carry on a detached discussion of the Chilean political experience when such vivid memories, images and feelings crowd together into one's mind. Nevertheless, this is what I have attempted in the present volume. The ardor of the three years of the Allende government with its profound mutations and the overwhelming sadness induced by the subsequent repression, torture and death may have blocked up the spirit, but they also make the mind work more lucidly. A sense of duty toward both the past and the present has impelled me to complete this study, a work whose apparent detachment is linked to the purest passion for my people's struggle for democracy, justice and liberty.

The vortex of events during the Allende years left little time for immediate reflection. The first questions emerged abruptly, after I was placed in prison by the military junta. Just what occurred during the Unidad Popular era that led to such a decisive defeat? How did such sharp economic disequilibria develop?

In the prison on Dawson Island, in the Straits of Magellan, we began to attempt the first answers to the questions that goaded us, and it seemed to me that the fact of sharing confinement with a group of 35 persons—including ministers, senators, deputies and party chiefs—was a unique opportunity to deepen the thinking on these matters.

In May 1974, our group was taken away from Dawson Island and split up among several different prison camps in Santiago and Valparaíso. In the camp at Ritoque I was able to continue with the work, forming a team with ex-Chancellor Clodomiro Almeyda and with Carlos Matus, former Minister of the Economy. I took daily notes and made steady progress in the analysis. The interchanges with the other two men were very valuable: Almeyda threw much light on complex political issues. Matus deepened the methodological approach; his originality and analytical sharpness opened the way to new ideas. Fernando Flores, former Minister of Finance, contributed greatly in matters such as systems theory and cybernetics.

As the months passed, the number of written pages grew. It was forbidden to remove them from the camp. How then could these notes be preserved? We discovered a way to sneak them to the outside and were thus able to save them. Valuable material had already been lost. I had been collecting documents and personal notes since 1971. After the coup, however, searches began of the homes of those who had participated in the Allende government. The searchers were out to locate material which might serve the junta in its press campaigns or in implicating in some way those who were already prisoners and could not defend themselves. Families and friends, therefore, decided to burn those documents that might be made to serve this purpose. I thus lost some material that would have been valuable in recounting the history of the regime.

In December 1974, I was expelled from Chile and left for the United States and Harvard University. The present work owes a great deal to the assistance of two friends and professors at Harvard: Albert Hirschman and Raymond Vernon. Many institutions made the final work possible. The Ford Foundation contributed to my trip to Harvard. I found a stimulating and affectionate atmosphere at the Harvard Institute for International Development, for which I must thank Lester Gordon, the Director, as well as the other investigators. It was there that I was able to dedicate more than a year to refining the manuscript for the present book.

In 1976, the exile's life led me to Venezuela. There, little by little, I was able to revise the entire study. In this task I counted on the collaboration of the Director of the Centro de Estudios de Desarrollo, José Agustín Silva, as well as that of other investigators at the center.

Abraham Lowenthal, Director of the Latin American Program of the Woodrow Wilson Center at the Smithsonian Institution, inspired the final revisions by convoking a group of authorities to comment upon the preliminary draft. My thanks and acknowledgments for their observations go to Clodomiro Almeyda, Edmar Bacha, Andrés Bianchi, Atilio Boron, Louis Duguid, Richard Fagen, Ricardo Ffrench-Davis, Alejandro Foxley, Celso Furtado, Albert Hirshman, Robert Kaufman, Stephen Marglin, Carlos Matus, Oscar Muñoz, Pedro Felipe Ramírez, Julio Silva Solar, Eugene Sofer, Barbara Stallings, Lance Taylor and Peter Winn.

Five years after the tragic termination of the Unidad Popular experience, many of its aspects now emerge in a different light, viewed from a perspective richer in analytical possibilities. What we affirm critically now points to facts and situations that we did not see then with the same clarity. The passage of time has allowed a more attentive and organized observation of the whole from which new conclusions have been derived.

To my wife, Maria-Eugenia, and to my children, who have always encouraged and recognized the importance of seeing this work published, must go the credit for the final materialization of the book.

I dedicate this work to the memory of the late President Allende, with the fullest acknowledgment. The moral example of his life, irrevocably dedicated to the popular cause, is imperishable.

SERGIO BITAR

Introduction

Few political experiences have had the resonance of the attempt in Chile to implement a democratic transition to socialism. World public opinion was focused on Chile throughout this unusual three-year period, when a political coalition of the Left—the Unidad Popular (UP)—won an electoral triumph and initiated a far-reaching process of transformations to be carried out within the existing institutional order. Nationalization of basic natural resources and of the large foreign corporations, agrarian reform, state expropriation of the banks and monopoly firms, and the redistribution of income—all took shape in Chile simultaneously, supported by a vast social movement. That these transformations occurred in the midst of a deepening of democracy, with full respect for fundamental rights, excited an additional interest in many countries in Latin America and Europe, as well as among numerous progressive movements in the rest of the world.

The tragic denouement and the subsequent installation in Chile of one of the most repressive regimes in the region revived interest in the Allende period. How could such an electoral victory be won and such transformations brought about? Why did the experiment collapse so abruptly? Was the intended project viable or was its failure predetermined? What lessons can be learned from this period?

No author can account for all the causes that explain the exact course of events. In this book we have advanced an interpretation of the economic phenomena at play and of their interaction with the political, taking as our general theme the problem of economic policy during a stage of transition to socialism.

To resort to the use of economic theory alone would be inadequate if we are to understand the dynamics of a transformational process. From this dynamic perspective, the ultimate significance of every economic measure is political and must be understood in relation to the overriding objective: changing the structures of power.

In order to elucidate the options that the UP government faced in Chile in the various stages of its administration, we must see these choices in the context of political priorities and limitations. The principal objectives were arranged hierarchically in such a way as to subordinate other political decisions. The been raised by reformist political movements. But the intensity, breadth and simultaneity of the transformations attempted by the UP have no historical precedent in a social and institutional context like that of Chile. Finally, what establishes the revolutionary character of a movement definitively is the resolution with which it moves to alter the structure of power. The UP attacked the dominant groups at their basis and opened the way for new forms of power and control on the part of the workers. The genuine resolve which the UP brought to this task derived from the deep popular roots of the principal parties of the government coalition, from their clear class orientation, and from the active and autonomous participation of workers' organizations.

No matter how revolutionary these objectives might be, another question altogether is how to attain them in a specific, complex reality. The confusion between means and ends begins, quite simply, when the revolutionary nature of the actors and their convictions is measured by each action and policy taken in isolation.[2] We must learn to distinguish between ultimate objectives and efficient means.

In order to assess the viability of the UP's endeavor, we ought to be precise about which objectives and which strategy we are discussing. For, alongside the central strategy of the Left, there existed elements of another, more radical approach. The result was confusion and a deviation from the main strategy.

The basic points of the central strategy were expounded in the Program of the UP, which proposed accelerated and simultaneous changes in the ownership of agricultural land, banks, mines and industries, together with active participation on the part of the workers. These objectives were anti-oligarchical and anti-imperialist, designed to prepare the way for a transition to socialism. The aims would be implemented democratically, carried out within the existing institutional order. The Allende government was conceived as the first stage in a long process. This stage was not supposed to lead to a total confrontation, nor to a revolutionary crisis in which the contention for power would be brought to a forced climax. It is the viability of this central strategy which we will discuss here.

Naturally, we cannot overlook the fact that within the UP, albeit as a minority, there existed different viewpoints, which foresaw a move toward confrontation and the immediate and total transformation of the state. These notions never amounted to a coherent vision. Instead they were simply the extremist attitudes of those who, in the face of every concrete action, tried to act out their "revolutionary principles." They succeeded only in pushing events in an impracticable direction, incompatible with existing historical conditions. This radicalizing impulse emerged as a threat to the main strategy of the UP. The Allende government and its supporting parties demonstrated a serious weakness in failing to address these deviations, which should have been combated from the beginning. If we were to concede that the failure of the Chilean experiment was predetermined because the institutional strategy was an illusion, any prolonged analysis of this strategy would, of course, be uninteresting. But such a simple, sweeping negative assessment does not square with the facts.

It can explain neither the electoral triumph nor the real accomplishments during the government's three years of the existence. Our initial assertion is that the coup d'état in Chile was not predetermined and, therefore, that the collapse was not inevitable.[3] Moreover, the conditions were favorable at the beginning for the implementation of the UP Program in its general outlines. There is no doubt that the process was viable at its starting point.

Granted that the original conditions were favorable and the coup was not inevitable, what were the failures of strategy and direction that led to the dissipation of this initial potential? How are we to understand the progressive isolation of the government? In order to grasp the Chilean reality, the process must be observed dynamically, in its diverse aspects, and at different moments. Viability is a matter of degree. This notion is central to political action. A simplistic, binary, black-and-white conception of proletariat and bourgeoisie obscures the problem. In the argument set forth here we intend to examine the causes of this loss of viability and to establish the conditions which had to be fulfilled in order to insure a greater probability of success.

Viable Trajectories

How can we order such a torrent of events so that they acquire rational meaning? In periods of crisis, reality is interpreted so diversely that an innocent reader might imagine that he is hearing about different countries. This is inevitable, given that there is no objectivity without reference to the point of view of the analyst with respect to the process he is observing. In the presence of intense social struggle, the explanation of the facts gains sense and coherence only when it is interpreted from the perspective of one of the parties to the conflict. It is one thing to analyse events from a position antagonistic to change; it is quite another thing to do so from a position favorable to change, taking as a reference point the crisis of the initial situation and the necessity for a transformation.

The author was, in fact, both a partisan of and a participant in the UP government, serving for a brief period as a Minister in Allende's Cabinet. This has a double significance for the contents of this book. In the first place, the facts are interpreted from a point of view favorable to the proposed transformations in Chilean society. Causal relationships, the sequence of and connection between events, and the broad movements are seen with reference to the goals pursued by the UP government. In the second place, direct experience causes one to attach greater importance to specific events and decisions, to the richness and complexity of the process. Furthermore, the author's experience has meant that the government and parties of the UP, in all of their strengths and weaknesses, are at the center of the analysis here. The difficulties encountered and the struggles with the opposition are seen from the point of view of the government, for whom the actions of its adversaries constituted a part of the reality upon which it had to act.

In so specifying the perspective of this work, we do not hope to reclaim its iron-clad objectivity. Rather we hope to clarify its character and avoid the pretension of a unique and impartial approach, something an analysis of this nature cannot claim.

A pre-existing analytical framework is indispensable in order to explain these events. The Chilean experience can be placed in a larger context: that of transition between two differently structured situations. The initial situation was characterized by certain historical-structural determinants and by an institutional, ideological and cultural reality that permitted the initiation of a transformational process and at the same time imposed limitations and restrictions. The objective was a new situation with different structural and conjunctural characteristics. Schematically speaking, the main question was how to get from the initial situation to the desired objective. There were several different trajectories, each made up of a different sequence of actions and reactions. Some of these trajectories, those with a greater probability of traversing this distance, were more viable than others. Understood in this way, viability is the probability of passing from one situation to another.

The conditions imposed on the process limited the number of possible trajectories. The characteristics of the Chilean system imposed certain limitations. The trajectory that would ultimately be traversed would be conditioned by the actions of the government, the response of the opposition, and the inertia of the system itself. This complex network of forces delimited the range of possibilities. We could, therefore, speak of a zone of viability, delimited by restrictions of power. The trajectories lying within this limits were possible ones.

Underlying the analysis advanced here are several concepts which should be noted briefly. First there is the notion of *situation* understood in an overall sense as integrating the structural and the conjunctural. These two levels interact and condition each other in order to make up the reality which confronts us. To conceive reality as that which is simply observable is to forestall an explanation of how a system evolves and hence to frustrate an understanding of the built-in margins of viability that govern all transitional experiments. To understand reality as a simple projection of the structural is an incorrect abstraction which overlooks fundamental elements. The "situation" synthesizes the structural and the functional.

At a later point we employ the concept of *initial situation* (the point of departure) and the *target situation* (the point of destination). A *strategy* lays out the principal guideposts marking the path of advance from one point to another, and these guideposts may allow for several possible trajectories. A single strategy cannot determine all actions in advance, because in terms of acute conflict one must allow for a considerable range for improvisation, necessary in order to adapt to unforeseen circumstances. Finally, by *trajectory* we mean simply a specific concatenation of events.

We have utilized the concept of *transition* here to identify the phase which leads from one situation to another, structurally distinct state of affairs. This is a restricted usage, of course, different from that notion of transition which refers to the passage from one mode of production to another.

The Democratic Transition

The Chilean endeavor amounted to an acting out of a hope latent in many political movements: to bring about profound social and economic changes within a democratic framework. The special theoretical and political interests which the Chilean experiment aroused throughout the world can perhaps be understood if we reflect on the dual character of the Chilean system: on the one hand a dependent and underdeveloped economic structure—with features shared in common with the majority of the poorer countries—and on the other a more advanced social formation and institutional organization with characteristics approximating those of certain developed countries, in particular the nations of Southern Europe.[4]

Many of the conclusions drawn from this experience, especially those advanced shortly after the coup d'état, are overly general and serve only to reinforce existing convictions. For some the collapse of the Allende regime simply reaffirmed the impossibility of positive progress within the institutional framework, hence arguing for the necessity of a prior, total rupture with existing institutions in order to effect any transition. Even among those in search of democratic political solutions, especially in Italy and France, there was disagreement. The Italians asserted that the Chilean experience demonstrated the necessity for a much wider social and political alliance than that which supported the UP. The French Left argued that the economic problems which Chile confronted were characteristically those of a poor economy; therefore any political conclusions are inapplicable to Europe. For conservative groups, on the contrary, what occurred in Chile reveals "one more time" that all radical change brings with it chaos, and that the outcome was proof of the technical and political incompetence of the Left.

Today it is both possible and necessary to carry out detailed studies which explore the intricacies involved, and elucidate the multiple aspects relevant for future experiences of this type. While the global view is of interest for the historical analysis of long time periods, a disaggregated and detailed analysis provides essential complementary knowledge for those who wish to manage a complex system in transformation. Agents of transformation require not only a general theory, but also a rigorous knowledge of specifics if they are to act effectively.

The central problem which continues to demand our interest is that of transition in complex socioeconomic systems, especially within a situation of shared power. In the political-economic field it is indispensable to move ahead in the elaboration of a theory of the functioning of systems undergoing rapid and profound structural change. The lack of more refined knowledge of this type was disturbingly evident among the UP leadership. The study of concrete events is a good place to start in filling this vacuum. We can be sure that the same problems will reassert themselves on the occasion of any new attempt at a democratic transition to socialism.

Notes

1. "Both categories of investigators [economists and political scientists] have become enamored of models that posit simplistic relationships [between economics and politics] in which a phenomenon pertaining to an outside discipline is introduced as a kind of prerequisite. . . ." See A. Hirschman, *A Bias for Hope* (New Haven: Yale University Press, 1971), p. 2. This theme is treated more extensively by Hirschman on pp. 1–37 of the same work.

2. The Program of the UP did not amount to just one more reformist scheme, nor did it represent a utopian attempt to alter radically the correlation of forces. President Allende expressed himself as follows on the subject of these limitations: "If we were to forget that our mission is to establish a humanist social project, all of the struggles of our people for socialism would become just one more reformist attempt. If we were to forget the concrete conditions from which we depart, attempting to create here and now something that exceeds our real possibilities, we would also fail." From the First Message of President Allende to the National Congress, May 21, 1971, in S. Allende, *Salvador Allende: Su Pensamiento político* (Santiago: Editorial Quimantu, 1972), p. 116.

3. Two of the most important political actors during the period studied, representatives of the majority forces in the country, have dealt with this question as follows: "Was it absolutely necessary that things happened as they did and that, in consequence, a successful military coup was bound to occur? If the response here were to be affirmative, this would mean that the political project of the UP was essentially unviable . . . If our reply is negative, or if it is argued that, notwithstanding the impossibility of indefinitely postponing the confrontation, it was possible to avoid military subversion, this means that the political project of the UP was a viable reality." See C. Almeyda, "El problema militar en la experiencia de la Unidad Popular," *Chile America*, Nos. 37–38 (1977). "Was the failure of the Chilean road to socialism inevitable? . . . We know that it did indeed fail—but we do not know that it had to fail . . . the decisive question now is to determine if the causes of the failure were unavoidable, or if the collapse was a consequence of errors that could have been avoided . . . To attempt the transformation of one social order to another without systematic violence is a very difficult and complex undertaking. I believe, as did Allende, that in Chile such a transformation was possible and that the favorable factors outweighed the unfavorable." See R. Tomic, "La Democracia Cristiana y el gobierno de la Unidad Popular," in F. Gil, et al., eds., *Chile 1970–1973: Lecciones de una experiencia* (Madrid: Editorial Tecnos, 1977), p. 218.

4. Commenting on the lessons of Chile for Europe, Schmitter notes: "Chile, because of its previous experimentation with popular fronts, its more advanced party organizations and the greater articulation of its Left, particularly the more or less balanced relationship between the CP and the socialists . . . came to be a prototype of experimentation in 'the unarmed transition to socialism.'" See P. Schmitter, "La Europa Latina y las lecciones de Chile," in Gil, et al., *Chile 1970–1973*, p. 345.

Contents

CHAPTER 1

Chile 1970:
Economic Underdevelopment
and Political Development

The initiation of the transformative process proposed by the UP was not a fortuitous event: objective conditions existed which made it possible.[1] But these same conditions imposed restrictions to which the chosen plan of action had to be adjusted. In order to evaluate the Chilean experience it will prove essential to identify both the conditions favorable to the transformative process, as well the restrictions which it was obliged to confront. Such is the object of this chapter, in which three principal themes are taken up: structural characteristics of the Chilean economy, political and economic evolution in the years prior to 1970, and the factors which would condition a democratic transition.

Basic Characteristics of the Chilean Economy

The Chilean economy exhibited a set of features held in common with most Latin American economies, even though it exceeded the norm in its level of development. Chile's population approximated ten million, and its annual per capita product was about $700.[2] The relatively superior level of economic development was evident in the larger share of total production held by industry and services, compared to agriculture, which accounted for only 10 percent of the total.[3] Industry and the tertiary sector in fact enjoyed a prominence relatively greater than in the case of any other Latin American economy. In Chile this feature was pivotal in establishing the economic and political features of a strategy of change. It also marked a clear difference from the conditions prevailing in those countries which had undergone the classic revolutionary process. In these countries agriculture and the peasantry constituted a much larger share of total production and of the labor force.[4]

The relative superiority of Chile's development could not, however, conceal structural features similar to those of other underdeveloped and dependent economies: high economic concentration, high concentration of property ownership, regressive income distribution, and growing external dependence.

1

These characteristics were basic to the diagnosis of the initial situation advanced by the UP, a diagnosis which can be outlined as follows: The economic concentration and the centralization of ownership placed control of the strategic decision-making centers in a few hands. The overlapping of political and economic power in a single small group led to the continual reproduction of the existing situation. From this feature a fundamental conclusion was deduced: to change the situation would require a modification in the relationships of ownership and control in the command centers of the economy.

Another conclusion also followed: given political conditions favorable for such a transformation, the very fact of high concentration meant that the strategic patterns of economic control could be altered by means of a change in the forms of ownership of only a limited number of large oligopolies and extensive agricultural estates. A massive and generalized economic intervention would be unnecessary.

In order to appreciate the dimensions of this concentration, it will be enough to refer briefly to the prevailing situation in each economic sector. In the agricultural sector in 1965, 2 percent of the estates held 55.4 percent of the total acreage.[5] This was the first year of Frei's agrarian reform, which achieved a partial alteration of the traditional patterns of property ownership and of the reigning power structure in the countryside. A breach had been opened which would permit the UP to move ahead rapidly; but new expectations had also been awakened, creating pressure for an even faster pace of change. In the mining sector, another area of great concentration, control rested in the hands of the three foreign companies dominating copper production. In 1970, sales of this metal accounted for 75 percent of all national exports. Thus the three North American firms in question handled 59 percent of Chile's total exports that year.[6] In both sectors, agriculture and copper, economic concentration was a long-standing phenomenon, consistently linked with concentration in property ownership. In the manufacturing industry and in commerce the same phenomenon emerged later.

In 1963, 3 percent of the industrial establishments controlled 51 percent of the value added, 44 percent of the employment, and 58 percent of the capital in this sector. In addition, 284 corporations held 78 percent of the country's corporate assets. Moreover, in the case of 230 of the 271 largest corporations, the ten largest stockholders held at least a 50 percent share.[7] These figures give no hint of the importance of groups of stockholders with interests in several different firms, nor of the interconnections between banking and industry. If such factors are considered as well, the consequences are even more striking. The figures suggest the same essential features in wholesale commerce: twelve distributing firms (0.5 percent of the total) handled 44 percent of the sales in 1967.[8]

Finally, concentration was also high in the private sector of the banking system, although the presence of the State Bank constituted a limiting factor. In 1970, the latter handled 46.4 percent of the deposits and 52 percent of the total credits in the entire banking system. Three of the 26 private banks which managed the remaining assets controlled more than 50 percent of this balance.[9]

The second characteristic feature of the Chilean economy was its concentration of income. Distribution of income was skewed, allowing an elite group, with a living standard similar to that of the upper and middle sectors of the advanced countries, to exist side by side with a larger proportion of the population which could not even buy the bare necessities of life. Table 1-1 shows this distribution.

Such data on personal income demonstrate that the poorest 10 percent of the population received incomes equal to 1.5 percent of the total incomes received, while the richest 10 percent took in 40.2 percent of the total. The coefficients of concentration were considerably higher in Chile than in developed countries, and close to the average for Latin America.

Moving from relative to absolute terms, in 1970 close to 25 percent of the population lived in conditions of extreme poverty. Two-thirds of this poorest group lived in urban areas.[10]

The unequal income distribution also reinforced the processes of economic and property-owning concentration, which in turn led to more inequality. These three factors thus formed a vicious circle.

The final factor to which we will refer in this section was the insertion of the Chilean economy into the international system and, in particular, its relation to the U.S. The mode of insertion began to change in the 1960s. The traditional dependent relationship, founded on control of natural resources and public services, was supplemented by rapid growth of the great multinational corporations in the industrial sector. Many subsidiaries of these giant corporations established themselves in Chile at this time and set about molding the overall pattern of industrialization.

In this phase industrialization was aimed toward imitating the consumption patterns of the most advanced economies. The prevailing income concentration permitted the manufacture of durable consumer goods intended for the high income groups; and, in turn, the growth of these activities demanded a high concentration of income.

In other words, a minority of the population was able to insert itself favorably into the world economy and reach a level of consumption close to the average for developed countries. To illustrate this state of affairs, it is enough to point out that in 1970 close to 7.0 percent of the population received the equivalent of $4290 per capita. At the other extreme, 54 percent of the population earned a per capita income of only $212. In short, two economies coexisted within the same system: the first with a consumption pattern similar to the U.S., the second with a subsistence level below the poverty threshold.

The technological and financial predominance of the international firms gave them sufficient power to impose their own forms of production and consumption. On the other hand, their impact on local industrialization did not bring about an increase in Chile's capacity to create or reproduce new

TABLE 1-1. Distribution of Personal Income in Chile, 1967

Percentage of Population	Percentage of Income
50	17.1
(20)	(4.0)
(30)	(13.1)
30	26.4
20	56.5
(10)	(40.2)
Total 100.0	100.0

Source: National Survey of CEDEM. These figures represent
disposable personal income, since direct taxes
have been subtracted, as well as social security
and union dues.

technologies, a precondition for local autonomy. Thus Chile's industrial sector was linked, through its most modern section, to the international system, but only as an appendage and not as a component of its own dynamic.

Concentration of income, concentration of property ownership, oligopoly and foreign penetration were all component parts of a single mechanism.[11] At the political level this linkage was reflected in a growing interpenetration of the interests of the large national proprietors with those of the foreign firms.

The features described above were at the base of the economic problems and of the political tensions prevailing in 1970. Such features, however, are by themselves insufficient to explain the actual course of events in Chile or the possibility of initiating a transformative process. The same kind of situation had prevailed—and still prevails—in many Latin American countries without the opening up of political possibilities similar to those which emerged in Chile.

In order to explain the political consequences of the structural features noted above, it is essential to contrast the weaknesses of the economic system with the demands exerted on it by organized social groups.

Slow Growth, Scanty Redistribution

The political conflict was not a direct consequence of the economic situation, since it depended first on the level of political consciousness and organization of the social groups composing the majority. The Chilean case was characterized by the coincidence of a slowly growing economy and a relatively advanced social organization, the latter evolving within an open political system. This contrast, which had been gestating over a long period, deepened during the 1960s, especially in the five years which preceded the UP government.

Let us examine first the capacity for growth and redistribution of the Chilean economy. The annual rate of growth of the national product reached an average of 4.4 percent in the 1961–70 period. In the last four years of the decade, this figure dropped to 3 percent. The overall 1961–70 average was attained thanks to rapid growth in the biennia 1961–62 and 1965–66. In both periods, the government stimulated economic activity by expanding public spending, especially on housing and public works. But on each of these two occasions, the expansive cycle was short; and the initial measures were followed by restrictive policies which slowed the rhythm of growth.

In these cycles the state was the decisive factor in the expansion. The private sector was not capable of sustaining a stable rate of growth. Its potential for expansion was weak; and, because it dominated the system as a whole, the overall dynamic was deficient. The rate of savings, for example, did not exceed an average of 15 percent in the whole decade of the sixties. The share of the private sector in savings actually dropped in this period, compensated only by an expansion in public savings.

In order to make up for this insufficiency, the state expanded its financial powers and also resorted to international financing, in the form of direct investments and credits. The external debt mounted steadily during the 1961–70 period. This demonstrated that the contracting of large debts was not a mere conjunctural necessity designed to deal with monetary difficulties. Rather, increasing debt was a structural requirement of the Chilean model of development. In sum the weakness of the private sector led to a swelling external debt and an expansion of public financing.

Apart from the slow growth rate, income distribution improved slightly, to the benefit of middle-income strata. In the 1965–70 period, thanks to more effective social and political organization these groups succeeded in enhancing their situation. Low-income people, meanwhile, were barely able to avoid a deterioration in their relative position. Included in this latter category were such groups as wage workers, peasants, and many self-employed workers. Table 1-2 shows clearly the increase in the share of income received by those in the category "salaried employee" during the 1960s. In the first half of this period (1959–64), the Alessandri government followed a policy of unconditional support of the private sector, hence benefiting only the employers. In the 1965–70 period, the Frei government, attempting to sustain itself from the support of the middle strata, promoted a redistribution in favor of salaried employees. In both of these periods, wage workers and self-employed workers lost out, or, at the most, maintained their position.

It can be concluded, therefore, that the Chilean economy was functioning in such a way as to give gradual access to certain middle-level urban groups; but it was not capable of absorbing the redistributive demands of the great mass of workers. A higher rate of economic growth would have allowed for a more

TABLE 1-2. Income Distribution in Chile According to Occupational Category, 1960-70

	1960	1964	1970
Employers	27.1%	36.1%	33.0%
Self-employed workers	21.2	17.1	12.4
Salaried employees	29.5	26.5	34.2
Wage workers	22.2	20.3	20.4
Total	100.0	100.0	100.0

Source: Unpublished calculations of H. Varela, Odeplán.

rapid incorporation of new groups. But the large contingents or organized urban workers which emerged at this time were very difficult to incorporate into the system. Their pressures in favor of an improved income distribution restricted an accumulation process which presupposed and fed off inequality. All this time, the slow growth rate increased the numbers of the discontented.

Social Pressures and Workers' Politics

A rapid broadening of the political system and an acceleration in the process of social organization took place simultaneously. One factor accounting for this development was the high degree of urbanization in Chile. The concentration of the population in cities facilitated political and social organization.

Two indicators reveal the extent of this process. First, the number of registered voters increased 136 percent between 1958 and 1970. The proportion of voters relative to the total population, which had held steady at 15 percent during the period 1920 to 1960, jumped to 28.3 percent in 1971.

Something similar occurred in the area of labor organization, which, particularly among peasants, increased sharply in the 1965–70 period. Agrarian reform and the policies of the Frei government helped clear away some of the obstacles which had until then discouraged such organization.[12]

The broadening of political participation and the strengthening of the labor organizations created strong demands on the system. The political parties and labor organizations, which had acquired greater autonomy, stimulated and gave direction to the new aspirations. As a result the social conflict intensified.

One indication of the scale of conflict is the number of strikes which took place in the period just before the Allende government. In 1960, there were 257 strikes involving 88,500 workers. By 1964, these figures had climbed to 564 and 138,500, respectively. During the Frei government, the situation was aggravated still more, culminating in 1970 with 1819 strikes involving 656,000 workers.[13] Other forms of conflict also intensified, including occupation of factories, large farms, and vacant urban sites (which were seized to accommodate squatter settlements).

With this intensification in the social conflict, the existing equilibrium between demands on the system and its capacity to respond altered decisively. Slow economic growth and widening social discontent fed on each other. Increased popular pressures limited the accumulative capacity of the private sector, and mounting social tension led to a change in underlying economic conduct. The "sense of uncertainty" remarked on by representatives of the private sector expressed itself in a preference for high-liquidity activities, a reduced interest in long-term investments, and an increase in the speculative behavior and capital flight. The growth potential of the private sector thus contracted even further, and its capacity to confront new demands was correspondingly reduced.

The established model of development required a high concentration of income in order to generate a modest rate of savings; and it also needed "se-

curity" in order to attract foreign capital. Both conditions presupposed re-
straints on the demands of labor and a restricted democracy. Without these
requisites being fulfilled, the contradictions sharpened, opening the way for a
more profound transformation.[14] In this context there existed one attenuating
factor: the expansion of state economic functions.

The State as a Socioeconomic Buffer

One fundamental historical feature of the Chilean economy was the steady
expansion of state economic activity. This occurred under governments of
different ideologies: progressives fortified its role more than conservatives, but
state economic intervention was always on the increase. The expansion of the
state apparatus served the regulate and moderate socioeconomic conflict. In the
attempt to reconcile the limited growth capacity of the economy on the one
hand, and workers' pressures on the other, the state acquired mounting importance in the spheres of production and redistribution.

In redistributive affairs the state expanded the supply of services and
generated new sources of employment. Public spending in health, education
and housing for the working class and middle class increased steadily. Likewise
subsidies for essential consumer products (and control of their prices) meant
greater public spending for the benefit of low-income groups.

The Chilean state also intervened in production. In order to stimulate the
economy, it extended its activity in three directions: public spending on wages
and salaries, public works, and housing; transfers of public funds to finance
investments in the private sector; and direct investment in state enterprises.
Both functions, redistributive and productive, permitted a lessening of the
tension between demands placed on the system and its capacity to respond.
Concomitantly, the importance of the state in the economy grew until reaching
its maximum level in 1970.

By that year, the state in Chile had attained an economic role larger than in
any other Latin American country, with the exception of Cuba. This situation
was evident in several indicators. Thus, for example, according to ECLA, the
share of the public sector in total investments in 1967 reached 58.6 percent, a
level matched only by Bolivia in the rest of nonsocialist Latin America. This
proportion was 40.8 percent in Mexico, 38.8 percent in Brazil, 37.1 percent in
Argentina, 34.1 percent in Peru, and 28.6 percent in Colombia.[15] The results
are similar if we compare the various levels of total spending by the central
government taken as a proportion of the national product. In the 1967–68
period, this proportion amounted to 36.1 percent in Chile, 27 percent in
Argentina and Brazil, 22 percent in Venezuela, 20 percent in Peru, 16.6 percent
in Mexico, 14.7 percent in Colombia, and even less for the remaining countries.[16]

In the 1961–70 period, the Chilean state expanded vigorously, especially
during the Frei government (1964–70).[17] Total fiscal spending as a percentage of
GNP grew from 16.9 percent in 1964 to 24.2 percent in 1970;[18] and public

spending as a percentage of GNP advanced from 35.7 percent in 1965 to 46.9 percent in 1970.[19] Direct and indirect investment by the state constituted a major component in this increase. As a percentage of total investment, direct public investment climbed from 39 percent in 1961 to 49.3 percent in 1969, while indirect public investment jumped from 7.6 percent to 25.5 percent over the same period. Following this course, public investment went from 46.9 percent to 74.8 percent of total investment in 1969.[20]

In addition to the straightforward financial backing traditionally granted to the private sector in order to stimulate its growth, new state-run enterprises were created. The first of these were set up in basic and intermediate activities: electricity, oil, steel and sugar. Later they were extended to export industries and to those employing more advanced technologies: cellulose, petrochemicals, metals and metal products, and electronics. The Corporación de Fomento (CORFO), owner and manager of these state enterprises, grew to significant proportions.

In the banking sector, something similar was underway. In 1970, through CORFO and the Banco del Estado, the public sector attained control of practically all the medium- and long-term credit in national and foreign currencies. As for short-term credit, in 1970 the Banco del Estado granted 52 percent of the credits and received 46 percent of the deposits.[21] Finally, it is sufficient to note the expansion of state functions involved in the creation of new institutions to implement the agrarian reform, as well as the closer supervision of copper-mining activity by the Corporación del Cobre.

In sum it can be said that of all the nations with mixed economies Chile possessed one of the most extensive state sectors. For an analysis of the situation prevailing in 1970, such a characteristic is fundamental and had many implications.

It is true that the state apparatus had contributed to the financing of the private sector and to the reinforcement of the prevailing socioeconomic system. At the same time, however, this apparatus generated its own growth dynamic, acquiring a relative autonomy from the private sector. It offered an opening to new social groups, whose power base consisted in the management and expansion of this very apparatus. The national bourgeoisie was subordinating its initiative and independence to direct controls imposed by the state and to the need for infusions of public credit. This process accentuated its weakness. In other words, to the extent that the state lavished financial and technical assistance on the local great bourgeoisie, it also created the possibility of itself assuming the functions of this class. The dialectical relationship between state and bourgeoisie began to undergo a qualitative change. The state had made itself into a powerful instrument, capable of replacing the large economic groups of the private sector in their accumulative and entrepreneurial roles, thus providing the basis for a process of socialization.

Last but not least, the growing presence of the state, its direct participation in the ownership of the means of production, had been legitimized. The fact that this expansion was occurring without provoking ideological resistance from the great majority of the population constituted a political condition favorable for the continuation of the process.

In summary, the evolution of the pre-Allende socioeconomic system in Chile was characterized by three main features: (1) a weakening of the principal dynamic element, the large firms of the private sector; (2) a buildup in the social and political organization of middle- and low-income groups; and (3) a significant expansion in the state apparatus.

Frei's Reforms and the Sharpening of Contradictions

The above characteristics were already in evidence at the beginning of the sixties (during the Alessandri government, 1958–64), and became more accentuated in the last half of the decade, during the Frei government (1964–70). In order to analyze what occurred in this period, we must emphasize the differences between these two administrations.

The Alessandri government, supported by the right-wing political parties, put into effect a program in the classical liberal style. Its plans assumed the existence of a vast and dynamic private sector whose initiatives, free of state "interference," would by themselves automatically generate economic growth. Improvement in the living conditions of low-income groups would be the result of growth alone, rendering any recourse to redistributive measures unnecessary. The actual economic and political effects of this program were such that, by the end of this administration, the rightist parties had been severely debilitated. Incapable of mounting a serious presidential candidacy on their own, they were reduced to supporting Frei.

With the Frei government, a process of reform was set underway, designed to remove the obstacles to growth and ameliorate income distribution—in short, a program of modernization of the existing system. Some of these objectives were obtained, but at the same time the underlying tendencies in the system became more pronounced. In the end, the events of this period served to encourage the emergence of conditions favoring the attempt at more radical change in 1970.

Let us briefly examine the political and economic dynamic set underway during the Frei period. It must be kept in mind that this government set out not merely to administer the status quo, but instead proposed a structural modification of the Chilean economy. In contrast to the Alessandri program, whose guiding conception was growth first and redistribution later, the Frei program held that both objectives could be attained simultaneously.

In its economic dimension this program envisaged a developmental model with three central points: agrarian reform, modernization of industry, and an increase in exports. Agrarian reform would break the traditionalistic stranglehold on production and draw significant numbers of peasants into the market. The industrial sector would be stimulated by means of new investments, particularly from the state and foreign sources, and by a broadening of internal demand which would follow an increase in the income of the middle sectors. Copper exports would generate a larger surplus to finance industrial investment. Growth in these exports would be attained by means of an agreement with the multinational firms which owned the large mines.

In the political field, the Christian Democrats tried to portray themselves as an alternative to the Left, arguing that they could achieve growth and equality without profound, systematic change. The Christian Democratic Party sought its primary political support from the modern sectors of the national bourgeoisie and the middle strata, while trying to attract the support of urban marginal groups and peasants as well. The goal of the CDs was to preside over a successful administration which would significantly weaken the Left.

This scenario could count on the support of the U.S. government and of the large North American corporations. For the former, the CD platform could be advanced as an alternative to the Cuban Revolution. This hope followed from the idea that the Latin American crisis could be resolved with a program of partial reforms, which would not attack large national and foreign private property, and which would not break with the prevailing institutional order. In accordance with this North American strategy, it would be necessary to effect certain reforms and grant considerable financial support to Frei in order to reduce the risk of a deep change. This program was implemented through the Alliance for Progress. On the other hand, while such reforms were underway, it would be essential to act through military, political and police channels to forestall a mass movement in favor of a radical change.[22]

U.S. backing for Frei was expressed, first, in the financing of his electoral campaign in order to prevent a win by Allende (his opponent as well in the 1964 elections). Later a vast flow of financial resources was put into play in order to support the Frei government's economic policies.[23]

The average annual disbursement in the 1961–64 period was $112 million. During the Frei government, the annual average reached $144 million. The volume of credits authorized grew at a rapid pace during the first phase of the government, only to diminish once the economic and political results disappointed the expectations of the Alliance for Progress.

Indeed events moved in another direction. Agrarian reform encouraged rapid peasant mobilization. Tension mounted on rural estates, new expectations arose, and the political conflict with the landlords sharpened. The CD government tried to limit the conflict, slowing down the pace of reform, but the grassroots pressures kept growing. This situation had some general consequences. The conservative economic elites had demonstrated their incapacity to contain the process, while the peasant organizations, the Left, and sectors of the CDP itself pointed out that the dilatory and poorly defined actions of the government threatened the success of rural reform.

A partial change, moreover, was difficult to isolate from the rest of the system. In this case it tended to permeate the whole economy. In the agricultural sector, workers on estates not initially affected by the reform demanded quick expropriation; and expectations for change emerged in industry as well.

Despite the financial backing granted by the government, industrial entrepreneurs did not feel secure. They looked on uneasily as the connections which had previously guaranteed the alignment of state decisions with their immediate interests began to weaken. Economically, they did not behave as foreseen. Their rate of savings declined, while the presence of the state and foreign firms was increasing.

The entrepreneurs reacted by pressuring the government to contain the agrarian reform, reduce price controls, hold down wages and salaries, stop the rise in taxes, and guarantee greater profits. Even though they had attained some of these goals by the last years of the Frei government, they decided to muster their political forces separately from the CD.

Along with this regroupment on the Right emerged a wide-open conflict between the government and labor. The CDs, in an effort to expand their popular base, tried to gain ground on four fronts: first, among middle-income sectors, principally salaried employees, professionals and technicians; second, among those peasants favored by the agrarian reform; third, among urban marginal groups which would receive certain state benefits; and, finally, among the owners and managers of small and medium businesses.

The quest for support among these groups encouraged their expectations. Salaried employees and peasants insisted that the government satisfy several demands, including an appeal for higher incomes. The Left parties in turn encouraged and coordinated the formulation of these demands, thus gaining rather than losing from the process as a whole.

In this political setting, the economic policy of the Frei government must be analyzed (see Table 1-3). In the first two years of Frei's administration, public spending was increased and the middle sectors and peasants enjoyed a rise in real income. The resulting increase in demand, encountering unutilized productive capacity, stimulated a rapid growth in production. At the same time, inflation began to diminish. However, both wages and salaries and public spending exceeded initially scheduled limits, thus threatening the whole economic program.

From its third year (1967), the government changed its policies and adopted restrictive measures. The pace of growth slowed considerably, while inflation accelerated, thus menacing the original redistributive advances. This development coincided with the high point of popular mobilization, exacerbating the conflict and intensifying the polarization. The essential problem, therefore, was to contain the expectations which had been aroused earlier.

In sum, the Frei government intensified the contradictions in the system by moving in opposed directions: on the one hand it fed popular mobilization and organization; on the other it attempted a course of economic development which left the economic structure practically intact.

At the political level, this process pushed the large bourgeoisie to look for its own way out, through a realignment of all the groups opposed to the changes. The same process also generated a broad, organized popular movement, represented by the parties which would later coalesce to form the UP. The CDP itself was affected. In 1969, one group (MAPU) split from the Party,

TABLE 1-3. Principal Economic Consequences of the Frei Government

	Rate of growth in the GDP[a]	Rate of inflation (12 months)[b]	Unemployment rate[c]	Rate of investment[d]
1965	5.0%	25.9%	4.7%	18.1%
1966	7.0	17.0	5.4	17.4
1967	2.3	21.9	6.4	15.7
1968	2.9	27.9	5.4	16.3
1969	3.1	29.3	5.4	17.1
1970	4.5	34.9	8.3	16.4

Sources: a. Odeplán.
b. Consumer Price Index, Instituto Nacional de Estadísticas.
c. Unemployment in Greater Santiago, Instituto de Economía y Planificación, Universidad de Chile.
d. Gross National Investment over GDP, Odeplán.

arguing that the latter was too weak to pursue its official objectives effectively. The most progressive group remaining in the Party in turn succeeded in imposing a platform for the 1970 presidential elections which proposed to step up the pace of change. No partial solutions seemed viable.

Thus the united Right, out to restore its old power, rejected an entente with the CDP, which was proposing an intensification of the initial changes. The strengthened Left was pushing for a yet more radical way out of the nation's impasse. Thus the economic and political conditions led very logically to an electoral field dominated by three distinct forces. These conditions made Allende's victory possible.[24]

The attempt to modernize the established order through partial reforms proved to be no substitute for basic change. It served instead as a catalyst.[25]

Economic Factors Conditioning a Transformative Program

Upon taking office, Allende had to deal with several underlying trends, some favorable to the implementation of his program, others jeopardizing it. In order to explain the process that unfolded over the three years of UP rule, it is essential to identify these specific characteristics, particular to the Chilean reality, which marked the initial situation and conditioned the possible courses of action. Keeping this aim in mind, we will first enumerate the principal economic conditioning factors and then turn to a discussion of the corresponding social and political conditions.

THE STATE IN THE ECONOMY

The size and diversity of the state apparatus were factors favoring the take-over of the great private firms. The existence of official bodies like the Corporación de Fomento (CORFO), the Corporación del Cobre (CODELCO), the Corporación de la Reforma Agraria (CORA), the Banco del Estado, and others, all with great influence in the Chilean economy, permitted the expansion of state economic activity without significantly altering the economic system. A starting point close to state capitalism is undoubtedly advantageous in initiating the socialization of the means of production. Furthermore, the high level of concentration in the economy made it possible to attain control of the basic economic decision-making centers through the take-over of only a few firms and organizations.

These same characteristics of the state apparatus, however, constituted a limiting factor: because of its vastness and complexity, it resisted the rapid modification required of it in order to carry out the revolutionary objectives proposed by the UP. A substantive change carried out over a short period could bring about serious disarticulations in the whole productive apparatus. Because of this it was necessary to recognize the rigidities and distortions involved and go about overcoming them gradually. There was no alternative: the whole potential of the state economic apparatus had to be utilized immediately; these mechanisms of action were indispensable to the new government, and a radical transformation undertaken beforehand was unthinkable.

Another limiting feature of the state apparatus rested in the fact that it had been developed to support the private sector financially; entrepreneurial initiative had always been left to the latter. The state's administrative capacity was restricted to a few large firms. Consequently, it could not immediately supplant the private sector and take on the responsibility for running a large number of enterprises in a very short time.

It was essential, therefore, to preserve the role of the market as an orienting mechanism for a considerable number of firms. The play of market forces would also be necessary to assure that middle-range entrepreneurs did not appreciably alter their conduct with respect to investment and replacement of equipment.

In addition, while public spending represented a large proportion of the GNP, its composition and level could not be altered substantially in the short run. Finally, up until 1970, workers had no share in economic decision-making at the level of nation, region or individual firms. The incorporation of workers into the different levels of decision-making would require a phase of adaptation and learning which would produce some maladjustments at the beginning.

In sum the state economic apparatus constituted an essential base of operations, but it was poorly adapted to fulfill a leadership function, and its transformation would require several years. Because of this a very rapid expansion of the state role could lead to a series of imbalances and a temporary failure in the mechanisms of control.

DEPENDENCY ON THE U.S. AND ITS CONSEQUENCES

In order to appreciate the conditions in which the Allende government had to function, it is of interest to point out two mechanisms of U.S. domination: direct ownership of firms and short-term external financing. Nationalization of foreign-owned property would chiefly affect the copper-producing companies. U.S. property was concentrated essentially in this sector and, as a result, nationalization would lead to conflict over a relatively delimited front. The confrontation with foreign interests could be isolated to one basic activity— copper—avoiding a generalized conflict in other activities and other firms. This was clearly an advantage.

North American ownership in the remaining sectors was less than in other Latin American countries. In the Chilean manufacturing industry the book value of U.S. investment was lower than elsewhere in the region.[26] Investments in individual firms, with the exception of copper, were relatively minor; and their nationalization could be managed through separate negotiations with the main offices.

The principal restriction stemmed from short-term external financing. Resources might become less available once the Chilean government took over management of the copper companies. Payments on and renegotiation of the enormous external debt with the U.S. and with European countries would also provide the occasion for the exertion of pressures from the U.S. This last consideration was of great importance, since Chile carried the highest per capita debt in Latin America, over 50 percent of which was owed to the U.S. Because of this, the level of imports, and hence the level of internal economic activity, was vulnerable to U.S. pressure. Another factor which had to be considered was Chile's dependence on certain particularly strategic imports— spare parts and some primary materials—which came from the U.S. and which could not be dispensed with right away. The most dependent activities in this sense were copper and petroleum.[27] Last, but still important, Chile was one of the few food-importing Latin American countries. A redistribution of income would cause these imports to rise, thus creating vulnerability on another flank.

In sum external economic conditions imposed serious restrictions. While the concentration of U.S. property in copper allowed for a relatively isolated and specific action, the magnitude of the external debt and the financial dependence on the U.S. constituted important short-run limiting factors, especially if the latter decided on a policy of total obstructionism.

THE GREATER COMPLEXITY OF CHILE'S ECONOMY

Unlike other countries which had undergone revolutionary change, Chile exhibited a relatively advanced level of development at the beginning of this process. This fact had several implications. The economic system was more tightly integrated, and the interactions between its different sectors were more finely tuned. Thus a change in one part of the system would spread rapidly to other areas. In simpler economies with less closely integrated sectors or subsystems, the effects of a determinate change can be isolated. For example, in those countries with a majority of subsistence-level cultivators, an alteration in the industrial or mining sector would have had fewer repercussions than in Chile.

The level of development was also reflected in the structure of consumption. While it was true that many Chileans could not even meet their basic needs, a considerable portion of the population was consuming at levels well above the minimal. This extent of diversification in demand required the market as a regulator. Furthermore, an increase in consumption would inspire an even faster rise in new expectations. This tendency is typically more pronounced in the highly urbanized economies like that of Chile, where the demonstration effect spreads quickly. In this kind of situation any eventual reduction in levels of consumption, caused by imbalances stemming from the transformations undertaken, would provoke fierce resistance. This reaction would be even stronger when, as was the case in Chile, middle-income groups had been improving their standard of living gradually over a relatively prolonged period.

Because the change process would be tested in an electoral setting and required a wide base of popular support, a stable economic conjuncture had to be maintained at every moment. The task of transforming a complex system was difficult, involving unpredictable factors and potentially critical developments on all fronts. If the multiple indirect effects were not to escape the control of the government, they would have to be foreseen and taken into consideration in the application of a single strategy with selective tactics acting over each sector.

Social and Political Conditioning Factors

The level of economic development achieved in Chile had a correspondingly complex social structure. While the great majority of the population consisted of salaried employees and wage workers, the distinct groups and social classes were interdependent and tied together at different levels. It was not possible to point to well-defined groups whose political behavior could be deduced from their location in the productive structure.

Such complexity was particularly evident in the case of the so-called middle class. The conformation of a broad social and political bloc demanded the participation of these groups. But at the same time, the distinct and at times contradictory interests of the component groups of the alliance had to be reconciled. This would limit the speed and intensity of change. It was essential to put together an alliance broad enough to initiate the changes yet homogeneous enough to deepen them. To attain this equilibrium was a delicate and difficult task.

In the political and institutional field the principal conditioning factors were the following:

1. The reform program of the Frei government led to a three-way polarization in the presidential elections. This tripolar configuration was a condition for both the electoral triumph and the implementation of the UP program. This fact in turn meant that political understandings would have to be pursued. A unified opposition, restoring the bipolar confrontation of Left and Right, had to be avoided.

2. Under such circumstances structural change required a flexible and stable institutional order. The prevailing idea was that the institutional order possessed sufficient flexibility to accommodate the scheduled transformations. In this sense it constituted a favorable condition. But the very stability of the established order also limited its malleability and made the system harder to modify. The process of change could proceed within the institutional order, but it could not depart from it. It constituted in this sense both a lower and an upper limit, both a floor and a ceiling, for the process of change.

3. The position of the armed forces was the determining factor. As long as they subordinated their actions to Constitutional limits, they would be a bulwark against seditious designs from within or without. But, in turn, this attitude determined a limit of power within which the transformative process would have to develop. This restriction would become more evident as the constitutional position came to be questioned by those sectors of the military ideologically opposed to the transformations.

4. Last, at the international level, the balance of power between the superpowers in 1970 allowed for the coexistence of ideologically diverse regimes. This was a favorable condition. But, at the same time, for the government and dominant economic interests of the U.S., a transformative process undertaken through institutional means amounted to an unacceptable challenge. UP was aware of the efforts exerted by the North American government to forestall an Allende victory in 1958 and 1964, so total opposition from this quarter was considered highly probable.

These factors defined the limits within which the UP had to function. The same factors that allowed for the viability of the program also imposed restrictions on it. Only a political course which took these characteristics into account would allow effective advance toward the ultimate objective.

The Roots of the UP

It is not possible to comprehend the difficulties faced later by the political leadership unless we remark on two principal traits of the UP which were already present in the initial situation. The UP and the parties which formed the axis of the coalition (the Socialist Party and the Communist Party) were not new political formations. Rather they had a long history of joint political action, and deep popular roots. Moreover, in the heart of the UP there were conflicting conceptions with respect to the institutional strategy. The first feature constituted a favorable condition, while the second was a limiting factor. We will examine them separately.

The UP was preceded by three political alliances of the Left: the Popular Front in 1938, in which the majority Radical Party joined with the Socialist and Communist Parties in a coalition that won the presidency; the People's Front in 1952, in which the first presidential candidacy of Salvador Allende was mounted by a coalition of the CP, a fraction of the SP, and the Democratic Party;[28] the Popular Action Front (FRAP), set up in 1956, which joined the Socialist and Communist Parties and sustained two presidential candidacies of Allende in 1958 and 1964.

There was a fundamental difference between the experience of the Popular Front in 1938 and that of the subsequent leftist coalitions. In the first, the majority Radical Party was dominant, and the Marxist parties served as support elements. By contrast, after 1956, with the formation of the FRAP, a separate political project of the Left parties was set in motion. This project culminated in 1969 with the formation of the UP, which also included the Radical Party, but this time under the hegemony of the socialists and the communists.

It is important also to take into account the long political life of the Communist Party and the Socialist Party. Their first traces date from 1900 in the nitrates mines where the Chilean proletariat first emerged. The Socialist Workers' Party was formed in 1912, changing its name to the Communist Party of Chile in 1921, after the creation of the Third International. This fact is relevant, inasmuch as the Chilean Communist Party had laid its foundations before the Bolshevik Revolution; and its origins were eminently proletarian, not petty-bourgeois.

The Socialist Party was founded in 1933. Thus, by the time of the victory of the UP it was already 37 years old. It was born out of the fusion of several political groups which had come to the fore during the economic crisis of the thirties. These groups had varied ideologies, from social democratic to anarchist. This diversity of ideological and strategic viewpoints continued to characterize the Socialist Party, right up until the 1973 coup.

In sum the parties of the Chilean Left possessed tradition, solidity and legitimacy. This allowed them a greater chance of success.

Another element which strengthened the UP was the incorporation of Christian sectors. Even though their initial quantitative importance was inconsiderable, the composition of their membership and their growth potential gave them much qualitative significance. The MAPU Party, a split of the CDs, joined the UP from its creation. A new group of similar origins, the Left Christians, was added in 1971. Such groups defined themselves as socialists and shared a similar policy of coalition with other progressive parties. They represented important contingents of intellectuals and opened the way to attracting new sectors of the middle class and proletariat refractory to traditional Marxist thinking. These groups brought with them new dimensions, ideas and values to the political project of the UP.

The strategic differences existing between the various parties of the UP were played out within the alliance and affected the subsequent course of events. The greatest departures from the general line of the UP came from within the Socialist Party. In order to explain this, we must refer to historical precedents in that party: the formulation of the "Workers' Front" political line in 1957 and the emphasis placed on the armed struggle in 1967. The first formulation had its origin in the frustrating results of the alliances with the Center parties over the period 1938 to 1952. As a result of its participation in the Popular Front and in the succeeding government of J. A. Ríos of the Radical Party, important sections of the Socialist Party concluded that their political position carried no weight in the Center-dominated coalition. This conviction led them first to withdraw from the Ríos government (1941–46) and then to refuse support to the next Radical Party candidate in the 1946 elections. The Workers' Front thesis, a political line which sought to restore the autonomy of the working-class parties, emerged from this experience.

The Communist Party, in contrast, persisted in a policy of broad alliances, under the banner of "national liberation" with which it sought to confront fascism in the years between 1930 and 1940. The differing lines led in the postwar period to a distancing between the two parties, which was only overcome in 1956 with the creation of the FRAP. Notwithstanding the latter agreement, however, the Socialist Party, consistent with its earlier positions, remained more reluctant to support political alliances which diluted its ultimate objectives. Thus the incorporation of the Radical Party into the UP encountered initial opposition from the Socialists.

The second precedent for the strategic divergences within the UP occurred in the discussions concerning the options or paths to power which occurred within the Socialist Party in its Congress of 1967. The statements approved there endorsed the armed struggle as the only appropriate response to the realities of Chilean power politics. The Cuban Revolution loomed large in these formulations, as well as Allende's two defeats in 1958 and 1964.

But this divergences did not, up until 1970, lead to a change in the fundamental commitment to the institutional strategy. The predominance of this outlook was not a last-minute agreement; rather it was the result of a prolonged political praxis, a reflection of the Chilean reality itself. The conflict within the UP did not mean that the outlook favoring armed struggle was gaining coherence and predominance; rather it meant a weakening of the capacity to implement the institutional alternative.

One last consideration must be mentioned: the UP did not contemplate a political alliance with the CDP, since the latter was an antagonist, a party proposing a model of reform fundamentally at odds with the project of the Left. Nevertheless, as a minority in parliament, the UP had not clarified how it would deal with the CDs in order to carry out its legislative functions. It was simply assumed that, as in the past, some kind of understanding could be reached with respect to each important project. But the CDP had, as a governing party, swung parliamentary agreements by virtue of its ability to maneuver to both the Right and the Left. This possibility was denied to the UP, which could only move to the Center. In 1970, a rigid attitude against political agreements prevailed in the UP. This was in spite of the existence of favorable conditions for reaching such agreements, conditions which stemmed from the momentary primacy of the progressive sectors within the CDP, led by the Party's candidate, Radomiro Tomic. The exclusion of an entente with the CDs was reflected as well at the tactical level, limiting specific agreements. The divergences within the UP and its rigidity with respect to the CD would emerge as obstacles for the success of the institutional strategy.

Notes

1. For a political analysis of the structural-historical conditions which led up to the UP, see A. Boron, "Notas sobre las raices historico-estructurales de la movilizacion politica en Chile," *Foro International,* Vol. 16, No. 1 (1975), pp. 64–121.
2. Chile's population was exactly 9,535,000. See Instituto Nacional de Estadistica, *Censo de población de 1970* (Santiago, 1971). With respect to the production per capita there are various estimates. According to a study by Odeplan, the GNP per capita was up to $700 in 1970. See Odeplán, *El desarrollo economico y social de Chile en la decada 1970–1980,* Book 1, Vol. 2 (Santiago, 1972). Another more recent work puts it at $868. See Odeplán, *Cuentas nacionales de Chile, 1965–1973* (Santiago, 1975), p. 30. CEPAL calculated the figure at $650 in 1969. See CEPAL, "Tendencias y estructura de la economía latinoamericana" (Santiago, 1971), p. 25.
3. In 1969, the composition of the GNP by sector was as follows: industry, 24.9 percent; services (commerce, banks, house ownership, public administration and all others), 44.1 percent; and agriculture, only 9.3 percent. See Odeplán, *Informe económico anual, 1970* (Santiago, 1971), p. 12.
4. In Russia and Cuba, for example, agriculture was the most important sector as far as employment was concerned. In Russia, in 1922, agriculture employed 74 percent of the economically active population. See Marodnje Khozjajstvo SSSP, 1952–1972, Central Statistical Office, Moscow, 1972, cited in P. Sylos Labini, *Saggio Sulle Classi Socialli,* 4th ed. (Rome: Laterza, 1975), p. 165. In Cuba, 40.9 percent of the economically active population was employed in agriculture. Thus, when the last national census of population completed before the Revolution took place in 1953, 807,514 persons in an economically active population of 1,972,276 were working in agriculture. See "Censo de Población 1953," Oficina del Censo, Republica de Cuba, La Habana, 1955, in J. Dominquez, *Governing Cuba* (Cambridge: Harvard University Press, 1977), pp. 204–205.
5. According to the agrarian reform law applied during the Frei administration, all estates with an irrigated area greater than 80 hectares were subject to expropriation. The use of "irrigated hectare" as a unit of measurement allowed land of different quality to be measured according to a common index. In 1965, only 4876

out of a total of 232,955 estates (i.e., 2 percent of the total) were greater in extent than 80 irrigated hectares.

6. Copper production in 1970 came to 692,000 tons, 541,000 of which were extracted by the Gran Mineria. The value of all exports (FOB) was $1,112,000,000; copper exports had a value of $840,000,000; and the production of the Gran Mineria brought in $657,000,000. Corporación del Cobre (CODELCO), "Indicadores del Cobre"; and Banco Central, *Boletin Mensual* (various issues).

7. Garreton and Cisternas, "Algunas caracteristicas del proceso de toma de decisiones en la gran empresa" (Santiago: Servicio de Cooperación Tecnica, 1970).

8. Seventy firms (2 percent of the total) were responsible for 76 percent of total sales. See Instituto Nacional de Estadisticas, *Encuesta continua de comercio y servicio* (Santiago, 1967).

9. Banco Central, *Boletin Mensual* (September 1971).

10. In a study begun in 1972, the conditions of extreme poverty were defined according to the type of housing. These conditions were crowding of inhabitants; housing in urban areas lacking appliances or with an inadequate sewage system; squatter settlements, shacks, huts, trailers with or without appliances, etc. See Instituto de Economia, Universidad Catolica de Chile, "Mapa de la extrema pobreza en Chile," No. 29 (Santiago, 1974).

11. So-called "dependency theory" approaches this problem in general terms. In addition there exist numerous quantitative works on Chile. On dependency theory, see F. Cardoso and E. Falletto, *Dependencia y desarrollo en America Latina* (Mexico: Siglo XXI, 1969); T. dos Santos, *Lucha de clases 6 dependencia en America Latina* (Bogota: Oveja Negra, 1970); O. Sunkel, "Transnational Capitalism and National Disintegration in Latin America," *Social and Economic Studies*, Vol. 22, No. 1 (1973). On Chile, see L. Pacheco, "La inversion extranjera y las corporaciones internacionales en el desarrollo industrial chileno," in O. Muñoz, *Proceso a la industrializacion chilena* (Santiago: Ediciones Nueva Universidad, 1972); and S. Bitar "La presencia de la empresa extranjera en la industria chilena," *Desarrollo Económico*, Vol. 13, No. 50 (July–September 1973).

12. Until 1967, unionization among farmworkers was practically prohibited. The prevailing law, dating from 1947, imposed numerous restrictions: only those who worked on the same estate could form a union; more than 20 workers had to join; leaders had to read and write, etc. See J. Chonchol, "Poder y Reforma Agraria," *Chile Hoy* (Mexico: Siglo XXI, 1970), p. 283.

13. For 1960–1967, see Instituto Nacional de Estadisticas, *Sintesis Estadistica* (various issues); for 1968–1970, see OAS, *America en Cifras. Situacion Social* (1972).

14. The conduct of the large foreign corporations in Chile confirms this dynamic. According to an executive of the Kennecott Company, the situation in the period 1965–69 was as follows: "Braden and other copper companies had come to be the sacrificial lambs in the political tumult normal to Latin America . . . Under these circumstances, there was a natural reluctance to invest additional capital, especially given that the Chilean government could not guarantee the investment. The best solution would have been to take Chilean partners into the enterprise . . . Nevertheless, the local partners would not be from the private sector. *The historical insecurity and instability of the Latin American economic system inhibited this kind of investment*" (author's emphasis). C. Michaelson, President of the Division of Metals and Mining of the Kennecott Company, speech in Salt Lake City, 1969. Cited in G. Martner, *El pensamiento económico del gobierno de Allende* (Santiago: Editorial Universitaria, 1971), pp. 187–188.

15. CEPAL, "Tendencias y estructura de la economía latinoamericana," p. 68.

16. CEPAL, "Tendencias y estructura," p. 73.

17. Figures on the importance of the Chilean state in economic activity vary according to the way in which the state's activities are classified. In various studies the

categories treasury, central government and public sector usually include different institutions. Hence the figures used to illustrate the evolution of the state's role are not all consistent with the foregoing data.

18. Calculated on the basis of data from the Direccion de Presupuesto, Ministerio de Hacienda. Cited in R. Ffrench-Davis, *Politicas economicas en Chile* (Santiago: Ediciones Nueva Universidad, 1973), pp. 252, 329. Public spending includes both fiscal spending and spending by the decentralized institutions.

19. Data from de Dirección de Presupuesto, Ministerio de Hacienda, "El Presupuesto Fiscal para el ano 1971," in S. Ramos, *Chile: Una economía en transicion?* (Santiago: Editorial Prensa Latinoamericana, 1976), p. 77.

20. Odeplan, "La inversion publica en el periodo 1961–1970" (Santiago, June 1971).

21. Banco Central, *Boletin Mensual* (September 1971).

22. These two components of U.S. strategy have been expressed clearly as follows: "Castro's presence led to a new U.S. hemispheric policy, with a special emphasis on Chile—the Alliance for Progress . . . The reaction of the U.S. to the new hemispheric peril—communist revolution—evolved in the direction of a dual response . . . The U.S. conceded credits for national development and supported reformist civilian regimes. But there was another component of U.S. policy towards Latin America . . . Development could not cure overnight the social ills that were seen as the seedbed of communism. In order to eliminate the immediate danger of communist subversion, it was often considered necessary to support the armed forces, even when it was frequently these same forces who helped to freeze the status quo which the Alliance for Progress was trying to alter." See United States Senate, *Covert Action in Chile, 1963–1973.* Staff Report of the Select Committee to Study Governmental Operations with respect to Intelligence Activities (Washington, D.C.: U.S. Government Printing Office, 1975), p. 4.

23. In the presidential elections of 1964, the two principal candidates were Frei and Allende. Concerning North American intervention in the elections, the following reference is explicit: "During the 1964 campaign, overt action consisted of two principal components. One was direct financial support to the Christian Democratic campaign. The CIA paid for more than half of the total campaign costs." See United States Senate, *Covert Action in Chile,* p. 15.

24. For a general analysis of the political conditions which preceded and conditioned the UP period, see J. Garces, *1970: La pugna politica por la presidencia en Chile* (Santiago: Editorial Universitaria, 1971). On the tripolar configuration, see p. 67.

25. "Reform, one could argue, can lead not to political stability but rather to greater instability and even to revolution itself. Reform can be a catalyst for revolution more than a substitute for it. Historically, as has been noted frequently, the great revolutions have followed periods of reform, and not periods of stagnation and repression. The fact that a regime undertakes reforms and grants concessions itself stimulates demands for greater changes, which can build up to a revolution." See S. Huntington, *Political Order in Changing Societies* (New Haven: Yale University Press, 1968), p. 363.

26. In 1972, the direct investment of North American corporations measured at book value, reached the sum of $2.505 billion in Brazil, $2.025 billion in Mexico, $1.403 billion in Argentina, $552 million in Venezuela, $262 million in Colombia, $89 million in Peru, and $46 million in Chile. United States Department of Commerce, *Survey of Current Business* (Washington, D.C.: U.S. Government Printing Office).

27. In 1970, 36.9 percent of Chilean imports originated in the United States, and this amount included 43.5 percent of all capital goods imported. In the copper and petroleum industries, more than 80 percent of the spare parts and replacements were of North American origin. For a brief analysis, see F. Fajnzylber, "El comercio externo en el gobierno de la Unidad Popular," mimeo, *Seminario Development*

and the International System: The Case of Chile 1970–73 (La Haya: Institute of Social Studies, 1976).

28.   On this occasion the Socialist Party suffered a split, with one sector supporting the Populist candidate Carlos Ibañez, who was elected president. This sector of the Socialist Party (the Popular Socialist Party) withdrew from the government after a few months; and it was not until 1957 that it reunited with the sector supporting Salvador Allende.

CHAPTER 2

Objectives and Strategy of the UP

In the official Program of the Unidad Popular, which constitutes the most complete formulation of its objectives, there was scant reference to any strategy of action. In order to render this strategy explicit, we must necessarily attempt some interpretations, based on the program itself and on other documents of the president and of the government parties. For the UP, Chilean society was faced with a global crisis which could only be overcome by means of profound structural transformations.[1] From this point of view previous attempts at partial reforms had left the economic control centers in the hands of the national great bourgeoisie and of external interests; consequently, these reforms had not resolved the most pressing problems of the majority of the population.

The diagnosis was based on a theoretical analysis which characterized the Chilean socioeconomic system as a species of underdeveloped and dependent capitalism, whose principal functional modalities were thought to be those described in Chapter 1. At the root of the situation in 1970 was the high concentration of property ownership and the consequent political and economic control of the society by a restricted group of large national capitalists and foreign firms.[2] According to the analysis of the UP, this structural feature imposed strict limits to the expansion of democracy. If the democratic process in Chile was to be extended and deepened, it would be necessary to alter fundamentally this distribution of decision-making power.

The UP defined its central objective in the initial phase as the elimination of latifundios, monopolies and the external control over basic wealth, all in order to open the way to building socialism. In this sense the program was eminently anti-imperialist, anti-monopolistic and anti-capitalist. It was accepted as well that in order to achieve these goals broad mobilization and popular participation would be required. Fundamentally, the UP relied on two elements which together would help create the conditions for launching a transition to socialism: socialization of the means of production and popular participation. The revolutionary character of the program derived from the UP's fundamental objective: to alter profoundly the socioeconomic bases of power, generating a new balance of forces in order to win control of the state apparatus and develop an ideological consensus.

Upon subjecting the program to critical analysis, it becomes apparent that, while it was indeed based on a coherent theoretical viewpoint, its character was overwhelmingly global and structural. This diminished its value as a guide to concrete actions and clear strategy. In particular the emphasis on structural objectives led to a relative neglect of the conjunctural aspects of the transition. However, in other, more finished policy formulations, a more flexible strategy was defined; and a sequence between transformations in the economic base and changes in the institutional superstructure was spelled out. It is this strategy which must be analyzed, first in its global characteristics and subsequently in its economic dimension.

The Global Strategy

The economic and institutional development of Chile and its degree of social and political organization permitted, in the words of President Allende, a "second path to socialism." The distinctiveness of this course rested in the attempt to transform the economic base and subsequently change the social relations of production without rupturing the given institutional framework.[3] The strategy of the UP presupposed that the ideological and institutional conditions prevailing in Chile provided an opening for introducing substantive modifications in both the ownership of the means of production and workers' participation. Once these transformations had been effected, conditions more propitious for a change in the prevailing legal order would be generated.

The exercise of executive power and the use of already available legal mechanisms would be adequate to carry out the major nationalizations and expropriations.[4] Later in the process new forms of popular organization would be built from the base up, forms which in subsequent stages would congeal into a new institutional order. In other words, the initially available power and the inherent flexibility of the Chilean institutional system would allow the economic changes to be effected; and concomitantly these changes would reinforce the power of the majority social groups, thus giving rise to a new juridical order. The interaction among ideological, institutional and economic structures was acknowledged. The transformation of these structures would follow a certain sequence in which economic change would precede and reinforce institutional change, and both would favorably modify the ideological sphere.

In order to differentiate the Chilean strategy from other transitional experiences it must first be observed that in the classical paths to socialism the sequence of changes was initiated in the institutional or political-legal sphere, which was always the critical point of the system. In these situations, the rigidity of the political order prohibited state-initiated economic transformations that might affect property ownership and the social relations of production: nor did it allow any room for a massive development of the ideology and consciousness of the proletariat. A break with the status quo could only be brought about by means of a frontal assault aimed at total control of the state apparatus. Once this control had been achieved, it became possible to direct an economic and ideological transformation and to advance progressively toward the construction of a new institutional order.

In the case of Chile, the system had evolved to the point of admitting an opening in the ideological field: full criticism of the system was allowed and change was legitimated. Furthermore, progressive modifications had been brought about in the economic structure: an extensive public sector, a relatively weak private sector, the preponderance of the urban-industrial component and agrarian reform. At the political-institutional level it was possible to win executive power through electoral means. According to its plan, the UP could use this initial quota of power as a springboard from which to launch progressive changes on the economic and ideological fronts, and, later on, in the institutional sphere.[5]

Just as in the case of previous socialist transitions, the Chilean road forward would also have to begin with a certain degree of control over the state apparatus. However, while the earlier transitional processes began with a political rupture followed by total control of the state, in this case only partial power would be won at first, through electoral means. This would be followed by incremental advances toward workers' hegemony, finally bringing about a qualitative change that would permanently alter the class character of the state.

Nevertheless, this strategy had important restrictions, recognized by the UP leaders. Its viability depended on the malleability of the National Congress and of the political parties as well as on the behavior of the armed forces. With respect to these factors, the UP acted on two basic assumptions: (1) institutional flexibility, in particular the possiblity of a tactical understanding with the Christian Democratic Party; and (2) noninterference on the part of the armed forces, especially their continued observance of institutionalist principles.

A third fundamental assumption was the possibility of forming an alliance between the proletariat and the middle classes—more specifically, among wage workers, salaried employees, self-employed workers, professionals and small businessmen. It should be noted that in the UP Program there was no mention of the specific steps that would be followed in order to put this alliance together.

With regard to the external context, it was considered that international conditions existed which allowed some leeway for the UP to advance its project.[6] American opposition, it was supposed, would be intense; but there would be no direct military intervention. Opposition would be expressed instead through all kinds of economic, political and propaganda pressures. External factors would impinge on internal developments, exacerbating or moderating them. But in the strategic conception of the UP, internal factors were considered to be ultimately determinant. The strategy was structured at a very general level, but it lacked a concrete and disaggregated analysis. This weakness was due in part to internecine theoretical differences concerning the historical stage which would be initiated with the electoral triumph of Salvador Allende.

Two positions were expressed from the initiation of the debate on the program. According to the principal and dominant position, the period would be above all anti-oligarchical and anti-imperialist: its objectives would consist in socializing the latifundios, basic wealth, banks and monopoly firms. The period which was starting would be one of preparation; it would precede the transition to socialism. The construction of socialism was itself not to begin in this period; rather there would be an advance toward situations more favorable for this task. In order to implant socialism, a more extensive control of the state would be required, as well as a more advanced level of popular organization and political consciousness. This position was propounded chiefly by the Communist Party, an important sector of the Socialist Party, the Radical Party, and by Allende himself.

The second position, even though a minority viewpoint, was pushed continually throughout this period. Its exponents argued that the initial stage ought to be the immediate construction of socialism. Their principal emphasis was on attaining total power and forcing an abrupt change in the nature of the state. They argued that a national bourgeoisie with any autonomous thrust was virtually nonexistent, since local entrepreneurs were almost totally dependent on international capital. For this reason the national bourgeoisie could play no role and ought to be displaced from the start. This line was sustained by sectors of the Socialist Party and, from outside the UP, by the MIR (the Revolutionary Left Movement).

In the period which preceded the elaboration of the program, this latter group had already expressed doubts concerning the possibility and the desirability of coming to power through elections. The logical consequence of this line of thinking was permanent questioning of the electoral option, both before and after Allende's victory. Underlying this discussion was a crucial problem: the paucity of existing theory concerning the political strategy which, the UP ultimately selected. Given the absence of similar previous experiences, the reference point remained the classical cases of socialist transition, historically distinct from that of Chile.

The Economic Strategy

From the global strategy there followed one fundamental objective in the economic sphere: the transfer to the state of the basic means of production in order to create an area of socialized property. The state would assume control of the key centers of economic decision-making; the political power of the dominant groups would be undermined; and a new model of development would be installed.

The control of the critical means of production would allow a greater surplus to be captured, a surplus which would be used to improve the distribution of income and to raise the rate of savings. Likewise investment resources would be reoriented toward the production of essential consumer goods and toward secondary industries based on those basic resources in which Chile enjoyed comparative advantages. This kind of investment would promote greater autonomy from external control and increased welfare for the general population.

Rejected from the start was a "developmentalist" conception, according to which the principal objective ought to be to increase the rate of growth in order to approach the level of the developed countries, attaining equality and national autonomy as an "automatic" by-product of growth. By contrast, the UP viewed Chile's underdevelopment as a situation historically and structurally distinct from that experienced at one time by contemporary developed countries. The underdevelopment of countries like Chile was seen as coexisting with—indeed inserted into and subordinated by—an international system dominated by the large advanced countries. This diagnosis was inspired by Latin American studies on dependency, at that time attracting great interest.

The UP held that the prevailing model of development in Chile was one of concentration and exclusion. The historical evolution of this model demonstrated that instead of extending economic benefits to new sectors of the population, concentration of income and property ownership persisted. The dynamic of growth in this model stemmed from the modern industrial sector, which in turn was sustained from the consumption of durable goods by the high-income strata. This dynamic was reinforced by the penetration of foreign firms, which continually imposed the pattern of consumption and the technology of their countries of origin, thus distorting Chile's productive structure. The same interpretative analysis led to explanations of technological dualism, regional imbalances and unequal income distribution. Using this conceptual framework the UP identified the elements causing the continual reproduction of the status quo: concentration of ownership of the means of production, external dependence in fundamental economic activities and the unequal distribution of income.[7]

The proposed economic strategy followed from this diagnosis. It looked to a shift to a new productive structure, one which would respond to a more equalitarian pattern of consumption. The expanded production of essential consumer goods would lead to a higher rate of economic growth and fuller employment of manpower and national resources. The product-capital relationship in this kind of activity would be higher; and the density of capital per person employed lower. Moreover, the requirements for imported primary materials could be reduced, since basic consumer goods would absorb fewer imports than durable consumer goods. On the other hand, standardized mass production would allow increased vertical integration in industry. These ideas had previously been advanced by CEPAL economists, some of whom later served on the UP's technical staffs.

It was concluded from this analysis that it would be necessary to begin by redistributing income and changing the composition of production and investment. Production and investment would be altered by means of several basic measures. Agrarian reform would open the way to expanded agricultural production by encouraging the application of new technology and a more rational use of water. Production would be redirected toward activities with a greater value-added component; agroindustrial activity would be encouraged and exports increased. Industrial production would become standardized and new products would be designed. Investments would be channeled toward expanding economic activity, toward more extensive use of existing capital equipment (through more shifts at factories) and toward projects with quick returns. In the mining sector, the nationalization of copper, iron and other natural resources would mean that a greater share of the total surplus would be retained within the country; and the increase in production would generate new export revenues. Finally, the state would expand services in health and education, and would augment housing construction.

While these proposals applied very well to the middle term, there was no corresponding economic policy to deal with short-run problems.

Structural Reform with Redistribution of Income

How were conjunctural measures joined to longer-term objectives? The two main objectives—state expropriation of the large firms and income redistributions—had to be reconciled with other, short-term goals: reduction in the rate of inflation, increase in employment and an acceleration of the growth rate. In the economic program it was estimated that movement toward the two principal objectives was compatible with these other short-term goals.

In accordance with the UP Program, socialization of the means of production—those measures we will label as structural changes—would extend to: (1) the latifundios; (2) the large copper, iron and nitrate mines, as well as other natural resources; (3) the banking system; (4) the chief monopoly firms in industry and distribution; and (5) foreign trade. All of the state-owned or cooperative enterprises would constitute together the area of social property, or social ownership, which would coexist with areas of mixed and private ownership. The mixed ownership sector would be made up of enterprises jointly owned by the state and by private interests, national or foreign. Income redistribution would also be pushed immediately. This decision was based on two main considerations: the existence of idle capacity, allowing considerable room for short-run economic growth, and the need to attract political support for the structural changes.

There was in fact unutilized productive capacity which could be harnessed to accelerate growth and redistribute income. By 1969, it was estimated that only 75.6 percent of total industrial capacity already in place was being utilized.[8] In 1968, the same measure was around 80.6 percent. The high unemployment rate, moreover, indicated that there was unutilized manpower ready to be put to work.[9] According to the UP, the low growth rate for the years 1967–70 was not due to limitations in productive capacity, but rather to a policy of restricting global demand. Significant restrictions stemming from balance of payments problems were not expected. The Frei administration had succeeded in accumulating a considerable quantity of international reserves, and an increase in revenue from copper exports was foreseen. It was also supposed that there would be greater access to sources of financing in Western Europe and the socialist countries. According to the calculations, these factors would together compensate for an eventual restriction of U.S. financing.

The second argument advanced by the UP was that redistribution and state expropriation were mutually reinforcing. The policies of redistribution and the expansion of public spending would furnish a base of political support for the projected changes in property ownership. Inversely, the creation of the social property area would furnish the instruments and the resources necessary to sustain the income redistribution. Structural transformations and redistributions would be accomplished simultaneously, not just for economic reasons, but for political reasons as well. There was a dialectical relationship between the two. This notion was decisive in orienting the economic policy of the UP.

Finally, the limitations imposed on economic policy stemming from the electoral campaign and the promises accompanying it ought to be pointed out. Along with structural changes, promises were made to adopt such measures as readjusting wages and salaries every six months, extending social security coverage, expanding and cheapening the cost of medical care and drugs, increasing the construction of low-income housing, scholarships for the education of workers' and peasants' children, more schools and obstetric centers. The electoral struggle pushed the UP political leadership to promise immediate satisfaction of the multiple necessities of the general population. This was reflected in the so-called Forty Measures which accompanied the Basic Program of Government of the UP.[10] Included in this list of promises were many ideas on the management of economic policy which lacked any technical basis and were of dubious political value.

The economic program of the UP had four principal foci: (1) the socialist idea that state expropriation of the means of production is a necessary condition in order to launch the transformation definitively; (2) the idea, deduced from dependency studies, that it was necessary to nationalize foreign firms, confront the multinational corporations, and reduce the financial influence of the U.S.; (3) a development strategy, drawn from the analyses of CEPAL, based on increasing the manufacture of essential consumer goods; and (4) a certain Keynesian bias, encouraging a strongly redistributive and stimulatory policy. The resulting schema had a global logic, but it lacked coherence in terms of specific policies.

The program of the UP would be viable only as long as certain conditions held true. In the first place, supply would have to react quickly in order to conform to the new demand. Because the policy instruments available to increase consumption would produce results almost immediately, production would have to keep pace. In the second place, in order to sustain income redistribution, public and private investments would have to be adjusted rapidly to the new demand.

The third condition which had to be fulfilled was that the structural changes could not be allowed to obstruct a short-run increase in production. Otherwise redistribution and structural change would not be compatible goals. The UP believed that any negative impact would be minor and that production would not only be maintained, but would in fact increase.[11] In sum it would be possible to redistribute wealth, transform and stimulate the economy without a drop in saving and without an inflationary surge.

Finally, the precondition of maintaining the social alliance between the proletariat and the middle classes carried one clear implication for the economic program: redistribution would have to be financed from funds extracted from upper income groups, whether from their personal incomes or from the profits generated from their enterprises. The surplus so captured would have to be enough to both redistribute income and maintain or even increase the national rate of savings. If not, conflict between low- and middle-income groups would be amplified, thereby frustrating the sought-after alliance. These conditions, present in the qualitative design of the program, were not subjected to quantification. This failure was an important source of later problems, especially with respect to monetary and financial matters.

Comparison with the Tomic Program

Inasmuch as the implementation of the UP Program demanded specific accords with the Christian Democrats, it is necessary to refer to the economic elements of the Christian Democratic program, in order to determine if the areas of agreement between the two were substantial enough to facilitate an eventual entente. Tomic's candidacy was pushed by the progressive sectors within the Christian Democratic Party, and several of his positions were consequently similar to those of the UP. In general terms the Tomic program also upheld the necessity to overcome existing difficulties by introducing important structural changes in the system. Essentially, he proposed to accelerate the changes introduced by Frei, rather than containing them.[12]

Compared with the Allende program, Tomic's put less emphasis on changes in property ownership and more on specific economic policies. His analysis was less structural and more instrumental, even though it explicitly acknowledged the necessity for profound transformation. Concerning changes in property ownership, the Tomic program contemplated the nationalization of copper and an acceleration in the agrarian reform. With respect to the banking system, it proposed new state controls, the nationalization of foreign banks and the progressive transformation of commercial banks into cooperatives. Concerning foreign trade, reference was made to its "Chileanization" without specifying the extent of this reform.

As far as the crucial problem of the mode of ownership of the large oligopolistic corporations, the Tomic program, in contrast with that of the UP, did not propose far-reaching and immediate state expropriation. It did foresee the expansion of the state apparatus through the creation of new enterprises which would be financed with the state funds hitherto transferred in the form of credits to the private sector. Also proposed was a policy restricting the entry of foreign subsidiaries, allotting a more dynamic role to the state in the ownership and management of these firms, and in the creation and diffusion of technology.

Workers' participation also had a fundamental place in the Tomic program. As distinct from the UP program, Tomic emphasized "workers' enterprises." A "Fund for Independence and Development" would be created which would acquire some large and medium private firms and create other, new enterprises—all in order to place management in the hands of workers and salaried employees.

With respect to general development policy and specific economic policies, the Tomic program possessed some elements in common with Allende's: income redistribution, increase in the production of essential consumer goods, more accelerated growth, control of inflation and reduction of external dependence. The proposed redistributive measures were also similar: better remuneration, health, education and housing, and a unitary social security plan. There was, however, an important difference in emphasis. For Tomic, the saving problem was of more concern, and the compatibility between redistribution and savings was established with more rigor. In short a more moderate estimate of the available surplus was assumed. Finally, this program paid more attention to efficiency, to concrete measures, taking care to preserve quantitative coherence.

In summary, a comparison of the economic programs of Allende and Tomic reveals an important area of convergence. The principal differences lay in the relative emphasis placed on expansion of state control of the industrial sector, in distribution—fundamental for the UP—and in efficiency and instrumental precision, more important for the Christian Democrats. But the areas of convergence could have allowed, at the least, for joint actions on specific matters.

Notes

1. The UP's diagnosis, its program and proposed strategy are all reviewed in Unidad Popular, *Programa basico de gobierno de la Unidad Popular* (Santiago, 1970); G. Martner, ed., *El pensamiento económico del gobierno de Allende* (Santiago: Editorial Universitaria, 1971); S. Allende, *Salvador Allende. Su pensamiento político* (Santiago: Editorial Quimantu, 1972); and R. Debray, *Conversación con Allende* (Mexico: Siglo XXI, 1971).
2. "Chile is a capitalist country, in a dependent relationship with imperialism, dominated by sectors of the bourgeoisie structurally linked to foreign capital. These sectors are unable to resolve the fundamental problems of the country; problems which derive precisely from the class privileges which these same sectors will never

give up voluntarily." Unidad Popular, *Programa básico de gobierno de la Unidad Popular.*

3. "Chile is confronted by the necessity to initiate a new way of building a socialist society. Social thinkers have heretofore supposed that the first to take this step would be the more developed nations, probably France and Italy, with their powerful Marxist-oriented workers' parties . . . Chile today is the first nation on earth called to mold the second model of transition to socialist society." From the First Presidential Message in Martner, *El pensamiento económico del gobierno de Allende,* p. 113. In March 1972, Allende noted: "We want . . . to utilize the bourgeois institutional order to make possible the changes this country needs and clamors for, changes in the political, economic, and social fields leading to socialism. In the case of Chile, the use of the institutional order is possible, because it is broad and open to such innovations." Speech reprinted in G. Palma and A. Zammit, *La via chilena al socialismo* (Mexico: Siglo XXI, 1973), pp. 7, 8.

4. In his first message to Congress, President Allende observed: "Even though the responsibility for a democratic transition rests not entirely with the Government, we hope that it will be shared by the Christian Democrats, who will be called upon to demonstrate consistent support of the principles and programs which they have so often propounded to the nation." See Martner, p. 122.

5. This notion of "institutional flexibility" had deep roots in the thinking of the Left, as can be seen in the words of President Allende in March 1972: "[T]he institutional regime has been shown to be not only open to revolutionary forces but also sufficiently flexible in its internal equilibrium to tolerate revolutionary changes and allow their realization . . . The supercession of the present institutional regime in Chile cannot be seen as the product of voluntaristic action by a daring minority. Instead, we must view such change as the fruit of conscious, organized action on the part of the great masses as they perceive the necessity of the transformations and create the mechanisms making these changes possible." Report to the National Plenum of the Socialist Party, March 1972. In Allende, *Salvador Allende,* p. 305.

6. The Minister of Foreign Affairs characterized the situation in these terms: "[I]n 1970, the political project of the UP from the point of view of the external context could be characterized as viable but difficult." See C. Almeyda, "La política internacional del Gobierno de la Unidad Popular," paper presented at the seminar on "Development and the International System: The Case of Chile, 1970–1973" (La Haya: Institute of Social Studies, 1976).

7. A summary of this interpretation can be found in Odeplán, *Resumen del Plan de la Economía Nacional, 1971–1976* (Santiago, 1971) and in P. Vuskovic, "Distribución del ingreso y opciones de desarrollo," in M. A. Garreton, ed., *Economia politica en la Unidad Popular* (Barcelona: Editorial Fontanella, 1976).

8. According to Odeplán, the utilization index of available capacity in 1969 for firms employing more than 50 workers was 78.7 percent in basic consumer goods industries, 86 percent for intermediate goods industry, and 76.1 percent for durable goods and capital goods industries. See Odeplán, *Plan anual, 1971* (Santiago, 1972), p. 6.

9. In 1970, Chile had high international reserves as a result, among other factors, of the high price of copper and an increase in the external debt. Net international reserves of the monetary system rose to $343.5 million in 1970, of which $300 million were liquid reserves. This figure had changed from -$27 million in 1960 to a minimum of -$264 million in 1963, later recovering to the maximum indicated for 1970. Figures taken from the Banco Central. For a detailed analysis, see R. Ffrench-Davis, *Políticas económicas en Chile* (Santiago: Ediciones Nueva Universidad, 1973), pp. 286–287.

10. Included as an appendix to the basic program was a list of 40 measures to be applied immediately by the government. To cite a few as illustration: Measure 9:

Pensions for all; Measures 13–15: Breakfast and lunch for all children, a daily pint of milk, free tuition, books and school supplies; Measure 16: Medical clinics in all communities; Measure 20: Mortgage payments will not be readjusted for inflation; Measure 21: Rent payments not to exceed 10 percent of family income. See "The First Forty Measures of the Popular Government," in Unidad Popular, *Programa básico de gobierno de la Unidad Popular.*

11.   This assumption led the Office of Planning to project a high rate of growth. "The consumption-oriented strategy, plus the programs in housing, health, education, public works in infrastructure and the concrete possibilities of exporting (especially copper) add up to a growth in total production of 50 percent for the period 1971–1976." See Odeplán, "Visión Perspectiva del plan de la economía nacional 1971–1976," in Martner, p. 77.

12.   "In spite of the efforts and achievements of the first Christian Democratic government, both juridical order and social reality continue to demonstrate a serious and unjust imbalance . . . It is imperative to advance a government program which will allow the basic necessities of all Chileans to be satisfied and which will include a significant redistribution of income, opportunities, and power. . . ." "The Tomic Program," *El Clarin* (Santiago, July 14, 1970), p. 6.

CHAPTER 3

The Initial Impulse in the Transformation Process

Once the experience of the Unidad Popular is viewed in its totality, the critical character of the first year of the government becomes obvious. In every political process involving accelerated change, the initial impulse has a decisive effect on the ultimate trajectory. By the later stages, the process has already acquired its own dynamic, and events occur with such speed that they sometimes exceed all powers of prediction and correction. Thus an extended study of the year 1971 is important—so important, in fact, that the next two chapters are devoted to it. In this chapter the general design of the UP policies in this first year and their outcomes are described. In Chapter 4, the factors which determined this course of events are analyzed in detail. In order to understand the initial policies adopted by the UP, we must take account both of the circumstances Chile faced in the last few months of the Christian Democratic government and of the events that occurred between the elections (September 1970) and President Allende's inauguration (November 1970).

The final period of the Frei government was marked by much general uneasiness and a growing number of labor conflicts. Inflation, which had diminished 21.9 percent in 1967, rose to 34.9 percent in 1970. The reductions in government spending on housing and public works affected the general level of economic activity.[1] The contraction in private investments in the pre-election period aggravated the situation. Unemployment in Santiago climbed from 5.5 percent in December 1969 to 6.8 percent in March 1970, and to 7.0 percent in June.[2]

The psychological climate of an election campaign preceded by a period of reforms stimulated pressures on the labor front. In the few months just before the election, several of the most powerful unions were on strike: copper and coal miners, port workers, and employees in banks and government offices. The CUT declared a national work stoppage to underline its demands for salary increases. Meanwhile, in the countryside, the social dynamic released by the agrarian reform proved difficult to control. Agricultural workers began to apply for wage increases and to seize estates that had not been expropriated by agrarian reform agencies. The apparent gravity of the situation was accentuated

by two very unusual labor actions occurring in this period. A grievance movement within the armed forces culminated in the insubordination of a regiment
in Santiago at the end of 1969. Second, in a historically unprecedented move,
judges in the national court system staged a work stoppage.

The country had reached a point of great tension, which only served to
reinforce the conviction of the Left that a profound crisis was underway, one
that demanded a radical political response. These preceptions, however, were
exaggerated. In reality these disequilibria all occurred within controllable
limits. It was an error to assume the existence of a state of general deterioration.
Inflation was not approaching unmanageable levels. Unemployment had
grown, but without attaining politically significant dimensions. Furthermore,
the balance of payments situation was the most favorable in the last few years,
and new revenue was expected from recent investments in the large copper-
mining enterprises.

The reformist policies of the Frei government had decisively influenced the
attitudes and expectations of many labor groups. For them the Christian
Democratic experience had demonstrated the possibility of effecting certain
changes in the structure of the system (including agrarian expropriations, tax
reform, expansion of spending on health and education, and agrarian unionization) without provoking major upsets in the functioning of the economy. This
meant that these groups were inclined to reject the unbalancing effects of an
extended period of change, the consequences of which might cause them to
shrink from this more arduous task.

The UP government did not initially confront an economic crisis in the
conjunctural sense of the term. Although the overall situation in the previous
years was one of latent structural crisis, its conjunctural manifestations had not
reached the boiling point of anarchy or breakup as was the case historically in
periods preceding episodes of revolutionary change. The mistaken diagnosis of
the situation, common among some sectors of the UP and accentuated by the
political struggle, only served to bias still further the initial tactical approach of
the Allende government.

Political Impact of the Election

The UP victory had an enormous impact in itself, aggravating the already
stressful situation existing in the final phase of the Frei government. In the two-
month lapse between the election and Allende's assumption of the presidency
(September to November 1970), the political forces of the Right, in league with
the United States government, attempted to prevent the transfer of power.

For the UP it was clear that the first obstacle that would have to be
overcome was a possible constitutional obstruction and a coup d'état. Fore-
seeing the actions which rightist groups could undertake, Allende and Tomic
had agreed before the elections to acknowledge publicly and prior to the congressional decision the victory of whichever candidate obtained a plurality. In
this way the vast majority of the electorate would be put on record in favor of

the traditional rules of the game, according to which whoever got the highest popular vote was elected by the Congress. This would also serve to dissuade those who might consider organizing a military coup.

Despite the attainment of this accord, the groups opposed to the UP put into effect three operations intended to block the consummation of the electoral outcome. First they got Alessandri, the second-place candidate, to make an appeal to Congress in favor of his own election, with the understanding that he would resign straightaway, thus bringing about new elections. It was further understood that the new candidate would be Frei, who could count on the support of the Right, in a replay of the bipolar scheme of 1964.[3]

Second, there was an attempt to foment a post-electoral economic crisis in order to intensify the general uncertainty and to demonstrate that it would be impossible for the UP to manage the economy in these conditions. Furthermore, the psychological climate for a coup d'état was being created. Frei's Minister of Finance contributed to this operation with a speech which called up in the public mind the image of a crisis flying out of control, despite all the efforts of the government to contain it.[4] Furthermore, according to evidence brought out later by the U.S. Senate itself, United States government agencies and some multinational corporations acted in concert with Chilean groups to activate the crisis.[5]

The third major anti-UP operation came two days before the proclamation of the National Congress, when it appeared that the previous efforts had failed. The Army commander-in-chief, General René Schneider, was assassinated. Schneider was considered by the extreme Right and the Nixon administration as a military professional of constitutionalist leanings, an opponent of those attempting to launch a coup prior to Allende's assumption of the presidency.[6] Meanwhile the UP and the Christian Democratic Party had arrived at a compromise agreement which assured that normal institutional procedures would be followed. This consisted in an amendment to the Constitution which specified a set of "constitutional guarantees," establishing additional rules, norms and procedures to insure that this document would be respected. This formula permitted the conciliation of divergent points of view within the Christian Democratic Party and was accepted by the UP. However, the political events already set in motion had seriously affected the functioning of the economic system.

Economic Impact of the Election

Allende's victory had barely registered when two economic trends struck with particular force: a sharp rise in the preference for cash and a sudden drop in construction and the demand for nonessential goods. Both phenomena began spontaneously among high-income social groups, but later both were stimulated deliberately by the anti-UP forces.

Pressures on the banks followed immediately. Demand for cash grew and deposits diminished. In just two weeks the volume of cash in hand in the private sector jumped by 35 percent.[7] The Banco Central was forced to transfer large sums to the commercial banks in order to meet this demand and avoid a collapse of the banking system. Similar pressures and transfers occurred with the savings and loan associations. Money was printed in enormous lots to deal with this demand, and purchases of foreign currency increased. The Central Bank had to take measures to limit remittances of profit and interest payments.[8]

The panic of the first few days appeared chiefly in Santiago, and only moderately in the provinces. Furthermore, the withdrawal of savings deposits was much more evident in the accounts of middle- and upper-income groups (savings and loan associations) than among low-income groups (Banco del Estado). Thus it was the upper-income groups who reacted most intensely.

The second phenomenon—drop in demand and suspension of private construction activity—went on through the first few months of 1971. The demand for durable consumer goods dropped much more sharply than the demand for everyday consumer items.[9] The Sociedad de Fomento Fabril, an association of industrial entrepreneurs, undertook a survey of 30 firms during the second week of September which revealed that sales had fallen 61 percent since the first week of the month before. Sales in electrical and metal products were off by 85 percent, while food sales were down only 7 percent. A later survey, covering the entire month of September, showed that total sales with respect to March 1970 had decreased by 22 percent—food sales dropped 2 percent, shoes and apparel 14.6 percent, and other categories 30 percent. Hardest hit sectors had been durable consumer goods and construction materials.[10]

In the construction industry, the contraction caused an immediate rise in unemployment. The sharp decline in sales did not have the same immediate effect on the level of activity in manufacturing. Nevertheless, inventories swelled, firms cut back in their purchases of primary materials, and some were forced to suspend payment on outstanding accounts, thus aggravating the financial crisis.

Another survey of eleven firms engaged in producing construction materials showed a 52 percent reduction in sales from March to September 1970, and an increase of 53 percent in inventories. Construction firms, linked directly to the National Savings and Loan System (SINAP), laid off 15 percent of their workers in September. The decrease in sales produced a very difficult cash-flow situation, and these firms encountered considerable difficulty in meeting their payrolls.

Yet another aspect of the post-electoral economic crisis was apparent on the Santiago Stock Market. The price index for stocks fell from 135 to 71 in the course of the month of September and stuck at this level in October.[11]

All of these observations show that the crisis originated among upper-income groups. The bank run, the drop in stock values, the decline in purchases of autos and other durable consumer goods, and the paralysis of private construction activity all derived from a reaction in part spontaneous, in part deliberately stimulated, on the part of wealthy Chileans. The majority of the country, made up of salaried employees and wage workers, did not change its behavior.

Faced with the magnitude of these events, the outgoing government was obliged to take measures to stimulate the economy, in order to sustain production and employment until November 1970, when the new president was to take office. For the UP it was essential that the Christian Democrats guarantee political normality up till this date, and this would require a degree of economic stability. Accordingly, the UP proposed a series of measures to the Frei government: expanding the amount of credits scheduled for September, especially for the most severely affected firms; facilitating the transfer of funds to the Banco del Estado and to government agencies and state-run enterprises in order to pay salaries and settle bills; allotting more resources to savings associations to finance housing. Certainly, these measures would have altered the fiscal and monetary program of the outgoing government. Not surprisingly the latter resisted a change in policy and reacted slowly to the situation.

A conflict between the UP's team of economists and the Frei government developed over the necessary volume of credit expansion. The group in power was reluctant to increase credit dramatically, arguing that this would not reactivate demand, which was the heart of the problem, but would instead only provoke greater inflationary pressures. This reasoning, correct under normal conditions, lost validity once the preference for liquidity had asserted itself. If credit was not expanded at this point, the crisis would sharpen, since the behavior of the affected groups, rather than settling down to normal, could become even more distorted. The argument of the Frei government, attributing the drop in demand to the election of Allende, left no way out and only fortified those rightist sectors determined to impede the transfer of power. The UP insisted on its position; and after a brief delay the Frei government proceeded to expand credits in appreciable volumes. Thus a final rupture was effected with the financial program sustained during the whole of the Frei period and especially throughout 1970. At this same point the economy fell into a recession which produced an abrupt jump in unemployment.

These events revealed that the mere perception of the possibility of structural changes gave rise to modifications in conduct which altered the functioning of the economic system. In such circumstances it proved difficult to carry out financial policy independently of the political situation. The experience of these two months in Chile demonstrates the need to take account of novel patterns of behavior of diverse social groups. Prediction of such conduct is central in the design of economic policy during a stage of transformation. Because of the lack of such foresight in Chile, the Allende government failed to cope effectively with abrupt swings in underlying economic behavior that frustrated many of its policy initiatives.

The economic situation confronting Allende upon his assumption of office revealed the following tendencies:

1. The Chilean economy had grown slowly during the previous five years.
2. In 1969 and 1970 idle capacity in industry increased, along with unemployment. These tendencies were accentuated by the post-electoral crisis.
3. On top of an already high rate of inflation in the first semester of 1970

came the strong expansion in public spending and in credits designed to relieve the post-electoral crisis. This swelling supply of money could later generate even greater inflationary pressures if it was not contracted as soon as the liquidity preference dropped to normal levels.

4. Labor turmoil continued throughout the post-electoral period. There were strikes and seizures of estates. The UP government would have to confront the demands of very large groups for pay increases, groups which saw in Allende's triumph the possibility of realizing long-postponed aspirations.

5. Lastly, international reserves were substantial, which allowed a certain leeway; but the price of copper had already begun to drop in August 1970.

Political Parameters of the Economic Program

The most important immediate objective of the government was to broaden its base of popular support and prepare itself for the nationwide municipal elections which would be held in April 1971. This overriding political objective required a policy of immediate reactivation as its economic precondition. Specific policies would be designed to gain support among the poorest groups—inhabitants of the squatter settlements of the large cities, workers and peasants—and also to improve the UP's standing among female voters.[12]

Secondly, it was considered indispensable to win the trust of small and middle businessmen, making clear to them that the government was contemplating changes in property ownership only for the very largest enterprises. It was necessary to isolate the dominant economic groups.

Once these immediate objectives had been attained, the next step would be to begin the nationalization of copper and the large foreign firms, state takeover of industry and banking, and agrarian reform. This was in order to weaken the economic power base of the main adversary: the local big bourgeoisie and the foreign economic interests.

With respect to the basic political aspects, the governing conception was as follows: First an agreement with the Christian Democrats was rejected. It was believed that the economic and political measures would attract the support of an important part of the popular base of the Christian Democratic Party without the necessity of a political accord. Second, with regard to the armed forces, the UP government decided on a general boost in pay scales, a demand which had been pushed with increasing vigor within the military. Furthermore, it was considered wise to involve the armed forces actively in economic development projects, especially those with a clear nationalist or national security content—including the management of the large copper enterprises. Concerning the mass media, a sector which would prove to be crucial in later stages, there existed no clear policy.

Finally, in matters of international relations, the dominant tendency in the government was to avoid secondary hostile actions which might provoke a global confrontation with the U.S. Of course, a conflict of interests was inevitable, and it was assumed that the U.S. government would move against the new regime in Chile.[13]

The government had to prepare for this situation, but it should not encourage it.[14] Relations with Latin American countries would be reinforced despite ideological differences. The government would maintain a neutral attitude toward the countries of Western Europe, avoiding unnecessary friction; and it would seek an active rapprochement with the socialist bloc nations. All of these political considerations had important implications for economic policy.

The Design of Short-Run Economic Policy

The central objective, that of broadening the government's base of support, was pursued through a program of economic reactivation based on income redistribution and an expansion of public spending. Unemployment would be reduced substantially, and at the same time worker's wages would be raised in order to increase consumption. As a consequence of the general rise in public and private demand, it was assumed that the economy would grow at higher rates than in the past.

The basic aim was to increase demand in order to spur the expansion of the productive apparatus. The two principal sources for the necessary corresponding increase in aggregate supply would be idle capacity in the industrial and construction sectors and disposable international reserves, which would begin to grow once copper production was stepped up.

It was estimated that the utilization of idle capacity already in place would allow the industrial sector to grow at a rate in excess of 10 percent during 1971. Even though the available figures were partial and of limited reliability, studies showed that in some activities significant increases could be attained. In addition to these estimates of underlying idle capacity there was a margin of unutilized productive capacity stemming from the post-electoral contraction.

Available international reserves at the mid-point in 1970 exceeded $300 million. This sum would permit higher levels of imports in food and primary materials, which would be in greater demand given the expected industrial expansion. However, it was further assumed that copper production would increase as a result of post-1966 investments, which according to the plans of U.S. companies should begin to bear fruit in 1971. By then production on the order of 900,000 tons was expected, 700,000 of which would be supplied from the largest mines. It was also considered that the increase in the demand for food provoked by the income redistribution could be satisfied in great measure with internal production, thanks to the favorable weather conditions prevailing in 1970 for the crop to be harvested in 1971. In sum it was estimated that the Chilean economy had an appreciable growth potential in the short run, which would permit both the absorption of more labor and the expansion of supply.

In order to stimulate demand, wages would be raised and increases would be effected in public spending for education, health, housing, and public works. Remunerations in the public sector would be readjusted in the same percentage as the rise in the cost of living for 1970. Low-income workers would receive a higher increase. Since inflation in 1971 was expected to be less than in 1970, the readjustment would bring an improvement in real income. Disposable income would grow, moreover, thanks to an increase in family allowances. These criteria were to be applied in the public sector, but they would also be taken as a benchmark for private-sector workers, who negotiated their wages independently.

Since there was considerable margin of growth for supply, it was concluded that the greater demand would not provoke a higher rate of inflation. On the cost side, a severe wage-price control policy would prevent business from passing along pay increases in the form of price boosts. Profits, not prices, would have to bear the burden of increased labor costs. Since sales would increase substantially, however, overall profit for each firm would be affected only slightly, even though the profit per unit would decrease.

The new fiscal spending in education, health, housing, and public works would be added to the greater outflows going to pay increases for public employees. In these conditions, a high fiscal deficit would be inevitable if there were no offsetting increase in revenues. A change in the structure of taxation was not under consideration for the first phase of the government, since it was estimated that the increase in overall economic activity would in itself yield greater revenue intakes. It was also estimated that the Treasury would acquire important additional resources deriving from the profits of those enterprises whose ownership would be assumed by the state. This surplus from the social ownership sector would offset the pressures on monetary expansion arising from the fiscal deficit.

Investment, it was assumed, would respond to the strong increase in demand. Income redistribution would entail higher consumption and enterprises would allot resources to expand production of essential consumer goods and thus satisfy this demand. For its part the state would augment its investment in construction and public works, and the state-run enterprises would implement new investment programs. It was understood, however, that this was a variable extremely sensitive to political changes. In order to forestall a drop in private investment the state would have to assume new powers, which would demand in turn state takeover of the large firms and banks.

The Policy of Structural Transformations

Even when recessive conditions at the end of 1970 called for an emphasis on economic reactivation, it was agreed to carry out an immediate socialization of private firms and banks and to move ahead with agrarian reform. There was initially some debate concerning the most effective combination of reactivation and structural reform measures. On the one hand, it was necessary to stimulate the economy in order to buttress the government's political and economic position before beginning the change in property ownership of the strategic firms. Without immediate reactivation, the post-electoral economic crisis might worsen. On the other hand, substantive reform measures could not be postponed, since the government would have to take advantage of the high degree of initial consensus.

The legal procedures to be employed in winning the objectives of the UP program were to be, to a large extent, improvised. There was no detailed definition set out in advance, except in certain areas. For the nationalization of copper, for example, it was agreed that a constitutional reform would be presented to Congress during the first year of the government. There was no fixed position concerning compensation. Even though the preliminary criterion was to pay as little as possible, this was considered a secondary aspect, a tactical question which would be settled at the proper moment.

The agrarian reform would be accelerated. Initially, it was thought best to propose a new law to Congress, but later it was agreed to operate with the existing law, approved during the previous administration. The goal was the expropriation over the presidential period (six years) of all estates defined as latifundia by the law.

The Program referred specifically to the expropriation of mining companies—iron, coal and nitrates. The expropriation of banking was also called for explicitly. In the industrial and commercial sector, by contrast, references were extremely general. There was no list of industrial enterprises to be transferred to state ownership. Neither the procedures to be followed nor the forms of compensation were defined precisely. These problems, it was established, would be worked out in the light of circumstances and would be left to ministerial initiative.

The state-run enterprises which would make up the social property area would have to become dominant in order to reorient production and investment. With this purpose in mind it was decided to introduce production guideline agreements between the state and private firms according to which the state would commit itself to a schedule of purchases of goods at a fixed price, thus providing for stability in sales.

It was considered essential to establish a policy favoring small and middle-level entrepreneurs in order that their activity could continue normally. The government would support them with credits, concede some tax advantages and prepare a Statute on Private Investment that would define the rules of the game applicable in this sector.

Foreign trade would be placed under state control in order to oversee capital movements, exports and imports more effectively. This goal would be attained through the expropriation of the large exporting firms, especially in mining. Imports, because of their diversified character, were more difficult to control. Direct government action would be concentrated in a few restricted areas. Many items of secondary importance could continue to be imported directly by the private sector, and regulation of this trade would be effected through the already established mechanism of the Banco Central.

Finally the whole process would have to be based on the active participation of the workers. There was general agreement to promote participation at every level: at the national level, at the regional level and in each unit of work. With respect to specific modalities no single position predominated. Certain sectors of the UP argued for a centralized scheme, which would allow the government to exercise more direct control. Other groups favored formulas conceding greater autonomy to grassroots initiatives. These were the guiding principles. Behind them one central problem was controlling: how to articulate a short-term economic policy simultaneously with measures implementing structural change, all within a democratic framework.

Traditional planning methods were of little assistance in this task. Their normative character was out of place in an accelerated process of transformation, where circumstances were changing rapidly. The theoretical assumptions of planning excluded political considerations and took structural stability as given. In Chile, by contrast, the critical problem areas for policymakers were the interaction between short-term economic policy and changes in property ownership and the decisive effect of political objectives on economic policy. As will be seen in the following pages, the failure of the government planners to come to grips with these problems meant that there was no coherent programming for this crucial period of transition.

Changes in Property Ownership in 1971

By the end of 1971, the large copper-mining firms had already been nationalized. As early as July, Congress approved unanimously a constitutional amendment which instituted the nationalization of copper. Within three months the president had set a figure for excess profits which would be deducted from the book value of the firms in order to arrive at the indemnification payment. The outcome was zero compensation for the subsidiaries of Kennecott and Anaconda, the two largest multinationals operating in Chile.

The large foreign-owned corporations producing iron, nitrates and coal were acquired by the state in 1971. Thus the basic extractive activities (petroleum had always been controlled by the state) came to be administered as a national trust. As a consequence the country acquired control of its basic export industries. The agrarian reform intensified, resulting in the expropriation during one year of a number of estates equal to all those expropriated during the entire term of the previous government. The pace of expropriations exceeded what had been scheduled. In mid-1971 a goal of 1000 new properties subject to expropriation was set. The number of estates actually expropriated came to 1379.

Expropriation of the banking industry also progressed quickly. Foreign banks were acquired by the state in the first half of 1971. At the same time, the state began purchasing the stock of private national banks. Of a total of 23 national banks the state attained a majority share in eleven, through which direct control over almost 90 percent of the total credits was established.[15] In sum, in three strategic sectors of the economy (minerals, agriculture and banking), goals were either close to realization or had been practically fulfilled by the end of 1971.

In manufacturing and commerce, important progress had also been achieved. In the first area, the state established definitive or provisional control over 68 private firms. The result was that, including private enterprises, 20 of the largest 23 manufacturing enterprises were in the hands of the state by the end of the first year of the government. State presence grew chiefly in the metal products sector, in construction materials and in the textile industry.

The largest distributors and wholesalers of consumer goods and construction materials had already been acquired by the first half of 1971. In their place the state set up a series of distributing agencies which would later play a fundamental role when market instability became more intense.

State takeover of foreign trade was effected by means of the nationalizations already noted and by the centralization of imports of food and primary materials for those enterprises which had been appended to the public sector.

Finally, workers' participation was stimulated by two principal measures: the creation of sectoral, regional and national organizations directly installed by the government, and the establishment of participatory norms agreed upon by representatives of the workers and the government, at the level of factories, mines and agrarian settlements. The first of these measures operated by decree and sought to include workers in policymaking discussions. This was undertaken in the National Council of Development, the Mining Councils, Peasants' Councils, Local Health Councils, and Supply and Price Directories. The second measure was implemented through the so-called Basic Norms for Participation drawn up by a commission which included representatives from the government and the CUT (the central labor council, to which most of the unions in Chile belonged). The results were more promising in the second case, since there the workers' participation was directed to the solution of concrete problems. By the end of 1971, some form of workers' participation had been established in 105 of a total of 125 firms surveyed in the public and mixed sectors.

Within private firms, the UP parties and the CUT sponsored the so-called Vigilance Committees in order to prevent irregularities. This was necessary because, faced with the uncertainty stemming from the socialization process, many firms suspended maintenance work, reduced the purchase of spare parts, and began to sell without proper billing in order to avoid paying taxes and to increase their liquidity. These practices had to be held to a minimum.

The Allende government accorded high priority to changes in property ownership. This commitment was reinforced from below by a popular mobilization which pushed for yet more radical change. The results were spectacular, even compared with other socialist transition experiences. Nevertheless, this emphasis on the transfer of ownership entailed two other consequences. In the first place it was not accompanied by a comparable advance in the administration of nationalized enterprises, which in fact declined in management quality. In the second place, short-term economic policy remained strictly subordinated to the structural goals, so that fundamental financial balances were neglected. Both consequences would manifest themselves in subsequent periods.

Economic Results

In addition to the important changes in property ownership, certain other positive economic advances were realized during the first year of the government:

1. Gross Domestic Product in 1971 grew by 7.7 percent, an unprecedented increase.[16] All of the sectors of the economy rebounded, especially industry.
2. The unemployment rate fell steadily over the course of the first year. In Greater Santiago it dropped from 8.3 percent in December 1970 to 3.8 percent in December 1971.[17]
3. The inflationary surge was blunted, the rate of increase declining from 34.9 percent in the period January–December 1970 to 22 percent over the same period in 1971.[18]
4. Income redistribution generated a substantial increase in the pay of the workers, peasants and salaried employees. The share of wage workers in national income went from 52.8 percent in 1970 to 61.7 percent in 1971.[19]

But together with these encouraging results, another series of indicators pointed to the existence of negative factors, the repercussions of which would be felt later. The expansion of consumption considerably exceeded growth in production. The fiscal deficit was greater than expected. The quantity of money held by the private sector increased by 119 percent over the year from December 1970 to December 1971. In the course of the year, the deficit in the balance of payments reached $341 million, producing a sharp drop in international reserves.[20] The country was increasingly losing its ability to make purchases in foreign markets.

Two contradictory perceptions emerged within the government. On the one hand, the advances achieved encouraged an even more intensive pursuit of the same policy; on the other, the financial imbalances provoked a certain disquiet. Nevertheless, even this early sense of alarm was very diffuse and did not reflect the magnitude of the accumulated imbalances and their potential for even greater disruption.

At the highest level of the UP, the economic forecast was not received with much concern. The underlying economic weaknesses caused concern only when they became manifested politically, as occurred with the "march of the empty saucepans," analyzed in the next section. In reality the financial imbalances had become unusually severe and their full significance was not understood. With historical hindsight it can now be established that the year 1971 was decisive and that the economic policy pursued in the first year generated consequences which considerably restricted the margin for action later.

Evolution of the Political Situation

In 1971, the government achieved its aim of increasing popular support. In the April municipal elections, the UP won 50 percent of the vote, and in subsequent elections the balance of power at the ballot box stayed at the same level. Many among the peasant and urban marginal groups who formerly had leaned toward the Christian Democrats switched their support to the UP. During this period the government maintained the initiative and faced a divided opposition. This fact boosted the confidence of the UP, but it also encouraged among its most radical factions the illusion of having within their grasp a decisive, almost undeniable power.

The dominant groups had lost a certain amount of their economic power as a result of the expropriations. This did not, however, mean a reduction in their political power over the short run. Smaller businessmen maintained a cautious attitude, one of apparent equanimity. Their profits increased as a consequence of the government's intensively expansionist economic policy; but the process of state expropriation had aroused a certain distrust in these circles.

Among the higher officials and employees in the public administration a dual reaction was evident. Pay increases satisfied their immediate interests; but the overbearing attitude of the UP party politicians, who frequently engineered demotions of middle-grade officers, provoked resentment in the bureaucracy. The spread of this "sectarian" climate disturbed more and more of those functionaries who were not partisans of the governing coalition.

The agrarian reform generated reactions of varying intensity. Landlords in the central zone, already weakened by the process initiated in 1966, offered scant resistance. In the southern area, by constrast, a more vigorous opposition to the agrarian reform emerged. In this region owners held medium-sized properties; and, unlike the traditional landlords, they themselves worked on their estates. These owners also exerted great ideological influence over the provincial middle class.

Behind the apparent weakness of the opposition, a new coalition was gestating, one clearly dominated by the Right. The National Party, conscious of its weakness, proposed an immediate entente with the Christian Democrats, an agreement which the latter accepted in practice. As a consequence the political picture shifted from a three-cornered balance of forces to a bipolar confrontation. The Right and the Christian Democrats were shaping a more and more homogeneous bloc. Over the course of 1971, the initial attempts on the part of the progressive wing of the CDP to arrange an opening towards the UP were totally frustated by the conservative Christian Democrats, opposed to any accord with the government forces. The hostile attitude of those UP parties which had already chosen to dispense with such agreements effectively eliminated the possibility of a tacit alliance among the progressive political tendencies in the country. The emerging bipolarization only served to sap the institutional framework of its flexibility, rigidifying it and contributing to later tensions. Meanwhile conservative economic and political interests promoted the organization and mobilization of the "gremios" groups of small businessmen, storekeepers, public employees, doctors, lawyers and technicians. These associations, financed by the Right, served as extraparliamentary pressure groups and as a major vehicle for an ever-growing anti-government ideological compaign.

This campaign denounced the presumed threats of the UP against the property, status and lifestyle of the middle class. It also seized on the breakdowns in the market which began to appear in mid-1971, turning them to great political advantage in the campaign against the government. Agitation over these issues culminated in the first mass movement of the Right in November 1971. The "march of the empty saucepans" activated and channeled the discontent of middle-class women over the supposed scarcity of consumer goods. It was the first time that these hitherto passive and unorganized groups had been mobilized. The march was a striking example of the political problems which the new rightist strategy would pose, and it demonstrated how economic maladjustments would be used to mobilize discontent against the government.

While this sharp social conflict was flaring, the armed forces demonstrated an apparent normality. The government had granted them important salary adjustments; it satisfied other institutional demands; and it appointed some high-ranking officers to important positions in state enterprises and agencies. Nonetheless, the popular mobilization, increasing demands for participation and the general social unrest produced a certain unease in military circles. Some spontaneous grassroots actions, incited by sectors of the extreme Left, led the military authorities to express their discontent directly to the president. The Right, of course, inflated these spontaneous actions in their propaganda, hoping to generate even more alarm.

One of the principal instruments used to this end was the rightist domination of important communications media. The UP parties gained control of some radio stations, newspapers and magazines in order to publicize its viewpoints and mobilize popular consciousness. But these media were operated without coordination or direction and did a poorer job than those of the Right in persuading and influencing public opinion. The opposition operated organically, thanks to the control exercised by one or two large firms which owned chains of newspapers. Its media campaign also benefited from better technical skills, some of them supplied by U.S. intelligence services.[21]

Finally, in the international field, Chile achieved in great measure what it had set out to do. Relations with Latin American countries were managed apart from ideological differences. The ties with Western Europe did not deteriorate, while relations with the socialist bloc countries warmed. Dealings with the United States had not led to open conflict, despite the nationalization of copper. But the decision to deduct for excess profits, leaving the two largest firms (Kennecott and Anaconda) without compensation, was raised as a pretext by the U.S. government to justify publicly its opposition to the Allende government and to obstruct access to external financing.

In sum the political position of the UP was strengthened during 1971, reaching its highest point in the three years of the Allende government. Nevertheless, just as on the economic front, grave tensions began to appear: internally, the opposition had polarized and solidified; and in the international field the United States was deploying increasingly active interventionist efforts. The financial imbalances and political tensions accumulated in this first year seriously conditioned subsequent events. By the end of 1971, the process had reached a critical point; the viability of the UP's project would henceforth diminish steadily.

Notes

1. In 1969, public spending for construction was cut back sharply. The total area under construction with public sector financing diminished from 1.85 million square meters in 1968 to 0.99 million in 1969, a decrease of 46 percent. Total construction for these two years came to 3.84 and 2.80 million square meters, respectively. Data from the Cámara Chilena de la Construcción. "La Coyuntura postelectoral," *Panorama Económico* (November 1970).

2. Figures from the Instituto de Economía y Planificación, University of Chile, in Banco Central, *Boletín Mensual* (March 1971).

3. According to the Constitution a president could not be elected to succeed himself, but in this case Frei could put himself forward as a candidate, since Alessandri would have served as president for a few days.

4. Minister A. Zaldivar, September 23, 1970. Reported in *El Mercurio* (September 24, 1970).

5. According to testimony given before the U.S. Senate by Mr. Broe of the CIA, an agreement was reached at a meeting on September 29, 1970 with Mr. Garrity of ITT on a plan "to accelerate economic chaos in Chile as a means of putting pressure on the Christian Democratic members of parliament to vote against Allende. . . ." Suggestions included having banks suspend or delay the transfer of credits, and applying pressures on savings and loans associations to force their closure. See United States Senate, *The International Telephone Co. and Chile, 1970–1971*, Report to the Committee on Foreign Relations (Washington, D.C.: U.S. Government Printing Office, 1973). Nixon himself, replying to the U.S. Congress, declared: "I was greatly concerned that Mr. Allende's presence in that office would directly and adversely affect the security interest of the U.S. . . . Therefore, I instructed Mr. Helms that the CIA should proceed covertly. I further instructed Mr. Helms and Dr. Kissinger that any action which the U.S. could take which might have an impact on the Chilean economy—such as terminating all foreign aid to Chile—should be taken as an additional step in preventing Mr. Allende from becoming President of Chile." *New York Times* (March 12, 1976), p. 14.

6. Some Army officers and rightist elements were found guilty of this crime by the Chilean military justice system itself. Later, hearings conducted by the U.S. Senate pointed to the active involvement of the U.S. government and its intelligence services. These hearings confirmed that the U.S. government made a decision to

provoke a coup d'état. "On September 15, President Richard Nixon informed CIA Director Richard Helms that an Allende regime would not be acceptable to the U.S. The CIA was instructed by President Nixon to play a direct role in organizing a coup d'état to prevent Allende's accession to the Presidency." See United States Senate, *Alleged Assassination Plots Involving Foreign Leaders,* an Interim Report of the Select Committee to Study Governmental Operations with respect to Intelligence Activities (Washington, D.C.: U.S. Government Printing Office, 1975), pp. 225, 227.

7. The quantity of paper currency and coins in circulation in the private sector rose from 3,092.8 million escudos to 4,195 million between August 31 and September 15, 1970. Banco Central, *Boletín Mensual* (January 1971).

8. Frei's finance minister, in the speech cited above, maintained that capital flight had occurred. Moreover, he pointed out that regular foreign credit lines for many private firms had been suspended. Thus the restrictive measures which were intensified under the Allende government appeared in the earliest days of the transition period. Two months later, Allende's finance minister, A. Zorrilla, stated in his report to the Congress on the state of public finances that the monthly average of dollars acquired for travel climbed from 5.3 million in 1970 (and 1.8 million in 1969) to 17.5 million in September 1970.

9. According to information presented by Frei's finance minister in his speech of September 23, food sales had remained steady; sales of shoes and apparel were off by 30 percent and auto sales fell from 650 to 180 vehicles—a drop of 75 percent. *El Mercurio* (September 24, 1970).

10. "La coyuntura postelectoral," *Panorama Económico* (November 1970).

11. "La coyuntura postelectoral."

12. The Left in Chile always received a lower vote among women than among men. In the presidential elections of 1970, Allende received less than 30 percent of the female vote.

13. "It was perfectly clear in the circles that designed and carried out international policy [in the UP government] . . . that the hostility of the U.S. was predetermined, dictated by deep political interests. But it was also clear that so long as our country maintained a reasonable, nonprovocative policy, this would neutralize not just the threat of armed U.S. intervention against us, but also the successful staging of a formal and declared blockade either financial or commercial, similar to that imposed on Cuba." See C. Almeyda, "La política international del Gobierno de la Unidad Popular," paper presented at the seminar on "Development and the International System: The Case of Chile, 1970–1973" (La Haya: Institute of Social Studies, 1976).

14. Despite the careful position adopted by the Chilean government, the U.S. government had already formulated an explicitly antagonistic line within a few days of the elections. On September 16, 1970, in a press report, Kissinger stated: "Now, it is fairly easy for one to predict that if Allende wins, there is a good chance that he will establish over a period of years some sort of communist government . . . So I don't think we should delude ourselves that an Allende takeover in Chile would not present massive problems for us and for democratic and pro-U.S. forces in Latin America and indeed in the whole Western Hemisphere." This statement was made one day after a meeting called by President Nixon, with Kissinger and the CIA Director in attendance, ordering the formulation of a plan to prevent Allende's taking office. United States Senate, *Multinational Corporations and U.S. Foreign Policy,* Hearings before the Subcommitee on Multinational Corporations of the Committee on Foreign Relations (Washington, D.C.: U.S. Government Printing Office, 1973), pp. 542–543. See also R. Fagen, "The United States and Chile: Roots and Branches," *Foreign Affairs* (May 1975).

15. Instituto de Economía, "La economía chilena en 1971. Perspectivas para 1972" (Santiago: Catholic University of Chile, 1972), p. 11.
16. This rate refers to the Gross Domestic Product. For the years 1967 through 1970, the percentage growth was 2.4, 3.0, 3.5 and 3.6, respectively. Odeplan, *Cuentas nacionales de Chile, 1965–1973* (Santiago, 1976).
17. Instituto de Economía y Planificación, *La economía chilena en 1971* (Santiago: University of Chile, 1972), p. 237.
18. Instituto National de Estadísticas, *Consumer Price Index.*
19. International Monetary Fund (May 25, 1976), p. 58.
20. Data from the Banco Central, cited in World Bank (October 1974), Vol. 3, Table 3-1.
21. The chain of newspapers belonging to *El Mercurio,* for example, included three of the five opposition dailies in Santiago. Concerning U.S. financial assistance, the evidence is abundant. U.S. Senate hearings have demonstrated CIA intervention in news reporting in Chile and financial contributions to *El Mercurio.* "The CIA spent $1.5 million in support of *El Mercurio,* the country's largest newspaper and the most important channel for anti-Allende propaganda. . . . The CIA developed material for placement in the *El Mercurio* chain, opposition party newspapers, two weekly newspapers, all radio stations controlled by opposition parties, and on several regular shows on three channels." United States Senate, *Covert Action in Chile 1963–1973,* Staff Report of the Select Committee to Study Governmental Operations with Respect to Intelligence Activities (Washington, D.C.: U.S. Government Printing Office, 1975), p. 29.

CHAPTER 4

Causes of the 1971 Outcomes

The first year of the new administration was so important in the history of the Unidad Popular that in this chapter we are obliged to attempt an exhaustive analysis of the developments. Let us begin with a look at the balance between supply and aggregate demand. Gross Domestic Product grew 7.7 percent, largely in response to the strong expansive measures. All sectors surged strongly. Manufacturing expanded by 13.7 percent; agriculture, forests and fisheries by 6.7 percent; construction by 11.4 percent; and mining by 2 percent.[1] Internal supply was even greater due to both the use of existing stocks and the increase in imports. Personal consumption expanded by 11.6 percent and government consumption by 9.3 percent, while fixed capital investments stayed practically constant (see Table 4-1).

By the second half of 1971, Chile had put its entire productive capacity to work. Despite this effort nominal demand had grown even faster than supply, exceeding available productive capacity. Consequently, the main disequilibrating factor proved to be the strong expansion in overall demand. Disposable personal income went up 49.8 percent in 1971 with respect to the previous year.[2] Prices advanced by 20.1 percent in the same period, leaving an increase in real disposable income of almost 30 percent. No economy in the world could have undergone such a breakneck expansion without suffering significant maladjustments.

Fiscal spending climbed sharply as well, in order to cover the pay increases for public employees and to underwrite greater activity in the areas of health, education, housing and public works. The pay hikes exceeded those planned by the government, which were in themselves ambitious. At the end of 1971, available data showed that remunerations in the public sector had gone up on the average by 40 percent instead of the 35 percent originally scheduled. Incomes below the official minimum, which were supposed to be increased by 39.3 percent, actually climbed 55.4 percent.

In the private sector government policies were not compulsory and served only as guidelines for negotiations between workers and owners. But here the expansive tendencies were even greater. By October 1971 the index of salaries

TABLE 4-1.   Chile: Aggregate Demand and Supply
             (in billions of 1965 escudos)

	1970	1971	Rate of Growth (%)
Aggregate Domestic Demand	23.23	25.29	8.9
Government consumption	2.59	2.83	9.3
Personal consumption	16.77	18.71	11.6
Fixed capital formation	3.41	3.45	1.2
Changes in stocks	0.46	0.30	-34.8
Supply	23.23	25.29	8.9
Gross Domestic Product	22.70	24.44	7.7
Imports of goods and services	3.65	3.82	4.7
Exports of goods and services	3.12	2.97	-4.8

Source: IMF, May 25, 1976, p. 32, Table II.

and wages had shot up 52 percent over the corresponding figure the year before. Family allowances, pensions and other fringe benefits had gone up even more. These increases in remunerations and in public spending led to a series of disarticulations in the market and the financial system.

The Fiscal and Monetary Situation

The augmented expenditures on wages and salaries, fringe benefits, and transfers to the public sector generated a sizable fiscal deficit. The increase in fiscal spending (72.5 percent) exceeded that in current revenues (29.1 percent), giving rise to a current account deficit. Counting capital expenditures, the total deficit amounted to 30.9 percent of total disbursements, an unprecedented figure.

Upon analysis it is clear that the most important factor in this deficit was the expansion of current expenditures, which went up 72.5 percent, while capital spending grew by only 36.1 percent. In absolute terms the increment in current expenditures was 11.1 billion escudos, while the increment in capital spending amounted to 2.8 billion. The three determining factors in this explosion in current expenditures were salaries and wages, social security and transfers to the public sector. Together these items accounted for 87.4 percent of the increase. Furthermore, current revenues grew only slightly and income from direct taxes actually dropped in real terms. This was due in part to the decline in tax payments from copper.[3] Fiscal revenues in national currency remained stagnant as well. The latter could have been increased through the implementation of a tax reform, but the Allende government failed to propose such a measure at the very beginning of its administration, which would have been the most opportune moment. In any case Congress was reluctant to consider even minor changes in existing taxation policies.

The government's efforts to link wage increases to new taxes on capital or on nonessential consumer goods were blocked in Congress. Thus the government had to support strong pressures on fiscal spending while its income remained stagnant. At the same time the jump in salaries and wages and the strict controls on prices caused enterprises in the social property area to suffer a sharp drop in profits. By the end of the year many of these enterprises were in the red. This dashed the earlier hopes that surpluses from this area would constitute another source of fiscal revenue.

The government deficit propelled a strong monetary expansion, the bulk of which derived from credits granted by the banking system to the Treasury and to public enterprises and agencies. Between December 1970 and December 1971 the money supply grew by 113.6 percent.

The initial predictions of the government proved mistaken here as well. Original estimates of the expansion in money supply, while they were greater than the combined effect of the price increases and the growth in production, were far below the expansion that had actually occurred by the end of the year.

This disequilibrium between aggregate supply and demand and the consequent monetary impact generated fierce political debate and favored the opposition. One segment of the opposition viewed the situation as proof of the technical incapacity of the UP government and its carelessness concerning financial affairs. Another, more reactionary group argued that the financial chaos was the result of a deliberate policy designed to destroy the economy to facilitate a later move to seize total control of the private sector through the state apparatus.

The emerging situation gave rise to intense discussions in government circles. But the initial necessity to reactivate the economy and the apparent success of the first few months inhibited criticism from within the UP. Since much of this criticism included assertions similar to those advanced by the opposition, it was dismissed as "technocratic" and rejected in the same terms as were the arguments of anti-government criticis. Only the political manifestations of economic disturbances towards the end of 1971 made possible a serious discussion of the underlying issues within UP.

The evidence is clear that severe fiscal and monetary disequilibria had already emerged by the end of 1971. Several questions must now be considered: Were these imbalances avoidable or were they inherent to the central project of the UP, transforming the very structure of the economy? Were the disturbances a consequence of the particular economic policy employed or were they caused by changes in the economic behavior of certain social groups? Finally, could the government be blamed for a failure of political or economic leadership?

Causes of the Initial Imbalances

The underlying conception of the original economic policy was coherent at a global level. Its basically Keynesian design did not depart radically from previous experiences in Chile, including that of the Frei government's first year (1965). The distinguishing features of UP policy consisted in the intensity and orientation of the expansive and redistributive measures. The UP planned larger wage increases and a higher level of fiscal deficit than in 1965. Policy orientations differed inasmuch as the UP aimed to increase the incomes of the poorest groups most and to extend services in health, education and housing.

Despite these differences in intensity and orientation there was no reason that Allende's policy should have given rise to the disequilibrium that emerged in the second half of 1971. The economy could in fact have grown over the short run and satisfied the additional demand. Any discrepancy stemming from the redistribution of income, between the composition of supply and the new pattern of demand could have been resolved through increased imports, financed ultimately by existing international reserves. The actual outcome, however, was far from this expectation.

The program of the Left paid scant attention to the design of short-term policies. Its emphasis was always on structural transformations, its perspective always long-run. For the highest leadership of the coalition, moreover, economic management remained a technical matter, to which they paid little attention. Economic considerations were delegated to others, with the understanding that they had to be subordinated to the overriding necessity of expanding the base of popular support. The economic program was not sufficiently elaborated, not subject to much discussion, and never solidified into a consistent and quantified plan.

The post-electoral events introduced new variables that complicated any attempt to achieve a more coherent approach. The government rapidly set about the tasks of income redistribution and economic reactivation, but it failed to impose a rigorous frame of reference. It did not establish critical thresholds, quantified indices which could function as warning signals when certain crucial limits were about to be surpassed.

A more coherent approach did not necessarily entail fixing strict numerical parameters. Such a rigid program could not have functioned in a situation where radical transformations were provoking changes in the underlying economic behavior of large social sectors. A flexible approach was called for, one capable of detecting the abrupt shifts in the political and economic system, and capable as well of generating a quick policy response. This kind of adaptability demanded efficient execution in several steps, including quick collection of information, rapid analysis in order to specify the necessary adjustments, and an administrative capacity sufficient to implement the new measures. The actual performance of the government, however, revealed serious deficiencies in all three stages of policy execution.

Information Lags and Tardy Countermeasures

Deficiencies in the gathering of data retarded the application of corrective measures. This weakness was especially damaging because any system, like Chile in 1971, that is experiencing abrupt changes will undergo a change in its ordinary reactions. Under normal conditions, for example, increases in wages and salaries and in public spending should have brought about a quick recovery in the economy. In the Chilean case, however, despite the strong expansive measures adopted in January 1971 with the intention of influencing the outcome of the April municipal elections, symptoms of recovery by the date of the election were minimal.

In fact, by April 1971, the industrial sector had only slightly augmented its production; private construction activity remained depressed; the public sector had not yet undertaken major construction projects; and the unemployment rate was still high. The only figures on unemployment in Greater Santiago available in March were those from December, which showed an 8.3 percent jobless rate. Data on industrial production available in April reflected activity in January. In September, five months after the April elections, the government was surprised that the recovery was still so sluggish, despite the fact that the quantity of money had doubled since September 1970. During the period from January to August 1971, new construction projects in the public sector had been initiated which were 700 percent greater in extent than those of the same period in the previous year. At the same time, however, private sector construction diminished considerably, and it was difficult to grasp the net effect on total activity. Available indicators on the level of economic activity were obtained only after considerable delay.

It was only at the start of the second half of 1971 that industrial and construction activity began to expand rapidly.[4] The unemployment rate began to fall noticeably in June. The index of unemployment for Greater Santiago registered the following changes: 8.3 percent in December 1970; 8.2 percent in March 1971; 5.2 percent in June; 4.8 percent in September; and 3.8 percent in December.[5] Despite the sustained expansion in money supply, prices rose only slightly, and inflation only became noticeable from November on.

The reactivation program, therefore, had a delayed effect. The combined effect of delays in the gathering of activity indicators and the real lag between the application of the program and the onset of the expected effects explains in part the tardy implementation of corrective measures. Clearly, by the time the indicators suggested improvements in the overall level of activity, the underlying imbalances had already reached alarming levels.

How can we explain the lapse between the first implementation of expansive measures and the onset of real economic recovery? One important fact was the existence of significant inventories accumulated by industry between September 1970 and March 1971. As a result of the decline in sales in the postelectoral period, firms had built up their stocks. The initial increase in consumption was satisfied in part from this stock on hand without an immediate growth in production. In the public works and construction area the state was slow in organizing its new programs, while the private sector failed throughout the whole year to regain its normal level of activity. Secondly, due to the prevailing political climate, middle and upper income groups chose to maintain a high level of liquidity, at least until the direction of events was clear. Furthermore, the inflationary expectations declined due to the government's decision to maintain a close control on prices. This preference for higher liquidity muffled the effects of the expansion of the money supply. Moreover, the liquidity was channeled toward activities which did not affect everyday consumption or impinge on the consumer price index.

Underestimation of the Disequilibrium

While these information lags retarded the implementation of corrective measures, this was no excuse for the inherent incongruency of short-term policy. There was a striking inadequacy in the general analytical framework. If it was thought that production could be made to expand by putting idle capacity to work, then it should also have been possible to estimate the range of increase in public spending compatible with the postulated growth in production and the expected rise in prices. Furthermore, the larger money supply could be kept from stimulating scarcity or inflationary pressures only to the extent that the demand for money changed or its velocity of circulation slowed down. But if money began to circulate more rapidly, strong pressures on prices would necessarily develop. Despite the importance of these monetary considerations, they were not prominent in the thinking of the government's economic staff, which was concerned with the "real" economy. Monetary and financial matters were thought of as secondary factors, as policy instruments subordinated to the attainment of structural transformations.

High government functionaries frequently argued in response to opposition criticism that in the new economic regime the system would function differently, that monetary and fiscal factors would not play the same role as in the past. This observation was in part true, since some of the underlying economic behavior had been modified in the short run. But as soon as behavior returned to normal, the resultant negative effects could only be offset by new measures, requiring greater reserves of power.

The lack of quantified framework impeded the integration of diverse policies into a consistent whole. Thus, to cite an important example, the remunerations policy for 1971 consisted in an upward adjustment equal to the inflation rate in 1970, but it was affirmed simultaneously that this rate would be drastically reduced in 1971. Since the rise in the consumer price index was on the order of 35 percent in 1970 and the readjustments in remunerations and family allowances for 1971 were even higher, the real increase in remunerations would be substantial, not really compatible with the expected expansion in supply. Inflationary pressures would inevitably exceed the government's estimates.

These disparities were also evident at a more specific level. It was believed from the start, on the strength of a survey carried out by the Office of National Planning, that an average of 32 percent of already installed industrial capacity was not in use. From this fact it was concluded that there was substantial room for growth. This conclusion overlooked two important considerations: the dubious meaning of an average value given the marked variation between the different branches of industry, and the fact that the high proportion of imported primary materials which would be absorbed in an expansion would exert great pressures on the balance of payments.

The tendency to underestimate financial phenomena was in part a product of ideological dogmatism. It was argued that centralized physical planning would replace the market mechanism. Once the state controlled a set of key enterprises, it would be easy to install the appropriate administrative regulatory mechanisms. This argument overlooked the degree of complexity of the Chilean economy in the structure of both production and consumption; it also misjudged the prevailing power conditions, which would not allow for total state control. Finally, the abundant contemporary experience of the socialist countries concerning central planning, administrative regulation and the role of prices was largely ignored. The mere fact of changed property ownership in a group of strategic enterprises could not alter the essential character of the Chilean economy over the short run.

Two influences seem to have affected the thinking of the government's economic team. First, there was the bent toward structural analysis, which underplayed the importance of conjunctural phenomena and of day-to-day economic management. Second, there was the Cuban experience. Several UP economists who had worked in Cuba had accustomed themselves to the extensive application of administrative measures and physical planning. But their technical activity in Cuba occurred in political circumstances very different from those in Chile, since the power question had already been resolved in Cuba. The complexity of the Chilean process demanded a meshing of structural analysis with a correct understanding of short-run phenomena.

Weakness in Implementing Decisions

The Chilean institutional apparatus was designed to administer the economic system by means of global regulatory instruments applied with maximum intensity. But the kind of programs undertaken by the government called for more precise mechanisms. For example, when the state assumed control of numerous private firms, it had to participate directly in wage negotiations. It no longer acted as a mediator, but became instead an immediate protagonist. This new function called for an extensive negotiation apparatus, and qualified personnel were scarce.

The redistributive policy entailed more extensive intervention in the process of commercialization in order to control inflationary pressures, the black market and speculation. The transfer of commercial, industrial, banking and mining firms to the public sector also required a renovated and expanded executive organization. These new tasks overloaded the decision-making apparatus, which soon began to waver and stall under the pressure. This phenomenon is inherent in all transformation processes: in periods of accelerated change an imbalance tends to emerge between the variety of situations generated and the capacity of the policymakers to confront and control each one of them.

Maladjustments of this sort were also amplified by political factors. As a coalition of different parties, the UP was marked by internal quarrels acted out at different levels. One divisive issue was the distribution of high public posts among the different parties. The method that was utilized consisted in designating a member of one party as minister, while assigning a member of another party to the position of undersecretary in the same office. Likewise one party would claim the position of vice-president or manager of state-run enterprise, while another party would tap one of its members for the next highest position. In the matter of specific appointments, the influence of each political group was decisive. Parties would frequently furnish several names, so that the head of an office or agency could choose among them; occasionally they would insist on a single nominee.

As a result bureaucratic loyalties became split between the government and the several political parties. This disturbed the decision-making process. Once the lines of authority became blurred, policy measures could not be executed effectively and confusion mounted. In order to by-pass this difficulty, a parallel system of decision-making began to emerge. Its status was occasionally informal, sometimes formalized; it operated by linking several functionaries of the same party background in a given sector.

The determination of the UP to maintain a balance of influences in the state apparatus led to the removal or shunting aside of functionaries who did not share the coalition's ideas, or of those who were sympathizers but lacked the political support of one party or another. As a result technical personnel were underutilized precisely at a moment when more professional skill was required to manage the ever-growing intervention of the state into the economy. Once the ranks of politically trustworthy technicians had been exhausted, there was increasing resort to unsuitable persons of questionable competence to fill important positions. This practice provoked anti-UP sentiment among a growing number of public officials, men who had not originally opposed the goals of the coalition.

Any transformation process demands great dedication, commitment and loyalty from the higher administrative echelons. In fact, many functionaries attempted to obstruct and weaken the government. As a reaction to this, political loyalty became an essential criterion in the selection of executives. Under normal, stable conditions, the everyday work of administration is carried out within a framework of restricted options, which limits the initiatives of high public officials. In periods of structural reform, by contrast, such procedures are upset and it is essential to act quickly and decisively in strategically important matters. This requirement caused political commitment to be over-valued relative to purely technical skill. Without underestimating the impor-tance of political considerations, however, it seems clear that the UP neglected technical functions and obscured the essential distinction between political orientation and policy execution.

In sum the economic leadership of the UP government faced three kinds of problems, each of which contributed to the unsatisfactory aspect of economic developments in the first year: a lag in the perception of the outcomes pro-duced by its policies; deficiences in the analytical framework necessary to foresee economic and political consequences and to articulate corrective mea-sures; and a lack of organizational cohesion in implementing those measures it agreed on.

The Wage Boom

During the first few months of 1971, the expansive economic policy fulfilled its essential purpose, widening the base of popular support for the April municipal elections. Once the electoral victory had been won, a moderation in the pace of expansion was expected. Instead the expansion continued. This continuation can be explained only if it is recalled that the government accelerated the process of structural change after the elections. The social and political struggle began to intensify. In these circumstances the support of the workers was essential. Hence a flexible attitude toward labor demands was adopted in order to eliminate the chance of strikes. This attitude had the political advantage of satisfying labor demands and maintaining the unquestioned support of workers and salaried employees, but it also gave rise to excessive pressures which the Chilean economy was in no condition to absorb in the short run.

The process had unleashed social forces which soon acquired their own momentum, exceeding the plans and intentions of the government. Union organizations were to a large extent autonomous. Their long struggle seemed to be culminating for the first time in the desired victories. For their part the parties of the Left continued their historic political commitment, supporting union demands and drawing workers into the state apparatus. Furthermore, the competition for grassroots ascendancy among the UP parties, and between them and the Christian Democrats, exacerbated the pressures for immediate benefits. As an easy tactic in their competition with the UP, the Christian Democrats began to push demands for pay increases even higher than those scheduled by the government.

These sociopolitical factors were amplified by the heterogeneity of the industrial structure. The coexistence of large and modern firms with small and traditional enterprises meant that the proletariat was composed of sectors with very different income levels.[6] These differentials were a driving force behind the wage demands. Low-income workers seized upon high-income workers as a reference group. The result was a chain reaction of demands for higher wages and more benefits.

This tendency was accentuated by the way in which private enterprises were transferred to the public sector. In several cases, unions came into conflict with owners and occupied the factories. The ensuing paralysis of activity forced the state to assume control and grant the pending demands of the workers. Private owners frequently conceded wage demands without delay, hoping to avoid a struggle that would culminate in state intervention. The government was obliged to make frequent appeals for moderation in wage petitions, and they were joined in this effort by the leadership of the UP parties. But the internal dynamic of the coalition, the permanent struggle with the Christian Democrats, and the Left tradition of union struggle all impeded an effective campaign for moderation.

Was this outcome inevitable, inherent to a transformative process? The forces at play were no doubt difficult for the political leadership to control. But the whole economic policy itself was based on two questionable assumptions: (1) the existence of a positive, mutually reinforcing relationship of redistribution, reactivation and electoral support; and (2) the belief that this electoral support was essential to carry out the structural transformations. Our judgment as to the inevitability of the outcomes of the government's first year depends to a great extent on whether or not these assumptions were valid. We will deal with this central issue below.

The Balance of Payments Situation

Internal conflicts were a determining factor in the deterioration of the economic situation. However the fluctuation in the level of foreign currency reserves also played a relevant role by dampening or intensifying the level of distress in the economy. By the end of 1971, the deficit in the balance of payments was amplifying the internal disequilibria and exerting a negative influence on the whole economic picture.

This situation had not been foreseen at the beginning. The prevailing conditions in 1970 suggested that the balance of payments would remain positive; it was even estimated that the international sector might compensate for strains elsewhere.

Several factors made this a reasonable expectation: the scheduled increases in copper production as a result of the Frei government's expansion plans, forecasts for a good year in agriculture, and the availability of considerable foreign currency reserves. At the same time, of course, other more uncertain factors had to be weighed. The U.S. would oppose the new government's economic program, especially the plan to nationalize copper. This opposition would certainly take the form of restrictions in the granting of credits, a measure the effects of which would certainly be significant, but difficult to estimate in advance. It was supposed, however, that the socialist countries would supply grants to counter any emergency situation. A surge in imports, necessary to meet the new demand stimulated by the programs of expansion and redistribution, had also been foreseen. Despite these advance considerations, the situa-

TABLE 4-2. Balance of Payments, 1970-71
            (millions of dollars)

	1970	1971
Exports	1,135	997
Copper	(862)	(701)
Others	(273)	(296)
Imports	1,001	1,085
Foodstuffs	(168.1)	(259.6)
Other consumer goods	(93.9)	(102.9)
Petroleum	(48.8)	(84.8)
Raw materials and intermediate goods	(395.3)	(390.1)
Capital goods	(294.9)	(248.0)
Trade balance	134	-88
Services and transfers	-203	-201
Current account balance	-69	-289
Capital movements	203	-74
Private	(12)	(-113)
Official	(191)	(39)
Debt relief	---	50
SDR	21	17
Errors and omissions	-64	-3
Overall balance	91	-299

Source: For 1970: IMF, March 1975, p. 38. Table 13; and p. 43, Table
        16. For 1971: IMF, May 1976, p. 87, Table CC; p. 88, Table
        DD; and p. 90, Table FF.

tion at the end of 1971 was radically different from what had been predicted, and the balance of payments showed a striking deficit. What brought about this negative balance?

The analysis must begin with an examination of the figures in Table 4–2. In the first place, a balance of payments surplus of $91 million in 1970 had become a deficit of $279 million by 1971. In other words, the balance of payments suffered a drop of $390 million in two years. This decline was caused, in roughly equal proportions, by both an unfavorable balance of trade and the movement of autonomous capital. In the second place, the deficit in the commercial balance stemmed principally from the drop in the value of exports, and to a lesser extent from the increase in imports.[7] In the third place, 1971 saw a net outflow of private capital and a sharp drop in the inflow of official capital. Why were the initial estimates so far off the mark? To what extent was the new situation due to the economic policy and to what extent to exogenous factors, beyond the control of the government?

The Balance of Trade Deficit

The decline in export revenues was chiefly the result of the fall in the price of copper. Production in this field actually increased from 691,500 to 698,700 metric tons,[8] but this was not enough to offset a decline of 23.5 percent in the value of copper in the world market (from 64.2 cents per pound in 1970 to 49.1 cents per pound in 1971). The drop in export revenues, therefore, was the result of an outside factor, uncontrollable by the Allende government. This variable, moreover, was difficult to anticipate. The price of copper is sensitive to a variety of factors on the international scene, and the short-run behavior of this index has always been difficult to predict. Despite the critical importance of this single product in the functioning of the Chilean economy, the country had never assembled a group of local experts capable of analyzing the copper market and forecasting its behavior. The uncertainty surrounding this key variable contributed to the delay in corrective countermeasures which might have brought other aspects of economic policy into line with the new situation.

In fact the UP government was aware of the situation, but it believed that even without a recovery in the price of copper, increases in production would be sufficient to finance the rise in imports and payments on external debt. Production itself, however, did not expand to the levels planned at the end of 1970.

At the beginning of 1971 another unforeseen factor arose: the production goals of the large copper mines could not be attained. In the two largest mines, Anaconda's Chuquicamata and Kennecott's El Teniente, the investment programs remained unfinished and were marred by numerous technical failures which prevented full utilization of the new facilities. Faced with the prospect of nationalization, the owners of Chuquicamata stepped up the pace of copper extraction, while at the same time they ceased removing spent ore and waste by-products. The development of the mine was adversely affected by this policy of short-run maximization in production, which caused the level of extraction in subsequent months to drop. Some of the new equipment, moreover, proved technically deficient upon installation. Production at Chuquicamata, which according to plan was supposed to reach 300,000 tons in 1971, never exceeded 250,000 tons. An extension of this mine, called Exótica, also failed to yield the expected results. In the latter case, the copper ores proved to be different from those of Chuquicamata, and the usual treatment process was ineffective. Production there reached 35,000 tons in 1971, instead of the 77,000 tons that were expected. In the case of the El Teniente mine, the plans for the extension underestimated necessary water supplies for processing, and difficulties arose with the new smelting furnaces. It was not until 1971 that these faults were partially corrected. Hence production at El Teniente suffered the most, yielding only 147,000 tons in place of the 260,000 tons anticipated in the original expansion program.[9]

Once these failures were evident, the government requested the assistance of foreign experts in evaluating and implementing the investment plan. Two technical missions, one French and one Soviet, released their reports during the first few months of 1971. They agreed in their conclusions: correcting the deficiencies would take more than a year's time and an additional investment of more than $100 million.[10]

Besides the technical failures and the drop in the price of copper—elements not subject to government control—other factors interceded which also explain the decline in the value of exports. The transfer of the nationalized copper companies to Chilean management and the reaction of their home offices to uncompensated expropriation affected the functioning of the large mines. The state had to assume responsibility for overseeing production, installing a new sales organization, supply of primary materials and spare parts, and overall management. All of this took some time in being organized. Information concerning the technical specifications of spare parts, their frequency of replacement and sources of supply had never been in the Chilean hands. Instead the foreign companies had always managed this component of the operation from their home offices in the United States. The vital information was not supplied to the government, a fact which caused numerous operational difficulties and delays. Furthermore, the copper companies blocked the sale of many spare parts of U.S. manufacture—in particular, trucks used to haul metal and ore, as well as some other items necessary to develop the mines. Chile was forced to resort to cash purchases through third parties.

The administrative transfer stimulated labor conflicts within the enterprises. Relationships with technicians and engineers deteriorated, particularly when the government suspended the traditional practice of paying its professional salaried workers in dollars. In addition the workers began to agitate for the dismissal of several executives who were identified with the former American management. Together these factors blurred and weakened the lines of command. It was a mistake on the part of the new administrators to permit such conflicts and antagonisms to develop and weaken technical capacity in an activity so crucial to the short-term success of the whole project. Pressure for wage increases began to mount, and the first symptoms of labor indiscipline and absenteeism began to appear. This was a clear consequence of the difficulty in reconciling a firm authority with greater worker participation and a change in traditional worker-management relations.

Returning to the larger analysis of the balance of trade, we must deal with the evolution of imports. The value of imported goods rose by $84 million, or 8.4 percent, in 1971. This increase stemmed principally from the growth in food imports, a result of the rapid expansion in consumption. The rise in food imports was in turn offset to some extent by a reduction in the importation of capital goods.

The income redistribution raised the level of consumption and stimulated imports, but with a slight lag. The increase was small in the first half of 1971, intensifying in the second half. The total value of imports as registered by the Banco Central grew by 9 percent in the first half of the year and by 36 percent the second half (both figures representing changes with respect to comparable periods in 1970). The value of imported primary goods for industrial use declined 1.8 percent in the first half and soared 66.1 percent in the second semester.

Food imports were concentrated among five main products: beef, milk, butter, sugar and corn. Except for the last product, destined for use as a primary material in the national development programs in the poultry and pork industries, these imports were strictly a response to the rise in demand. The sizable purchases of milk were the result of the national program, promised by President Allende, to supply a half liter of milk per day to every child in the country.

The largest volume of imports thus occurred in the second half of 1971, just when restrictions became tighter as a result of the decline in the value of copper exports and the reduction in the inflow of capital funds and external credits.

Capital Movements

In March 1971 the UP government envisioned a net inflow of $67 million in autonomous capital funds.[11] In November the Minister of Finance corrected this figure, estimating a net outflow greater than $100 million.[12] This change altered the situation completely. The government had not foreseen and was not prepared for a reversal of this magnitude. U.S. banks restricted credit abruptly, and they were joined in this policy by the international financial agencies, who were subject to decisive influence from the U.S. government. This international reaction could have been foreseen to some extent; something of this sort was unavoidable given the ongoing policy of nationalizations and structural changes. But the extreme intensity of the reaction was very much the result of deliberate, planned actions on the part of the Nixon administration.

The Reaction of the Chilean Government

It is essential to point out what the government could have done to confront these unexpected developments and contain their negative impact. In the first place the initial estimates concerning a possible drop in the value of copper exports should have indicated clearly that the available external resources did not allow for such an intense program of reactivation and redistribution. The economic plans of the new regime were very vulnerable on the external front; once developments in this sector passed a critical threshold, the whole economic process would be in jeopardy. There should have been, but there was not, a maximum awareness of this weakness.

In the second place the government continued to pay off its foreign debts in 1971.[13] When the situation became critical, it was decided (in November 1971) to suspend payments and renegotiate the debt. A correct evaluation of the balance of payments situation and of its possible political effects, however, would have resulted in an earlier decision to renegotiate.[14]

In the third place, the decision to deduct past excessive profits from the compensation to be paid to expropriated copper companies amounted to handing a powerful weapon to the UP's main foreign adversary. Once the two largest companies had been denied any compensation, the U.S. government could publicly justify its financial pressures against Chile. Likewise the companies themselves could thereafter proceed quite blatantly to block sales of Chilean copper. A strictly tactical consideration, which should have been secondary to the accumulation of the forces necessary for the struggle ahead, became instead a matter of principle.

Certain populist features in the UP program imposed an absurd restriction on foreign trade policy: the freezing of the rate of exchange. The devaluation policy implemented by the previous government had been the object of fierce criticism by the Left in its opposition role. The continued readjustments in exchange rates had been a matter of public debate; their supposed inflationary effects had been much exaggerated. This idea, much bruited in Left political circles, led to the proposal that such devaluations should be ended in order to slow down or reduce the pace of inflation. From a technical viewpoint this measure was justified on the grounds that the bulk of export revenue, that deriving from copper, was inelastic with respect to the rate of exchange, since all mineral wealth would be in the hands of state enterprises that would be obliged to produce according to a centralized plan. Foreign trade in general would be subject to progressive controls: the principal imports would be managed by state-run agencies, and the other items would be regulated by tariffs and similar administrative measures. In the first half of 1971, inflation advanced slowly and the import registers showed no significant increases. In the second semester, in contrast, inflationary expectations grew, and imported products became absurdly cheap.

The crisis situations led to a modification of the fixed-exchange policy in December. The government suspended exchange operations and carried out a differentiated devaluation, implementing a policy of multiple exchange.[15] This was a clear example of a reaction that was too little and too late. In fact the determining causes of the situation emerging at the end of 1971 had little to do with the rate of exchange. Nevertheless, the stabilization of the exchange rate had important consequences on the price structure. The scarcity of foreign currency led progressively to the establishment of new administrative controls, overloading the state apparatus with minor control tasks, which were, however, important for the functioning of many small and medium-sized enterprises. The rate of exchange lost its regulatory role, and administrative controls had to be elaborated to compensate. The economic impact of the deterioration in relations with the United States was soon manifested in the balance of payments situation. The original UP strategy had counted heavily on some room for maneuver in this critical area; instead, options diminished in 1971.

The factors analyzed above explain in part why the reaction was delayed. But they cannot explain either the intensity of the accumulated imbalances or the inadequacy of the government's reactions. The central failure was in the economic leadership, which foresaw neither the magnitude of the accumulated economic imbalances nor the political effects which they would provoke. The original design for short-term economic policy included much room for improvisation, a characteristic which became more dominant as the process accelerated. The crucial importance of the first steps in an attempted transformation process only becomes evident a few years later. These initial steps were inadequately prepared for in Chile.

The Conflict in the Countryside

The process of agrarian reform began to pick up speed with the inauguration of the UP government. The process went all the faster for the fact that a law and an ad hoc institutional structure already existed, both set in place by the previous government. The law legitimated reform and the institutions provided an administrative and technical base. Opposition to the reform from landowners had been debilitated over four years of struggle with the Christian Democratic government and by the successful organization of the peasantry. The latifundist class no longer had the support of the industrial bourgeoisie, much less of the Christian Democrats.

Nevertheless, new problems soon emerged to confront the Allende government. In the southern region, where proprietors personally managed the working of their land, the expropriations faced the stiffest resistance. On the other hand the militant peasant organizations began pressuring the government for faster and more extensive seizures, demanding in many cases the expropriation of estates below the legal minimum. This mobilization, propelled by some factions of the UP and by extreme leftist groups, soon led to a growing number of spontaneous occupations of estates.[16] At the same time the UP decided to correct certain deficiencies in the reform process, one of them being the exclusion of a whole group of peasants. The existing law granted rights to administer and share in the profits of expropriated estates only to tenants; part-time workers were excluded. Furthermore, a paternalistic style had been imposed by the state administrative apparatus on existing *asentamientos,* or settlements.[17] Finally, expropriation did not alter the original territorial division of property; the whole area of the former latifundio was included in the new productive unit.

In order to correct these faults the government established the Agrarian Reform Centers (CERA), which were supposed to facilitate the participation of the workers in the management of the enterprise, granting autonomy and a larger voice in the Workers' Assembly to peasants, and merging different estates to establish units more suitable for rational exploitation.

These new organizations made slow progress; only 25 of the CERA centers were set up in 1971. The whole process was held up by an interminable debate on the best way of organizing the area under reform, the role of state enterprises, the Agrarian Reform Centers, the settlements, and the scope to be given to individual property. This debate succeeded only in sowing confusion and weakening the total action of the government in the countryside.

The social tensions excited by the agrarian reform were in turn stimulated by the opposition. The UP and the CDP engaged in a fierce competition for influence among the peasantry, which was daily becoming more organized. The percentage of unionized peasants among all agricultural workers rose from 39.1 percent in 1970 to 62 percent in 1971.[18] The Christian Democrats, who had won significant support among the peasantry during their administration, began to see their position threatened by the UP. They did not delay in launching a counterattack, mobilizing their supporters with the argument that the Allende government was imposing a collectivist approach which excluded individual ownership of the land. For its part the Right attacked the agrarian reform with the same argument that had been used against the Frei government—that it would cause production to fall severely. The Right was assisted in its anti-reform campaign by the judicial system, which interfered with the government's policy by questioning the legality of some expropriations.

The conflict in the countryside had important economic and political consequences. Even though production grew in 1971, private-sector investment diminished and the reorganization of the expropriated estates was delayed. These developments coincided with the strong surge in food consumption. This contrast between slow agricultural growth and a sudden acceleration in the demand for food led to supply difficulties, above all in the key urban areas. Politically, the reform did not face great obstacles. Nevertheless, the split between CD and UP factions within the peasantry could only strengthen the hand of the Right and the landlords. In sum, at the end of 1971, the main problem for the Allende government on the agrarian front was to secure an increase in production without compromising a reform process that was reaching its climax.

State Control of Banking

State expropriation of the banking system also progressed rapidly. The first step was to negotiate with foreign banks, which accounted for only a small percentage of total banking activity. The state soon arrived at an agreement with these banks, compensating them with credits granted by their own home offices.

Take-over of locally owned private banks proceeded in a different manner. The most common practice was the purchase of stock by the state. In some cases, however, the owners refused to sell their stock shares. This occurred especially with those banks closely tied to the most powerful political and economic groups. Using its legal powers the UP government intervened in those banks where financial infractions could be proved or where normal functioning had been hindered by labor conflicts.

The owners' opposition was stiffened by the Christian Democrats, who fought state expropriation with all of their strength in the unions and in Congress. In the second half of 1971, the CDP presented to Congress a constitutional amendment designed to regulate the creation of the social property area. In the same proposal they announced their opposition to state expropriations, and proposed a formula whereby banks would be subject to the control of a mixed group of bank workers, clients and representatives of the state—the latter in a minority position. The Christian Democrats rested their argument on the dangers for a pluralist system of consigning to state hands alone the enormous economic power of the banking system. The government and the UP replied that state control ruled out management by the workers of individual banks. Because of its strategic nature, banking had to be coordinated centrally if it was to be used as an instrument in a policy of planned development.

Mistakes on the part of the government in its management of the political situation worsened the conflict. The government had committed itself at the beginning of 1971 to introduce a law regulating state operation of the banking system, but this project was delayed by disagreements within the UP. Some felt that to introduce such a bill in a legislature where the government was in the minority would put an early halt to the whole process and at the least lend itself to distortions. Those advancing this argument favored other approaches which they thought would be faster. Bank stocks should be bought up, and the state should intervene legally in bank administration. Once these advances had been secured, negotiation with the legislature could begin.

In the first few months of the new regime, the government won control of several banks, apparently confirming the correctness of the latter approach. But when sufficient strength was not accumulated later on, the legitimacy of these interventions was questioned. Even though it appeared that the balance was positive and the government had approximated its original goals, the possibilities for consolidating its position in future negotiations began to diminish. It seems evident that the failure to broach the matter formally in Congress, as had been, and taking the direct route instead worsened the chances for an eventual agreement with the Christian Democrats on this matter.

Nationalization and Compensation

Both the UP and the CDP had advocated nationalization in their presidential platforms, so the political conditions for taking this step were favorable. Immediately upon taking office, the Allende government introduced a constitutional amendment in Congress providing for the nationalization of the largest mines. It was passed unanimously in July 1971 (see Table 4-3).

The Executive, anticipating a confrontation with the United States, sought to assemble the widest possible national support for this measure. With this purpose in mind it tried to involve other branches of the state, besides Congress, in the decision to nationalize and in the subsequent arrangements for indemnification. The presidential initiative proposed that the controller-

TABLE 4-3. Nationalization of Copper, Indemnity Calculations
(millions of dollars)

	Chuquicamata	El Salvador	Exótica	El Teniente	Andina
Book value	241.96	68.37	14.81	318.80	20.13
Deductions for mineral rights	5.40	0.35	0.25	0.22	1.53
Goods in poor condition	13.06	5.60	4.55	20.52	0.34
Revaluation of assets after December 31, 1964*	0.00	0.00	0.00	198.58	0.00
Indemnity	233.50	62.42	10.01	99.48	18.27
Deduction for excessive profits	300.00	64.00	0.00	410.00	0.00

* This discount was put into effect in order to negate the revaluation of assets carried out by Kennecott in 1964 when it negotiated the sale of part of its assets to the Chilean government.

Source: Decreto Supremo 92, signed by the president on September 28, 1971.

general should determine the final amount to be paid in compensation.[19] But this proposal was altered during Congressional discussion of the measure. It was decided that the controller would determine the discounts for mining rights (the state did not even recognize such a claim), for property in poor physical condition, and for revaluations of assets occurring after 1964. These sums would be discounted from the 1970 book value. But the most important item to be discounted—excessive profits—was left in the hands of the president.[20]

This decision was crucial. In effect Congress had simply dumped the whole question of compensation into the president's lap, exposing him to the conflict and controversy which such a decision would inevitably provoke. If the amount of compensation was too high, the president would be subject to the bitter censure of some opposition sectors, the extreme Left, and even of the UP itself. If the amount was too low, the government would be blamed for the consequences of U.S. retaliation. This change in the original bill proposed by the Executive robbed the president of sufficient room to maneuver and prevented him from pursuing agreements with sectors of the opposition.[21]

The UP did not have a preconceived position on this question when it came to power. Nevertheless, pressure from one sector of the UP to refuse any compensation mounted as the time for the president to announce his decision approached. This sector pushed two arguments: that no matter what the Chilean decision was, the United States would try to enforce a financial blockade; and that the balance of payments situation required that as much of the reserves as possible be retained, and hence available funds could not be diverted to indemnify the copper companies.

In November 1971, President Allende announced the compensation decided upon after calculating the discounts.[22] With the exception of the two smallest firms, none of the others received any indemnity at all. It is difficult to hypothesize the outcomes of a different decision. There was, however, an alternative which would have left more room for maneuver in the negotiations with financial agencies that would have to be undertaken in 1972. From the strategic point of view, what was essential was not the compensation paid but the control of basic wealth. This control signified the elimination of a strongpoint of foreign political and economic power; it would mean the chance to manage autonomously the exploitation and commercialization of an essential resource; and it would bring with it the capacity to divert the surplus toward internal development and a change in the productive structure. Winning this control was vital, and its importance rendered quarrels about the exact amount of compensation relatively insignificant.

Furthermore, it seems clear that internal political support stemmed chiefly from the nationalization itself and did not depend on the amount given in compensation. Thus the decision to refuse compensation did not produce any new favorable political dividends. From the international point of view, the no-compensation decision and the principle of deducting for excessive profits were unacceptable to the U.S. government, both because of the loss they represented in themselves, and because of the precedent they set. There was little advantage in thus linking the nationalization of copper with a larger problem, one with international implications and consequences beyond Chile's control.

It is true, of course, that U.S. hostility toward the Chilean experiment had its own dynamic and had been set in motion before the subject of indemnity arose. It also seems true, however, that the decision to deny indemnity served to reinforce the most reactionary sectors in the United States. The prevailing viewpoint of the Chilean Left cast the U.S. as a monolithic imperialist entity, thereby ignoring the variety of viewpoints and internal conflicts in that country, which might have allowed for greater freedom of maneuver on the part of the Chilean government. A simple-minded ideological interpretation necessarily led to hasty conclusions. Our own conclusion is that the decision to deny compensation, even though juridically unobjectionable, robbed the Allende government of flexibility at a critical moment.

State Control of Industry

The flashpoint of internal conflict was the expropriation of the largest industrial enterprises. This was inevitable: for the Chilean bourgeoisie the large firms constituted the primary pillar of support. For the UP this front was strategically decisive. Nevertheless, its initial formulations were very general; they did not specify the scope of the expropriation program. Active policy was defined according to circumstances, as events evolved. Right after the April 1971 minicipal elections, the government launched a two-pronged campaign to take over the large firms: negotiation and requisition.[23]

Negotiation was the principal instrument in the metal products branch of industry. Its first application began with the purchase acquisition of stock in the Compañia de Acero del Pacífico, the monopoly steel producer. The state already held a majority of the company's shares in 1970, and it went on to purchase the entire stock in 1971. After this, a large number of mostly foreign-owned firms, producers of metal items used as intermediate and capital goods, were purchased. This line of action yielded immediate results, making possible the formation of a state-directed conglomerate centered in the Compañia de Acero del Pacífico.

The second procedure—outright requisition—was applied chiefly to textile and construction material firms and later generalized to other areas. According to already existing legal provisions, the state had the power to take over the management of any firms which had been prevented by prolonged labor conflict from supplying essential products. Over the course of 1971, some such conflicts emerged naturally, as a result of unsatisfied wage demands. In others cases, however, workers deliberately initiated disputes in order to force state intervention. The government was thus obliged to move farther and faster than it had originally planned.

The procedures followed by the government as well as the reaction of the firms involved varied according to whether the latter were foreign-owned or local. Foreign-owned firms were mostly subsidiaries of multinational corporations. They represented only marginal investments for the home offices of these giant firms, and their purchase or takeover by the state could be negotiated easily. This was not at all the case with local firms, which constituted the economic and political power base of the Chilean capitalists. Expropriation constituted a deadly threat to this class. The negotiating position of these firms and their owners was also weaker vis-à-vis the state, and they ran the risk of receiving very low compensation. As a result there was a clear understanding in this quarter that a united front, a refusal to negotiate or sell stock, was necessary. This attitude caused the government and the unions to search for different approaches.

At the end of 1971, the UP government began to employ a third method: the opening up of stock purchasing funds working through the Corporación de Fomento de la Producción, the autonomous state agency which owned most of the public enterprises. In order to win positions in those companies where the large stockholders proved to be intransigent, the government sought to persuade smaller stockholders to sell by offering them an attractive price.

But by the end of 1971 all the approaches had reached the point of diminishing returns. Negotiations declined because of the refusal of some firms and because of disapproval on the part of certain groups within the UP who objected to paying what they regarded as excessively high indemnities. The state stock purchasing funds yielded limited results and did not gain a majority position for the state in any of the corporations. The requisition and expropriation of firms also met with new institutional problems.

In order to explain this shift, the moves of the opposition will have to be analyzed. The Right was thrown off balance by the initial success and consolidation of the new government. It was forced to proceed cautiously because of the fact that no one knew exactly which firms the government would attempt to annex to the area of social ownership. The first move, therefore, was to demand that the government publish the list of firms to be taken over. This demand was supported with the argument that the prevailing uncertainty was unnecessarily upsetting to business owners and was hurting the business climate. The next step was the initiation of a campaign accusing the government of planning to seize all of industry, starting with the largest firms and going on to the small and middle-sized companies. Later it was charged that the government was acting illegally; specifically, the Executive branch was accused of enforcing the laws in violation of the spirit in which Congress had passed them.

The Christian Democrats as distinct from the Right, pursued another line of attack. Once they became aware of the government's advances, they reacted unfavorably, objecting to the procedure employed and not to the ends pursued. At least two positions were expressed within the CDP. The progressives, who had played the pivotal role in the presidential campaign, objected to the government's methods. The conservatives saw in the UP program the threat of a qualitative change in the structure of the economy and the conditions of power. They argued that a statist program was being pushed and that the government would progressively impose total control on economic and political life. This posture was almost coincidental with that of the National Party, which occupied the right wing of the Chilean political spectrum.

The CDP channeled its opposition through Congress, where it presented in July 1971 a proposal for amending the Constitution to establish definite guidelines for the private, mixed ownership, and public sectors of the economy. The key areas of the Christian Democratic proposal were also the most controversial. In the first place state takeover of banking was rejected. Secondly, the proposal included a requirement that a specific law would have to be passed in the case of each firm which the government sought to annex to the public or mixed-ownership sector. Third, existing legal powers to requisition or intervene in private firms were eliminated, and the authority of the Corporación de Fomento to acquire stock in private firms was curtailed. Fourth, all of the government's acquisitions of stock from private corporations were declared null and void after October 1971. Finally, it was established that as a general rule management ought to pass directly to the workers in each enterprise—the only exceptions to this provision being a few firms, like the large copper mines, where the state would have the chief responsibility. In sum the proposal represented an attempt to transfer all power for setting up the area of social and mixed ownership to Congress, where the opposition held a majority. Independent action by the Executive would be blocked. This proposal led to the absurd prospect of a UP government, which aimed to bring about structural change within the existing institutional framework, wielding fewer legal powers than the preceding governments, which had attempted simply to administer the system.

Why did the government prefer the policy of requisition to that of negotiation? One basic reason has already been given: the increasing refusal of the largest Chilean property owners to negotiate the sale of their firms with the state. Furthermore, it was argued within the UP that the amounts of indemnity agreed upon in the negotiations were too high; and it was held that better terms could be won if the government adopted a tougher position. From another point of view it was thought that the active participation of the workers in the phase of state intervention was essential to assure the success of the process. Such participation, it was argued, would awaken political consciousness.

Furthermore, why didn't the government gain a step on the opposition by presenting its own proposal for constitutional amendment, as it had in the case of copper? The president did announce that he would send a proposal to Congress to regulate the establishment of the social property area. But this proposal suffered successive delays due to disagreements within the UP. Those opposed to sending up the bill pointed out that it would be subjected to prolonged debate in Congress and that its contents would be distorted, thus running the risk of holding up the whole process and leaving the Executive branch without any capacity for action. Pressures exerted by the workers would converge on the government, provoking a cooling of the relationship with the popular base. Congress would succeed in limiting the extent of the social property area, discouraging the organization and activism of the workers, and wresting away legal powers the Executive still possessed. These internal controversies paralyzed the government, which finally opted for postponing a decision. In practice it was decided to move ahead employing the narrow leeway allowed within the existing institutional framework, and to negotiate later with Congress once the government had won a better position.

The introduction of the Christian Democrats' constitutional amendment, however, changed the picture. Based on this change in the legal situation, the Right fortified its position, extending its influence over the controller's office and the courts, both potentially opposed to the government. The controller's office began to hold up the Executive's intervention decrees and question their legitimacy. The Judicial branch upheld the claims brought by private firms against the Executive's intervention attempts. Both of these branches of the state apparatus began to alter legal criteria which they had always upheld before, turning on the government once they perceived that the balance of power had begun to shift in favor of the opposition. At the same time the opposition took advantage of the inevitable errors and wanderings of the UP to gain a strong influence over public opinion. The government was accused of acting arbitrarily, of failing to specify the criteria for the selection of strategic enterprises subject to expropriation, and of pressuring workers to force the requisition of unimportant middle-sized firms.

Once this whole period is seen in its proper perspective, it seems clear that the UP's delay in introducing its own bill for regulating the social property area was a mistake. Even though the lack of legal guidelines allowed for more freedom of maneuver initially, it also made the advances that were won transitory and open to question. The simultaneous introduction of one bill proposing the nationalization of copper and another setting up the social property area could have been advantageous. In the first few months of its rule, the government could muster more political force; it enjoyed a stronger bargaining position. The Executive could have faced the struggle with Congress with a firmer base. Moreover, the CDP and the National Party had not yet put together an alliance. Later on the Allende government was forced to negotiate in increasingly unfavorable conditions.

Another central consideration in every process altering the structure of property ownership is the advantage or disadvantage in making public the list of firms to be expropriated. This problem in fact produced much debate within the UP and the government. On the one hand, it was thought that publication of such a list would clarify the government's intentions, helping to counteract the scare campaign aimed at smaller businessmen by the associations of large entrepreneurs. Furthermore, the matter would be cleared up definitively within coalition and government circles. On the other hand, several important disadvantages were cited. The firms on the list would react by cutting production, ceasing investment, and slacking off on the maintenance of equipment. The state was in no position to take over all factories immediately, nor did it have enough personnel on hand to assume the duties involved. Moreover, it was further pointed out that announcing the limitations on expropriation ahead of time would serve to freeze the larger process by discouraging and demobilizing those workers, in fact a majority, employed in firms not on the initial list.

Since the discussion did not result in a consensus among the parties of the UP, the government abstained from publishing any such list. It was not until October 1971, after the Christian Democrats had already introduced their amendment, that the government proposed a bill regulating expropriation. The proposed law set a limit on future expropriations: only those firms whose capital and reserves in 1969 together exceeded 14 million escudos would be subject to transfer to the public or mixed-ownership sector. Include within this limit were 254 firms, more than the government intended to take over, but enough to allow it some leeway in choosing a smaller number later on. The list was thus finally made public, but not until one year after the start of the process. It seems evident that this action should have been undertaken sooner.

In order to offset the negative political effect of the interventions and expropriations on smaller businessmen, the government adopted several policies designed to conciliate this sector. Easy credits on favorable terms were granted to smaller businesses, and the government established production contracts to insure a steady demand for their output. However, the promise to pass a statute governing the private sector and establishing guarantees for its normal functioning was never fulfilled.

Two facts conspired against the hoped-for neutrality on the part of smaller businessmen. First, the Executive branch intervened in some 50 small and middle-sized businesses during 1971, contradicting its own guidelines. In some cases the interventions were caused by the owners' abandonment of factories, but the most common reason was the paralysis of enterprises arising from labor conflicts. In the second place, the extended controversy on the limits of the social ownership sector provoked doubts and, later, discontent. Because of this uncertainty, the Right was able to persuade the middle sectors that the government's expropriation plans would not stop with the largest firms.

Could an agreement have been reached between the Christian Democrats and the UP concerning the establishment of the social property area? We must refer to the parliamentary debate on this issue. The greatest disagreements emerged around the questions of which enterprises would be included in the social ownership area and what kind of role the state would have in their administration. In order to get around the restriction imposed by the Christian Democrats requiring a separate law for each firm expropriated, the UP proposed in its own constitutional amendment the inclusion of a list of firms whose expropriation would be approved all at one time. With this in mind the Executive sent up a new list in November. The original list of 245 firms scheduled for transfer to the public and mixed-ownership sectors had been pared down to 91.

The Christian Democrats wanted enterprises in these two sectors, with a few exceptions, to be administered by the workers in each firm. They hoped in this way to give some concrete form to their statements in favor of "participation," but basically they sought to inhibit state control and maintain their political presence in the unions. For the Allende government, the Christian Democrats' proposal was unacceptable. In the UP's thinking, the large state-run enterprises were to be guided by the central planning apparatus. Their activities were to reflect the interest of all workers, not simply those the workers in each firm. This debate intensified, and the positions become polarized. The Christian Democrats accused the government of pushing for the traditional statist brand of socialism, while the UP argued that the Christian Democrats were only trying to incorporate a restricted group of workers into a modernized capitalism.

Regarding the issue of workers' participation and the various forms of self-management, there was some overlap between the two positions; but this was outweighed by the pressure of ideological rigidity. The possibility of an accord on this issue began to be explored at a later point; but by then it was already too late. The proposed constitutional amendment remained under consideration while tensions heightened. Despite the differences between the two sides, it seems evident that this period presented one of the few opportunities for attaining a compromise agreement between the UP and the Christian Democrats on a law covering the creation of the social ownership sector.

Short-Term Economic Policy and Structural Change

At first the UP's economic policy created political conditions which favored the accompanying changes in property-ownership. The wage increases and the expansionist policy of the first few months made the government stronger and neutralized the opposition. This atmosphere facilitated a speedup of the larger process without producing major resistance. The pursuit of this policy, however, began to yield diminishing returns at the end of 1971. The excessive demand produced the first symptoms of scarcity and black markets and increased inflationary pressures. The actual political consequences of economic policy measures began to deviate radically from the expected results.

But how did changes in property ownership affect the level of production? Normally, structural change does have a short-run negative effect on production. But despite the fact that production in 1971 was going on in rapidly changing circumstances, levels did not decline in any economic sector. This leads us to believe that the structural transformations were not a significant factor in the maladjustments that became evident by the end of the year.

Production in agriculture and livestock actually increased, even while the agrarian reform was being speeded up. The strong expansion in demand and the relative improvement in agricultural prices stimulated production. Political tension in the countryside affected the size of the 1971 harvest; but in spite of this, more crops were sown this year than in 1970.

Mining activity also went up. The large mines augmented copper production by 5.7 percent over 1970. The restrictions emerging in the balance of payments were in large part unrelated to the management of the mines. A more efficient management, one paying maximum attention to technical quality and administrative stability, probably would have yielded a higher level of output. But the balance of payments difficulties of 1971 arose from factors that were outside the control of the government: the fall in the price of copper, failures in investment plans and capital flight.

The incorporation of the first manufacturing enterprises into the public sector coincided with a marked expansion of industrial production. All of the enterprises that passed under state control increased their activity. The chief negative effect was a drop in levels of investment. But this phenomenon, while it would have serious consequences in two or three years' time, could not have affected the production levels for 1971.

In summary, the setting up of the social property area had no effect on the short-run imbalances that appeared in 1971. Instead the main cause of imbalances in this first period was the abrupt surge in demand. This understood, the fundamental issue is whether or not the expansive policy was indispensable in initiating structural changes.

The Interaction Between Economics and Politics

At the end of 1971, despite the substantial growth in supply, there emerged temporary scarcities of some essential products. Overall consumption had reached a historical high point, and all social groups had benefited. Nevertheless, the Right succeeded in using the emerging shortages in focusing middle-class discontent against the government. The employers' and professionals' associations had consolidated their organization, and the CDP was coming together with the National Party to form an intransigently anti-Allende opposition.

This situation enflamed the internal debate within the UP concerning the economic measures. The negative political effects which the hyperexpansive program was beginning to generate forced many to question whether such a policy was necessary to support structural changes. The backers of the 1971 economic program attempted to rationalize the outcome, but their premises in doing so were not consistent with the general political line of the government. The basic premise in their argument was that the economic policy would create favorable conditions for a plebiscite which would alter the institutional framework. The underlying goal was to create, at the cost of exhausting all of the economy's reserves, an optimal situation for generating drastic political change. If this could be attained, the government and the UP would dispose of powers sufficient to bring the economic imbalances under control and carry out the strategic objectives.

The UP's political leadership, however, entertained no such radical intentions. The idea of a plebiscite in 1971 was debated, but it was not approved. It was considered unnecessary to risk so much of the program on an uncertain outcome, a contest as likely to be won by the opposition as by the UP. Besides, even a plebiscite victory could not produce an alteration in the balance of forces sufficient to underwrite a qualitative change in the institutional order.

The political assumptions implicit in the economic policy were thus inconsistent with the gradualist criteria dominant from the beginning among the political leadership. The political rationalization for the economic policy was in fact *ex post facto*, since it was never rendered explicit during the course of the year and many unforeseen factors came together to produce the final situation in 1971. This basic inconsistency was in part the consequence of the almost total separation of the economic and political leaderships. There simply did not exist adequate means of coordination in 1971. The economic authorities operated independently, while the political leadership was preoccupied principally with institutional and party problems. The consequences of economic policy were perceived by the politicians only when they were expressed politically, as criticism, grievances and mobilizations by the opposition. And by the time they reached this level, the accumulated imbalances were considerable indeed.

In summary, the economic variables had a significant political impact in 1971. The economic leadership acted independently with considerable room to maneuver this year. But the new situation which emerged in the last few months restricted the field of choices. It became harder to continue redistributing, extracting resources from middle- and upper-class groups, and moving ahead with the social property area. The economic leadership was confronted with new limitations stemming from the intensification of the social and political conflict, which it had not had to deal with before. In the subsequent stages, political requirements became pressing and began to impose themselves on the general process.

Notes

1. International Monetary Fund (May 1976), p. 33, Table 12.
2. Disposable personal income grew from 60.849 billion escudos in 1970 to 91.162 billion in 1971. Figures from Odeplan and the International Monetary Fund (May 1976), p. 80, Table 6.
3. As a consequence of the fall in price of copper and of the "freezing" of the exchange rate, book profits of the larger mines dropped from $373 to $108 million and fiscal revenues were reduced from $313 to $108 million between 1970 and 1971. Had the price of copper and the real value of the dollar remained constant, book profits would have reached $377 million in 1971. Since the companies had already been nationalized, the whole of this sum would have gone to the state. Data from the Directory of Finance, Corporacion del Cobre (CODELCO). See J. Estevez, "La nacionalización del cobre, una experiencia positiva," in Secretaría Ejecutiva de la Unidad Popular, *Documentos y materiales económicos*, No. 22 (Berlin: RDA, November 1977).
4. Industrial production grew, with respect to the same period in the previous year, by 2.2 percent in the first trimester; while it experienced an increase of 9.3 percent in the second trimester, and 17.8 percent in the last trimester, an especially high figure. Data from the Sociedad de Fomento Fabril.

5. Instituto de Economía y Planificación, Encuesta de Ocupación y Desocupación en el Gran Santiago (Santiago: University of Chile, 1972).

6. According to estimates for the last few years of the 1960s, the wage differential between high- and low-paid workers in the industrial sector was on the order of 1:6.5; while income differentials for the economy as a whole were 1:12. See Odeplán, *Antecedentes sobre el desarrollo chileno, 1960–1970* (Santiago, 1971), p. xxxv.

7. Of the $222 million loss in income in the balance of trade between 1970 and 1971, 62 percent was accounted for by a reduction in the value of exports and 38 percent in an increase in imports.

8. The production of the large copper mines grew from 541,100 tons in 1970 to 571,000 tons in 1971. Production in the smaller mines fell from 151,000 tons in 1970 to 137,000 tons in 1971. Corporación del Cobre (CODELCO), "Proyección de producciones del cobre y molibdeno" (Santiago, December 1971). See also World Bank (October 1974), Vol. 3, p. 47.

9. CODELCO, (December 1973).

10. For a detailed analysis of these failures, see World Bank (October 1974), pp. 8–14.

11. Consejo Interamericano de la Alianza para el Progreso, "Informe sobre la economía de Chile" (Washington, D.C.: OEA, February 1971), p. 63.

12. Presentation to the National Congress on the State of Public Finances (Santiago, November 1971).

13. Between interest on the external debt and its amortization, Chile paid the sum of $237 million in 1971. World Bank (October 1974), Vol. 3, Table 3–10.

14. The government carried a large debt with the Club of Paris: $2.2 billion, of which $1.3 billion were owed to the United States. E. Trabuco, "Analisis de los principales problemas de financiamiento de corto plazo: El caso chileno 1970–1973" (Buenos Aires: Friedrich Ebert Foundation, 1974).

15. The average devaluation was 30 percent. Exchange at the original rate was allowed for food imports; a 57 percent devaluation was imposed on currency exchanges to pay for machinery and raw materials; while luxury goods could only be bought with currency subjected to a 100 percent devaluation.

16. The number of estates occupied spontaneously by peasants increased at the following pace: 2 in 1967, 2 in 1968, 89 in 1969, 103 in 1970, and 560 in 1971. Instituto de Economía y Planificación, *La economía chilena en 1971* (Santiago: University of Chile, 1972), p. 519.

17. The *asentamientos* were transitional organizations created by the agrarian reform law. They were to prevail until the definitive character of property ownership, whether individual or cooperative could be decided on. The settlements were run on cooperativist lines under state control.

18. Figures from the Corporación de la Reforma Agraria in Instituto de Economía y Planificación, *La economía chilena en 1971*, p. 518.

19. The controller-general's office was an autonomous branch of government whose purpose was to rule on the constitutionality and legality of executive acts as well as exercising auditing and financial controls over the Treasury. The head of the office, the controller, was designated by agreement between the president and the senate, and his term of office was for life.

20. According to the amendment approved by Congress indemnification would be calculated on the basis of book value as of December 31, 1970. Later the following items would be discounted: (1) revaluations carried out by the companies after December 31, 1964; (2) the value of mining rights; (3) an amount for goods found in poor condition. Finally the president was empowered to direct the controller to deduct from the resulting indemnity all or part of the excessive profits earned after May 5, 1955 up to December 31, 1970. A complete analysis of the constitutional

provisions can be found in E. Silva, *El tribunal constitucional de chile (1971–1973)* (Caracas: Editorial Juridica Venezolana, 1977), pp. 149–155.

21. For an analysis of this problem, see J. Faundez, "Una decisión sin estrategia: la deducción de utiladades excesivas en la nacionalización del cobre," *Foro Internacional* (October–December, 1974).

22. The criterion used by the president defined excessive profits as those exceeding 12 percent of the book value. This percentage was based on the average profits earned in the world operations of the nationalized companies.

23. Requisition consisted in the seizure of control by the state when an important economic activity was being prejudiced by hoarding, speculation, paralysis, or other causes affecting the public interest. This takeover was to be temporary and did not affect property ownership, which continued in private hands. Requisition had been authorized in Decreto 520 of 1932, a law passed during the "100-day socialist republic." It was later refined and extended with further provisions in 1945 and 1953. See Silva, *El tribunal constitucional de chile,* p. 160; and E. Novoa, "Vias legales para avanzar hacia el socialismo," *Mensaje* (March–April 1971).

CHAPTER 5

Economic Policy:
The Search for Options

The political and economic course pursued by the Unidad Popular continued unchanged through the first few months of 1972. The central economic policy was still in force, and the confrontation with the opposition reached new levels of intensity. It was not until June that a break came, when the Ministers of the Economy and Finance were relieved and new measures were adopted.

The economic policy had already been subject to serious questioning beginning in December 1971. Despite this growing skepticism, neither the government nor the UP were able to decide on a new orientation. With the situation becoming more confused, important debates on possible options took place within the government. But the differences among the leftist parties delayed the adoption of corrective measures, and hence the government's room for maneuver was steadily reduced.

Reevaluation of the Political Situation

Once aware that its viability was diminishing the government undertook a reevaluation of the economic and political situation. On the political front, the opposition, both from inside the country and from the United States, had stiffened. In December 1971, rightwing forces began to organize groups of smaller businessmen into the newly created National Front of the Private Sector. They thus succeeded for the first time in joining together in the same organization both owners of large firms (which the government had already announced would become part of the public and mixed sector of the economy) and owners of small and middle-sized firms in industry and commerce. Similarly, the rightists gained influence in many professional associations and, for the first time, put together a broad front of white-collar professionals and technicians with a clear conservative orientation. All of this activity among the middle sectors was supported by an intense ideological campaign against the government and against socialism.

Also in December 1971, the Right and the Christian Democrats undertook the first of a series of impeachment procedures against state ministers. This practice, which was expanded intensively in subsequent periods, was designed to create an image of instability and illegitimacy, and to sap the administrative capacities of the government. The National Party brought an impeachment charge against the Minister of the Economy, Pedro Vuskovic, on the grounds of presumed legal violations in the establishment of the social property area. The CDP sought to impeach the Minister of the Interior, José Tohá, accusing him of nonfeasance and failure to preserve public order.[1]

The CDP-National Party alliance also made progress on the electoral front. In January 1972, the two parties united in a by-election campaign (for Deputy and Senator) in central Chile. The combined opposition won both offices. The Christian Democrats' opposition stance was increasingly hardened and its alliance with the Right consolidated, thus isolating the UP and leaving fewer possibilities for an eventual Center-Left accommodation. At the same time, however, several distinct viewpoints persisted within the CDP. The impeachment charge against Tohá was opposed by some within the Party, including members of its national committee. Furthermore, during the parliamentary by-election campaign some of the Christian Democratic leaders, unhappy with the National Party alliance, emphasized that the electoral accord did not compromise the fundamental non-rightist line of their party. But the conservative faction within the Party had won effective control. This faction used the argument that the alliance with the Right was tactical and that their opposition to the Allende government had more to do with procedural differences than programmatic content as a smokescreen to disguise its imposition of a political orientation of total opposition.

At the same time an openly hostile opposition to the Chilean government was assumed by the large American companies, the U.S. government and the international agencies within which the latter exercised decisive influence. By the middle of 1971, the flow of credits from Eximbank and the private U.S. banks had already diminished considerably. The U.S. government had, however, not yet expressed public opposition. Once the Chilean decision to discount for excessive profits was announced, this situation changed radically. The White House stated publicly its decision to suspend economic aid to any country expropriating U.S. firms without compensation. In December 1971, the Nixon administration instructed its representatives in the World Bank and the Inter-American Development Bank to oppose credits for Chile.

In January 1972, the Kennecott Corporation began a suit against the Chilean government for nonpayment of a promissory note which had fallen due the previous month. The note was for purchase of some stock in the El Teniente mine which had been acquired by the Frei government. Kennecott won a ruling in New York State courts subjecting all bank accounts of Chilean government agencies in New York to embargo.

Thus the domestic and foreign opposition forces were quickly passing over to the offensive. At the same time, in Chile, the extreme Left and some minority factions within the UP intensified their activist campaign, creating increasingly difficult situations for the Executive. They provoked occupations and seizures of farmland, urban building sites, and of firms not subject to expropriation according to the UP's program. The net effect was to contradict and throw into question the procedures which the government had already publicly established.

The UP was aware of this change in the opposition's strength; but it also knew that its own base of support among workers, salaried employees, and peasants had been fortified both qualitatively and in numbers and organization. Now that an intense social struggle was approaching, the central question was the relative speed with which the government and the opposition could accumulate the greater force. From this point of view, the alignment of the middle classes was crucial.

The New Economic Situation

In contrast with the year before, the Chilean economy began the year 1972 without the reserves to sustain short-term growth. The former assumption of idle capacity was no longer valid. Even though there was still leeway in some areas, bottlenecks had appeared in others, the effects of which were spreading throughout the whole economy. Foreign currency reserves were minimal and forbade the resort to imports in order to overcome the limitations on internal supply. Nor could the economy count on the inventories which had existed at the beginning of 1971 and which had served to meet demand that year.

The program to set up the social property area also encountered different circumstances. The expansion of supply in 1972 would depend to a large extent on the productivity of these enterprises. Accordingly, the efficiency of management in the production units of the public sector, especially in copper and agriculture, would be a crucial factor. The slightest dip in production for one of these enterprises, especially if it held a monopoly position, would have immediate repercussions.

Confronted with this reality, substantial sectors in the government decided it would be impossible to continue with the policy of expansion and redistribution. They considered it essential to avoid pay increases exceeding the rise in the cost of living for the previous year. The necessity to raise the rate of investment was also stressed. This attempt to impose a new direction was justified by the argument that 1971 had been the "year of redistribution," while 1972 would be the "year of accumulation."

Despite these concerns the policies were not, in fact, modified. It turned out to be very difficult to contain the forces unleashed in 1971. The sequential conception of redistribution followed by accumulation assumed that basic political and social conduct could be altered and popular expectations changed virtually instantaneously. In the next few months it proved impossible to apply this thinking with the facility that had been hoped for. In order to grasp what happened it will be useful to review at some length the forecasts made by the Allende government and then compare them with the actual outcomes.

The fiscal budget sent up to Congress by the Executive in December 1971 proposed a deficit of 10 billion escudos out of a total fiscal expenditure of 52 billion escudos—a deficit of 19.2 percent. At the conclusion of congressional debate the government's budgetary proposals had suffered considerable changes. The cost of the annual pay readjustment for public sector employees went up and, at the same time, Congress cut back the funding requested by the Executive. With these changes the deficit rose to 12.3 billion escudos, or 23.8 percent of total expenditures. The UP government knew that in the prevailing political circumstances it would be very difficult to restrain spending within budgetary guidelines: the final deficit would be even greater, as had been the case in 1971.

In the second critical area, the balance of payments, the projections for 1972 also showed that the same tendencies which prevailed in 1971 would grow more acute. At the beginning of 1972 it was estimated that production in the larger copper mines would increase to 630,000 tons per year and that the world market price would remain at 1971 levels. It was further assumed that agricultural exports would decline, industrial exports would hold steady, and food imports would ebb. Finally, net outflows of capital funds were expected to reach $100 million. Based on these assumptions, which would prove to be overly optimistic, a deficit of $362 million was anticipated in the balance of payments, $150 million of which would be subject to renegotiation.[2] It was understood that in the event that the necessary funding could not be obtained, consumption levels would be seriously affected, inhibiting the consolidation of the income redistribution achieved in 1971.

The perspectives for 1972 stimulated much debate within the UP and the government. In this climate of growing concern an important political conference was called to debate the economic situation. The president, the UP party leaders and government staff experts took part, at the beginning of February 1972, in the so-called El Arrayán meeting.

The El Arrayán Meeting

Much public attention was focused on the importance of this meeting. The central question was whether the government would decide to continue pushing its program with the same intensity or whether it would opt to consolidate its position. At the beginning of the meeting the president and the party chiefs underlined the gravity of the situation and warned of the risks of weakening the government. All of the party representatives stressed their preoccupation over scarcities, inflationary pressures, and the institutional impasse; they urged drastic adjustments in economic policy. But at the same time they tried to impose a set of conditions which were so discordant as to be almost mutually incompatible. Once again the political leaders exhibited a poor grasp of economic phenomena and a deficient sense of the interactions between economics and politics in a period of accelerated changes. Thus, for example, it was imagined that the following objectives could be approached simultaneously: (1) to reduce scarcities and undercut the black market; (2) to avoid an inflationary surge; (3) to avoid any retreat in income redistribution; (4) to maintain favorable conditions for extending the area of social ownership; and (5) to avoid provoking negative reactions among smaller business owners.

These contradictory goals stemmed from the very nature of the political project: to effect profound transformations while maintaining a favorable conjunctural situation. Thus the intensity of the struggle with the opposition obliged the government to rely on the undeviating support of workers and salaried employees. Therefore it had to minimize labor conflicts provoked by wage demands in order to avoid strikes which might turn out to the advantage of the opposition. But at the same time the excessive demands for higher wages aggravated the economic situation. A difficult problem was emerging: how to control wages and salaries in such a way as to conserve the advances in income distribution while at the same time maintaining labor discipline.

This was a complex dilemma. If abrupt price increases were put into effect, the inflation would provoke even more pressures on the labor front. But if adjustments in prices were not allowed, inflationary pressures would build up which would strike the economy with even greater force later on. In the meantime scarcities would worsen and the black market would flourish all the more openly.

All of the UP parties agreed that these conflicts could not be overcome purely by means of adjustments in prices and wages or by strictly fiscal and monetary measures. Administrative controls would have to be utilized more intensively. To this end it was essential to push even more rapidly the task of completing the social property area, which would provide an organic and efficient system of control with which to fight the emerging distortions in the market.

But what relative emphasis should be placed on administrative control measures as opposed to those aimed at financial adjustments? On this matter there were several different opinions. The thesis that state control of the economy should be extended rapidly was subject to some questioning. In the first place, it was argued that rapid expansion of the social property area, while indeed providing new control mechanisms, would also cause short-run maladjustments. The productivity of the enterprises involved could diminish, damaging production at a moment when there was no idle capacity to use in increasing supply. The lack of suitable personnel to manage the new factories was another objective fact. Moreover, the smaller business owners might react unfavorably and reduce their investments. Conflicts in Congress would worsen, since the opposition was already demanding the suspension of new expropriations until a suitable constitutional amendment was approved.

Those favoring a resort to administrative controls argued that a lid on wages and an increase in prices would reduce real income. In order to limit the growth of demand, resources should be extracted from the large private firms which had not yet been expropriated and a greater control should be established over the commercialization of intermediate and basic consumer goods.

This position was supported by one faction of the Socialist Party and by a group headed by the Minister of the Economy, Pedro Vuskovic.

Both positions were aimed at resolving the difficult problem of carrying out the strategic objectives in a situation of permanent electoral struggle. Elections were an indication of legitimacy and popular support. In the coming months the UP would have to weather a by-election for the Chamber of Deputies, a general election in the CUT, and an election in the University of Chile—not to mention the continuing elections in unions, neighborhood associations and high schools.

Those within the UP who favored financial adjustments argued that it was essential to avoid a massive shift of the middle sectors against the government. They held that it was necessary to accumulate more forces if the advance was to continue. Those favoring direct administrative controls argued that the first priority was to maintain the support of workers and employees, and that the social property area had to be constituted rapidly, because it would be impossible to do so later on.

None of these positions was put forth within a coherent and convincing framework, and the majority opinion finally crystallized in favor of a policy combining both points of view and thus assuring a consensus. The outcome was a compromise of poorly articulated measures which did not amount to a clear line of action. The principal components were:

1. *Wages and salaries:* It was agreed to limit increases to the rise in the cost of living during 1971, even though some differences persisted concerning how much effort the government and the parties ought to exert in holding workers to these guidelines. The economic staff responsible for the policy put into effect in 1971 was softer on this issue and more inclined to avoid conflicts. This meant that it was disposed to accede to higher pay raises if the rate of inflation stepped up in 1972.
2. *Prices:* There was agreement to authorize some increases, limited according to the following criteria: reduction of the level of real demand; higher increases for nonessential consumer items and minimal increments for items of necessary and popular consumption; price increases to enterprises in the social area in order to reduce their losses. This would cut down on the monetary expansion caused by the expansion of credits necessary to finance operating expenses in these enterprises.
3. *Foreign exchange policy:* The arguments for modifying the fixed-exchange policy were subject to much analysis, since a serious distortion in prices was being caused under the prevailing inflationary conditions. The economic staff of the government argued that a shift in the rate of exchange would accelerate inflation; instead imports could be controlled administratively. Their views on this matter prevailed, and the rate of exchange remained frozen.
4. *Monetary and fiscal policy:* There was a consensus that the fiscal deficit

should be reduced, or at least contained, in order to diminish its impact on monetary expansion. Two courses of action were suggested to fulfill this goal. The first involved adopting immediate measures, using financial mechanisms. The second involved extracting liquid funds from middle and upper income groups. Partisans of this approach feared that contracting public spending to reduce the deficit would also provoke a setback in redistribution and in the general level of economic activity. Thus the costs of the readjustment process would not fall on the workers; nor would public investment be prejudiced. The suggested measures included stiffer taxes on capital gains, on stockholders, on real estate and on automobile purchases.

5. *The agrarian reform and the area of social ownership:* There was a consensus on the urgency of pursuing these goals to their completion. Differences centered on the intensity of action and specific procedures to be followed. The minister of the economy advocated maximum priority for these tasks, a position consistent with the rest of his approach. Once financial devices (adjustments in prices, pay and fiscal spending) were set aside, administrative measures had to be resorted to in depth. In order to inhibit speculation it would be necessary to control distributors; in order to assure the distribution of essential goods it would be necessary to establish controls on production and commercialization; in order to plan production it was essential to bring the strategic firms under control as soon as possible. Those in favor of the second approach emphasized the possibility of a political agreement; they called attention to the disruption in production which might arise from hasty action; and they warned of the risk, which had to be avoided, of absorbing into the social area firms or estates not entered on the list submitted by the government or covered under the agrarian reform law. In addition they reiterated their firm opposition to unauthorized seizures. No general agreement was reached on this matter.

6. *Balance of payments:* Here agreement was unanimous: it was a matter of extreme urgency to renegotiate the debt and obtain more funds from the socialist countries. Interpreted in this way, however, the matter was reduced to its political dimensions. Neither the problem of how to deal with the demand for food deriving from the income redistribution nor the issue of how to adjust the rate of exchange was discussed.

7. *Workers' participation:* The existing difficulties and the impossibility of returning to the normal operation of the market led to the conclusion that it was necessary to support all of the popular organizations of workers and poor people. It was resolved by general consensus to encourage more popular participation in the management of enterprises, in the distribution of products, and in vigilance over production and commercialization.

The disagreements that arose concerning several of these points produced a general paralysis, and the subsequent inertia meant that the 1971 policy remained in effect. At this point, there was no clear alternative proposal nor did there exist an authority strong enough to resolve the controversies. As is always the case in politics, when two opposing positions confront each other and a mixture of both options is decided on, the result is a poorly defined hybrid policy that lacks a central thrust and turns out to be less effective than either of the original choices.

A CRITICAL ANALYSIS OF THE EL ARRAYÁN MEETING

The following conclusions derive from the author's personal participation in the El Arrayán meeting and a subsequent analysis of the proceedings there. The meeting revealed once more the inadequacy of the theoretical base used to interpret the situation. The economic options advanced were simply not in tune with prevailing political reality; their immediate and short-term political effects were not considered. At the level of strictly economic policy there was a general incapacity to formulate a coherent alternative approach, and the old policy was maintained with only slight modifications.

The lack of coherent political leadership was also evident at this conclave. The fundamental questions remained unresolved. No clear position was decided on vis-à-vis the Christian Democrats, nor on the formation of the social property area, nor with respect to the MIR and its strategy of property seizures. What resulted was a delay of six months between the reevaluation of the situation and the change of policy in June 1972.

The economic proposals raised by the minister of the economy at El Arrayán underestimated the power of the opposition and overestimated the capacity of the existing state apparatus to overcome the disarticulation of the market. The regulatory role of the price system and of financial mechanisms was undervalued in favor of more extensive administrative controls. Obviously, market mechanisms could not by themselves reorient the structure of production and consumption; this would have to involve the activation of the social property area and control of the means of production. The question was how to assess correctly the available political and administrative capacity in order to establish the speed and extent of the changes to be effected at any moment.

To impose massive state control in a very short time was an impracticable task. The Chilean administrative apparatus, strained to the limits, had begun to reach its breaking point. The number of prices subject to controls increased rapidly. Shortages forced even more regulatory measures on both consumer goods and intermediate goods in order to control speculation and hoarding. In an economy as relatively complex as that of Chile, such phenomena had to be considered in order to select the right combination of market and administrative regulatory mechanisms.

Underlying the different technical options there was one central problem: the difficulty of achieving a rapid increase in real income for the great majority, given the limitations on the size of the overall surplus available for redistribution.

The Widening Financial Disequilibrium

Economic problems worsened in the months following the El Arrayán meeting. Those urging corrective measures failed to implement their ideas. Their approach demanded decisive political strength in order to contain pay raises. They were faced with the difficult task of explaining to the workers that income redistribution would have to be limited to the 1971 levels, and consumption could not increase at all.

The pressures for higher incomes made themselves felt with considerable force. As inflation resurged, wage demands grew apace; and the increases agreed to exceeded the rise in prices in 1971. Workers in the large enterprises won additional benefits not included in the wage proposals suggested by the government. These fringe benefits included production premiums, profit-sharing and seniority incentives. Further demands were advanced for vacation bonuses, Christmas bonuses and scholarships for workers' children. These extra demands, popularly known as *colgajos* ("fringes"), amounted to significant increases.

The persistence of such demands had several different causes. First, the redistributive character of the initial economic policy could not be brought to a sudden halt; it had, in fact, aroused new expectations. This atmosphere stimulated a marked populist spirit always latent in the Chilean party system. In the second place, electoral pressures imposed a short-run outlook on policy. The parliamentary election in January 1972 was followed by CUT elections in June and yet another parliamentary election in July.

In the third place, the Christian Democrats began to push a populist political line from the start of the year. In an attempt to win more backing among wage earners and salaries employees, the Christian Democrats supported the most exorbitant pay demands, and directed their union members to reject the government's offers. The extreme Left joined this campaign, agitating especially among the urban marginal population and the peasantry, whose needs were most pressing. These groups began to flex their political muscles, demonstrating actively for more housing, services and land.

The motor forces of inflation shifted. In the first part of 1971 the growth in demand had been satisfied by an increase in both domestic production and imports. In the second semester, all of the available productive capacity had been put to work and foreign currency reserves exhausted. Bottlenecks began to form in many activities, and the pressure was left on prices. The strong state controls contained price increases, but the excess demand produced shortages. By the first few months of 1972, however, it was no longer production bottlenecks deriving from the sudden jump in demand that were causing inflation. Price controls were becoming less and less effective. This stimulated the demands for hikes in wages and salaries. The main cause of inflation had become the price-wage-price spiral.

The new pay levels in the public sector led to an increase in the fiscal deficit originally planned in December 1971. At the same time the government did not succeed in extracting more liquid resources from the upper- and middle-income groups. Between January and July the total deficit soared to −9 billion escudos or 90 percent of what had been originally scheduled for the whole year.[3]

The UP government had anticipated an increased flow of revenues deriving from new taxes on the income and consumption of upper- and middle-income groups (taxes on profits, real estate, capital gains and luxury consumption). But Congress voted these tax bills down, leaving an underfunded budget. At the same time the public agencies responsible for implementing the agrarian reform and setting up the area of social ownership had their funds cut back. Confronted with this parliamentary obstructionism, the Allende government had to opt either for (1) reducing pay increases, slowing down the agrarian reform, and cutting back on stock purchases (in the campaign to assemble the social property area); or (2) continuing all of these programs at the cost of a larger deficit. It was decided to adopt the second course.

In the enterprises of the social area, operating deficits continued to mount. While prices were held under strict controls in order to avoid an inflationary surge, wages and salaries and the cost of raw materials went up. Both this deficit and the fiscal imbalance were financed with internal credits, which led to even more monetary expansion. Between January and June 1972, the quantity of money in the hands of the private sector grew by 34.5 percent. The consumer price index jumped 27.5 percent in the same period. With production stalled, an increase in the money supply greater than an increase in the price index could only lead to yet more market disequilibria. The renewed monetary expansion was accompanied by a new phenomenon: a downward shift in the preference for liquidity occasioned by greater inflationary expectations. The circulation of money accelerated, provoking more demand pressures.

The balance of payments also deteriorated. The demand for consumer goods led to increased imports of food and raw materials; and, simultaneously, world market prices for these items went up. The combined effect of these two factors—increases in quantity and prices—was translated into a 27.5 percent increment in the import registers over the January to June 1972 period, compared with the same period the year before.[4] Total exports underwent a slight decline in value, even when copper production increased. Industrial and agricultural exports fell as one consequence of the greater domestic demand. The resurgence of imports and the slight reduction in exports yielded a deficit in the balance of trade higher than what had been predicted. Outflows of capital funds followed the same tendency as in 1971; as a result the total balance of payments deficit surged to dangerous levels.

The government focused its energies on the renegotiation of the external debt and the acquisition of new credits from the socialist countries. In April 1972, Chile won a postponement on the payment of some obligations, amounting to $165 million, which were to fall due that year. The creditor countries agreed to refinance only the sums payable in 1972, despite the fact that Chile had asked for a more extended period. The United States resisted this solution on principle as long as there was no agreement to compensate the copper companies, and it attempted to impose this criterion generally. The Western European countries exhibited more flexibility, and it was finally agreed to renegotiate the 1972 debt.[5]

Contacts with the socialist countries also paid off. Credits were conceded for machinery, raw materials and freely disposable resources. Chile especially needed this latter kind of support. The Soviet Union granted credits for $102 million, and China provided $52 million. Adding to these the credits supplied by the Eastern European countries, Chile received in 1972 a total volume of $226.3 million from the socialist bloc.[6] While these credits from the socialist countries amounted to significant aid, they could not resolve the most acute balance of payments problems at this point—problems that demanded above all freely disposable funds rather than credits for specific merchandise. Those who had entertained excessive expectations, imagining a kind of unlimited socialist aid, now understood that the crisis would have to be overcome mainly through a national effort and by changing domestic policies.

U.S. banks did not slacken in their effort to reduce funding to Chile: the $220 million in import credits available in November 1970 fell to $88 million in November 1972, and to $36 million in January of 1972. In order to deal with this deficit, the government was forced to resort to new measures. A system of strict administrative controls over imports was established. The Banco Central began to schedule all purchases and supervise all import transactions. This measure was inevitable given the magnitude of the problem, but it led to numerous bureaucratic obstacles, delayed necessary imports, and was incapable of discriminating the degree of urgency of imports.

With such a balance of payments deficit and surging inflation, the fixed-exchange policy caused the rate of exchange to lose all economic meaning. In May 1972, the Banco Central decided on a new devaluation which applied only to the brokers' market in currency, leaving unchanged the exchange policy for food and raw materials. The rigidity of the economic staff, its reluctance to implement new policies, had caused it once more to move in a partial and ultimately ineffective manner.

The main argument against devaluation was its inflationary impact. The regulatory value of a devaluation was underestimated; it was argued instead that most exports were inelastic with respect to the rate of exchange and that those categories which it was designed to encourage would receive subsidies. Imports would be ordered according to schedules drawn up by the state-run enterprises or by the Banco Central itself. This reasoning was more and more open to objection. On the one hand, imports became practically free, which meant a flood of requests for imports with which the administrative machinery could barely handle. Industrial or agricultural exports whose production depended on discretionary decisions for or against subsidies began to diminish. Products with imported components became very cheap, suited to the flourishing speculation, as occurred in the case of medicines and automobile replacements, which were traded as contraband to neighboring countries.

Finally, it is important to point out that in the midst of all these imbalances and disequilibria, total production continued to grow, reaching its highest point in the whole government period in the middle of 1972. The index of industrial production for the period January to June 1972 rose 13.7 percent with respect to the same period in 1971. Industry was working at top capacity. From this point on, any significant increase would require a considerable investment effort. The high level of production, in addition to enormous imports, fed an ample domestic supply of goods; but this was still insufficient to respond to the persistent increase in demand.

Ambiguities in Social Property

The area of social ownership continued as the source of the most intense disputes. The meeting at El Arrayán failed to resolve the question of whether to go ahead with the expropriations or to seek a parliamentary accord with the Christian Democrats. The result was that both courses were pursued at once, creating subsequent confusion.

In February 1972, Congress passed the constitutional amendment governing the social property area introduced by the Christian Democrats. This bill established criteria quite different from those of the government: (1) manufacturing enterprises were left outside the social area and their inclusion in this sector could only be brought about by passing a separate law for each expropriation or requisition; (2) the legal powers of the state to buy stock in private companies were abolished; (3) all state acquisitions of private firms subsequent to October 1971 were nullified; and (4) the general practice would be to turn over the ownership and management of all socialized firms and banks to their workers. In order to escape this impasse, the government decided to continue to acquire the stock of larger firms through public offerings. It was considered necessary to move quickly, and this procedure of bulk stock purchases at least allowed the government to reinforce positions already won.

The passage of the constitutional amendment and the intense anti-government campaign aggravated the conflict between the Executive and Congress. The government announced that it would veto those provisions of the constitutional amendment with which it was in disagreement. The opposition replied that the Executive's vetos could be overridden in Congress by a simple majority. This assertion created a new obstruction. According to the 1925 Constitution, then in effect, Congress needed to muster a two-thirds majority in order to override an Executive veto of a law it had passed. The government argued that this rule was all the more valid in the case of a constitutional amendment, so that such measures could not take effect unless vetos were rejected by a two-thirds vote in Congress. The opposition majority stuck to its position that a 51 percent vote should decide the issue. In order to resolve this difference, the Allende government proposed submitting the case to the Constitutional Tribunal, the court charged with deciding such disputes between the Executive and Congress. No understanding, however, was reached; and the question remained to haunt later developments. It should be observed that the opposition in this period did not present a united front with respect to the social area. One group within the CDP was still inclined to negotiate; while the National Party was unanimous in insisting that all government acts not in accord with the opposition-passed amendment should be declared illegal.

In the midst of the debate concerning the constitutional amendment and the legality of the government's activities, the government itself acted ambiguously. On the one hand, the Minister of Justice initiated discussions with the Christian Democrats in order to arrive at a common agreement. These conversations were hopeful, and the controversy was close to resolution. In the midst of this process, however, the Ministry of the Economy began an energetic attack on several firms accused of speculation and hoarding. These firms were requisitioned, which led to the breaking off of the UP-CDP discussions; the attempt to reach a wider agreement was frustrated.

Given this outcome the differences within the UP began to be expressed more openly. The most radical sector regarded any accord with the Christian Democrats as a sign of weakness. The groups in the majority within the coalition believed it was essential to reach some kind of wider political understanding in order to overcome the stalemate. Meanwhile the Radical Left Party, that faction of the Radical Party most concerned to effect a quick agreement with the Christian Democrats, decided to break with the UP and withdrew from the government in April 1972. The alternative positions in the crisis of the coalition became even more sharply defined.

With the strengthening of the opposition, the neutral and legalistic performance of the controller-general and the judiciary system began to change into a clear bias against the Executive branch. The controller's office began to reject the government's decrees of intervention in private firms, thus changing the line it had followed in 1971 and altering the criteria it had upheld before 1970. Similarly, the courts chose to rule against the Executive in arbitrary suits brought by the large property owners, entering at the same time into matters in which they lacked competence and had never before sought to rule. It was becoming clear that the degree of flexibility of the Chilean institutional order did not depend on the letter of the law, but instead on the political power which each of the forces struggling within the state apparatus could muster up. Confronted with this new reality, the UP resolved to pursue yet again an accord with the Christian Democrats. This attempt was initiated again in June, and with these efforts a new stage of the larger process was begun.

The economic importance of the 90 firms which the UP wanted to integrate into the social area accounted for the intensity of the institutional conflict. If the government succeeded, the power base of the Right in Chile would be substantially eroded. What was at issue was nothing less than a revolutionary transformation, one which was changing the structure of power and would open the way for control by the state and the workers over a decisive sector of the economy. Of the 90 firms, 74 were industrial, 6 commercial, 4 involved in transport and communications, and 6 in electricity, gas and water. The 74 industrial firms constituted the critical point, since the Christian Democrats were in agreement that the others on the list of 90 should be absorbed into the social area. Even when their quantitative importance was not spectacular, the enterprises involved controlled the production of widely used intermediate goods, and most of them were either monopolies or dominant in their sector.

Advances in Agrarian Reform and Banking

While the social property area seemed bogged down in numerous difficulties, the government had almost fulfilled its goals in other areas. By July 1972, the state had achieved control of 85 percent of bank credits in domestic currency and 95 percent of credits in foreign currency. The agrarian reform continued at the same rapid pace that it had achieved in 1971. But the headlong speed of the reform generated new problems. Landowners began to utilize several devices, both legal and extralegal, to prevent the state from taking possession of expropriated lands. In the first place they mobilized peasants on their estates against the reform, using the argument that the government would create state enterprises rather than cooperative farms. This line was effective among some groups of farmworkers, who began to occupy the estates on which they worked in order to prevent the entry of government officials from the Agrarian Reform Corporation. In the second place, landlords resorted to judicial measures to contest the applicability of the law to their estates. The provincial courts upheld these demands with some frequency, blocking the takeover of the estates and delaying productive work. The same tactics used in fighting the social property area were thus employed on the agrarian front: the institutional devices wielded by the government were challenged, both to obstruct its performance and create the suspicion of illegality.

The political and social agitation provided opportunities for the extreme Left to create de facto situations, seizing estates and thus pushing the government beyond its stated intentions. These occupations frequently involved land not included in the agrarian reform law, leaving the government the dilemma of either evicting the peasants or conceding the attack on small and medium landowners, whose interests were not supposed to be at stake in the agrarian reform. In this situation the organization of the estates already subject to reform suffered, and yields fell. The government could not clearly define its policies of productive organization, supply, incentives, forms of ownership and management. The speed of the process surpassed the existing organizational capacity.

In sum, the UP government had made progress toward its strategic objectives, but the institutional channels were almost completely blocked. The Right concentrated all of its forces in combating the changes in property ownership, blaming all failures in the functioning of the market on these reforms. For the

Right, therefore, the root of all problems confronting the national economy lay in the social property area.

The Opposition Goes on the Offensive

By June 1972, a bipolar political framework had crystallized. The CDP-National Party alliance led to new accords. Even though the differences between these two parties were steadily diminishing, the purposes that each of them pursued in the alliance were distinct. For the National Party, the very program of the UP constituted a dire menace. Its objective was to halt the program, even at the cost of a collapse of the democratic system. Within the CDP, one faction was assuming positions similar to those of the National Party, but a significant sector still sought only to limit the advances of the government program. The Center-Right alliance served the purposes of both opposition groups. For the National Party and the conservative wing of the CDP, the alliance facilitated the blocking of the institutional apparatus and the inhibition of government action. The constant accusations of illegality helped create the climate for a coup. In the case of the progressive Christian Democrats, the alliance served to bolster their negotiating position and would allow them to impose their viewpoints in any eventual agreement with the UP.

This polarization and the growing gap between government and the opposition led the UP to revise its political line with respect to the Christian Democrats. The opinion of that UP sector opposed to any accord continued to predominate; but the growing difficulties confronting the government reinforced the viewpoint of others who were in favor of limited agreements on specific issues, as in the case of the constitutional amendment regulating the public sector. The oscillation between these positions continued and led to contradictory situations. Meanwhile, in the society at large, middle-class groups switched their affiliation to the rightwing parties and their positions. By the middle of 1972, a supposedly key point in the UP strategy—the alliance of wage workers and salaried employees with the middle classes—had been invalidated. The Right had already sealed its alliance with smaller business owners and had thoroughly penetrated their major trade associations. The government could not counteract this turn of events.

A majority of the technicians and professionals also assumed an antigovernment stance. Thus, for example, the national association of doctors sponsored a national work stoppage in May 1972, protesting supposed affronts to the authority of doctors in provincial hospitals on the part of local residents. For professional people just as for many public employees, rank and position in the bureaucratic career ladder had a very important influence on political behavior.

The growing opposition of the middle sectors to the government's program led to an intensified debate within the UP concerning the kind of policy that could most effectively regain their support. The prevailing thinking, which emphasized conceding more economic advantages, was subject to question.

The most radical sectors of the UP, opposed to such concessions, upheld the thesis that the sociopolitical alignment of the middle classes was basically conditioned by their perception of the balance of power between the large property owners and the Right on the one hand, and the workers and the Left on the other. This opinion was widespread among the hardliners, who opposed any accords with moderates outside the UP. Those in the UP opposing the radicals argued that middle-class groups would turn on the government in the event of a total polarization, and that it was thus necessary to grant them concessions to avoid this possibility. The latter position, of course, would lose its force once the confrontation intensified and the active support of low-income workers and salaried employees became indispensable for the government's survival.

And this is in fact what happened. As a response to the Right-inspired agitations of the *gremios* (trade associations), the UP encouraged even more direct participation by workers in the tasks of the government. At this point a new stage in the process was begun: the direct, unmediated involvement of the masses in political action. Given the obstruction of the legal-institutional framework and its growing uselessness in channeling political conflict, the opposed social forces began to come into open conflict with each other in the larger political arena, outside the sphere of formal governmental institutions and procedures. Finally, groups of impatient officers began to maneuver within the armed forces. In March 1972, the government turned back an attempted coup and detained one of the conspirators.

The "Lo Curro Conclave"

Faced with the evident exhaustion of the existing economic policy, the president issued a call to the political parties to open a new debate aimed at deciding definitively on a change. Another round of meetings was opened in June 1972, which became generally known as the "Lo Curro conclave." Once more two approaches were proposed, but this time the options were stated in a firmer and more coherent manner. In substantive matters the two options considered were as follows:

Option 1	Option 2
1. Consolidate what had been attained so far in the area of social ownership, pushing forward only in the case of those firms appearing on the list made public by the government.	1. Continue moving ahead rapidly in the order to maintain and increase popular support. Extend the area of social ownership in order to augment administrative control mechanisms. Economic imbalances (inflation, speculation, supply failures) to be met with growing state intervention.

2. Launch a great effort to increase production in the public sector enterprises, especially in copper and agriculture. Maximize conservation of foreign currency reserves.

3. Effect a general financial readjustment through (1) price increases, especially for the goods and services of public sector enterprises in order to reduce their deficits; (2) strict wage controls; and (3) a new foreign exchange rate.

4. Impose greater labor discipline, consolidation of the lines of authority, gradual increase in workers' participation.

2. Production in socialized enterprises should be pushed, but not so much as to jeopardize worker mobilization.

3. Financial adjustments should be effected, but with less reliance on market mechanism. Distribution and prices should be supervised by a administrative controls and direct popular organization. Liquid resources should be extracted from middle- and upper-income groups, and less emphasis should be placed on wage controls.

4. Participation should be emphasized above all, with confidence that workers would create their own solutions to overcome difficulties.

With regard to international support, both sides affirmed the urgent necessity of obtaining greater resources from the socialist countries, Latin America and Western Europe.

Option 1 was favored by the president and supported principally by the Communist Party and the Radical Party. Option 2 was preferred by the Socialist Party. The government finally settled on the first approach. On June 19, 1972, President Allende designated a new cabinet.[7] The ministers of economy and finance were changed.[8] The initial economic policy was buried and a new stage in the process was set in motion.

Notes

1. Since the Right did not command the parliamentary majority necessary to press its charges, it needed the support of the CDP. But the latter discarded the accusations against the minister of the economy and concentrated on the minister of the interior, who was dismissed from office. This set the precedent for what amounted to political trails against the minister, a procedure which violated the spirit of the Constitution.

2. Figures from the Banco Central de Chile. See Consejo Interamericano de la Alianza para el Progreso, "El esfuerzo interno y las necesidades de financiamiento externo para el desarrollo de Chile" (Washington, D.C.: OEA, April 1972).

3. The current account deficit mounted to 3.01 billion escudos between January and July 1972, despite expectations of a 1.33 billion escudo surplus for the whole year. The deficit for the first seven months came to 9.05 billion escudos, whereas the total deficit for all of 1972 (current and capital accounts) had been planned in December 1971 to reach 10 billion escudos. Data from the Ministry of Finance.

4. Banco Central, *Boletín Mensual* (September 1972).
5. The debt renegotiation meant postponing payments falling due between November 1971 and December 1972. It covered 70 percent of the indebtedness to government agencies of 14 countries.
6. Data from SEREX. Directory of External Credits, cited in Consejo Interamericano de la Alianza para el Progreso, "El esfuerzo interno y las necesidades de financiamiento externo para el desarrollo de Chile" (Washington, D.C.: OEA, June 1973), p. 159.
7. The Communist Party affirmed the necessity of consolidating positions. Its viewpoint was that "what characterizes the present conjuncture, in our opinion, is that the balance of forces has turned against the working class and the Popular Government because of political and economic errors . . . it would be fatal to continue to expand the numbers of our enemies; to the contrary, concessions will have to be made in order to neutralize at least some of the specific social groups; mistaken tactics will have to be changed." O. Millas, "La clase obrera en las condiciones del Gobierno Popular," *Principios,* 145(May–June 1972), p. 39. Orlando Millas became Minister of Finance in June 1972 and was later appointed Minister of the Economy.
8. Pedro Vuskovic was replaced by Carlos Matus as Minister of the Economy, and Orlando Millas succeeded Américo Zorrilla in the Ministry of Finance.

CHAPTER 6

Attempt at Readjustment

Over the first year and a half of the Allende government, social and political conflicts had spread and intensified. The massive presence of the unions, the participation of workers in the factories and peasants in the countryside, the supervision of prices and distribution by neighborhood associations, and the firm resolve of the government to change the forms of property ownership were all unequivocal signs of the revolutionary nature of the process. The social groups who had wielded economic power and the parties of the Right understood that only a frontal opposition would suffice. The ultimate cause of the tensions rested in the basic contradiction between the interests of the dominant groups and the profound changes sought by the UP government. Nevertheless, the intensity of the struggle had sharpened unnecessarily. Anti-government sentiment permeated ever wider sectors of the middle class, largely as a consequence of the economic situation and of the absence of minimal operating agreements with the legislature.

In July 1972, the government decided to confront these weaknesses, and it proceeded to move in two directions: pursuing an accord with the Christian Democrats on the legal framework of the social property area, and modifying its economic policy. By four months later, in October 1972, both attempts had failed. That month the opposition succeeded in staging a stoppage of transport owners that qualitatively changed the forms of the political struggle. This crisis gave rise in November to the first Cabinet to include members of the armed forces, thus initiating a new phase. From this point on, economic policy lost any element of choice and became almost entirely constrained by strong political limitations.

This chapter analyzes the period between July and the first part of November 1972. The outcome of negotiations with the Christian Democrats is discussed, as well as the economic policies that were applied and the political context that engendered the "October stoppage" and the opposition offensive.

The Search for Political Accord on Social Ownership

In 20 months the UP had placed under state control, either permanently or temporarily, almost all of the banks and many industrial firms. The institutional mechanisms it utilized to effect these transfers, however, were increasingly subjected to legal and political challenges. The Christian Democrats, with the support of the National Party, had passed a Constitutional amendment which restricted the Executive's powers and attempted to force the return of some of the socialized firms. The government had reacted by vetoing some of the provisions of the amendment and adding others. Specifically, it attached a new and shorter list of firms, as proof of its intentions to limit expropriations to those established in its program. In April 1972, the government had entered into another round of discussions with the CDP, but without success.

New conversations were begun in June, supported by the progressive wing of the CDP. The rest of the Party, however, was awaiting a favorable moment to sabotage any chance of an agreement. The National Party and the business associations attacked and pressured the Christian Democrats in order to undermine the discussions and prevent the implementation of a reform which would definitively alter their base of economic power.

Several weeks of discussions between the UP and the Christian Democrats led to the following agreements:

1. With respect to the extension of the social property area, the Christian Democrats had exempted most industrial firms and asserted that a change in ownership for any particular firm could only be accomplished through the passage of a specific law. The UP, in contrast, insisted on socializing the 90 largest firms in the country all at once. A compromise agreement was reached, allowing for expropriation of about 80 companies. The UP accepted the requirement of a separate law for every firm, and the Christian Democrats agreed to include in the constitutional amendment a list of firms which would immediately enter the social area. One specific difference arose with relation to the largest paper-producing firm, controlled by the Matte-Alessandri group.[1] The Allende government insisted on its expropriation and proposed that the distribution of paper to the press be regulated by law, in order to assure a fair supply to all sectors. The Christian Democrats rejected this provision, and insisted on leaving this firm in private hands. Finally, the president accepted the Christian Democrat position, promising to press the point at a later stage.[2]

2. As for the banks, the UP argued the necessity to expropriate them, while allowing for the participation of their workers in management. The Christian Democrats wanted both the ownership and the management of the banks to be turned over to their employees. For the UP, this meant granting excessive power to a restricted number of workers, as well as limiting the capacity of the state to plan and implement its policies. The Christian Democrats, on the other hand, argued that state takeover of banking would provide the government with excessive political power. A compromise agreement was reached allowing for state ownership and administration by boards consisting of five representatives of the state, five workers' delegates and a manager designated by the state. Four

banks, in which the workers would elect seven representatives and the state would appoint three, were excluded from this general rule.[3]

3. The issue of "workers' enterprises," or self-management, was also debated. The Christian Democrats proposed that, apart from ownership, a procedure be established allowing workers to manage their own enterprises. The Christian Democrats were by no means unanimous on this issue. One current in the party wanted the ownership of each particular enterprise to rest with the set of all workers in self-managed firms. Another group argued that ownership should be cooperative, restricted to workers in each individual enterprise. Yet a third group, less inclined to alter the forms of property ownership, suggested that it would be enough if workers assumed management powers and paid an annual rent on capital to the private owner. In general the Christian Democrats argued that the larger firms also ought to be managed by their workers and not by the state. For the UP, administration of the large enterprises of the social area had to rest with the state, supplemented by participation of the workers. Concerning medium-sized enterprises, the UP was prepared to accept self-management; but several different viewpoints predominated within the coalition rather than one definitive opinion. Some upheld a strictly statist and centralist position. Others believed in a more participatory approach, allowing for worker control of management in some cases. For most of the UP parties, worker self-management was not of central importance in this phase. Since this kind of organization could only be extended at the cost of the private sector, it would augment the uncertainty and resistance of smaller business owners. Those UP groups who had split from the CDP, however, were strong supporters of self-managed enterprises. An agreement was reached as well on this issue, based on the following criteria: ownership would be socialized, but those enterprises included in the self-managed area would not fall under the authority of the Corporación de Fomento (the agency which held formal title to and directed the activities of the state enterprises), but instead would be guided by a new corporation, one in which workers would have an equal representation with state representatives. The Allende government also agreed that some of the 80 largest enterprises would be organized according to the Christian Democrats' thinking on self-management.

4. The Christian Democrats proposed that workers share in the profits of those state enterprises in which they were employed. The UP objected, arguing that such a policy would give rise to a privileged elite of high-income workers in the largest, most capital-intensive enterprises. It was finally agreed that a restricted proportion of the profits should be distributed in the form of welfare services and items of collective consumption. The bulk of the profits would be reinvested in a social fund serving all of the worker-run enterprises.

5. With regard to the state's powers to intervene and requisition private firms, the government agreed to more rigorous definition and a limitation

on the length of time such actions could last. Finally the government promised to introduce a bill specifying guarantees for the owners of small and medium-sized businesses.

These negotiations laid the groundwork for a satisfactory solution, one conciliating the two viewpoints which together commanded a political majority in Chile. Nevertheless, the Right and the conservative wing of the CDP managed ultimately to frustrate the accord.

When agreement was complete except for a few secondary issues, the UP requested from the Christian Democrats a postponement in the date which had initially been set for introducing the agreement in Congress. Surprisingly, this request was rejected; the Christian Democrats insisted that the congressional debate begin right away. In the next few days, in order to prevent parliamentary obstruction by the Right and a consequent setback, the president signed all of the new bills, withholding his veto in some cases; all went ahead exactly according to the agreement with the Christian Democrats' leadership. Nevertheless, the Christian Democrats in Congress broke with the accord and proceeded to vote, together with the Right, for their original proposals. The progressive wing of the Party, which had led the negotiations, was in the end subordinated by the conservatives.

The institutional conflict gathered new force. The opposition overrode the Executive veto of its constitutional amendment by a simple majority and asserted that the government was obligated to promulgate the new law. The president responded that this action violated the Constitution: given that a simple statute required the support of a two-thirds vote of Congress to be promulgated over Executive veto, it was absurd to hold that a constitutional amendment of greater scope need only attract a simple majority vote. If this were the case, it would be easier to legislate through constant amendments to the Constitution—a patent irrationality.[4] In order to resolve the legal dilemma, the government held that the conflict between the two branches of state should be decided by the Constitutional Tribunal.[5] The opposition retorted that the only solution lay in a plebiscite. The question was left pending, and it was not until May 10, 1973 that the government appealed to the Constitutional Tribunal. In the meantime the political tensions kept building.

A New Economic Policy

In July 1972, the Allende government made its first and last serious attempt to change its economic policy. The central purpose of the measures adopted at this point was to reduce the imbalance between aggregate demand and supply. A price increase was approved in the belief that although inflation would initially worsen as a result of the price hikes, they would ultimately produce stability and fewer shortfalls in supply. The price increases would be differentiated. First priority would go to the enterprises in the social area, in order to curtail their losses. The objective was to put these enterprises on a self-financing basis, thus eliminating the pressures on the money supply stemming from bank credits granted to finance their running operations. New price levels would be conceded to small and medium private firms in order to allow them to operate at normal rates of return. On the other hand, those firms which had been marked by the government for socialization but which still remained in the private sector would be authorized to raise prices only to the extent strictly necessary to cover operating costs.

The price policy was also designed to differentiate among products, and one problem was to make this aspect of the policy compatible with the bias in favor of the social property area. Price increments for commodities of a less vital nature would be relatively greater than the increases for essential goods and services. Telephone rates, for example, would be subjected to a readjustment differentiated according to urban zones: middle- and upper-class residential areas, as well as international calls, would experience higher rate hikes than the rest of the city. Similarly, durable consumer goods would go up more than foodstuffs.

The second priority would go to agricultural prices, in order to stimulate larger crops, particularly since the planting season was just getting underway. Furthermore, the state, through its purchasing funds, would be able to buy up food before it could be channeled to the black market. The higher prices would also allow for the self-financing of the agrarian reform sector, which had been absorbing excessive fiscal resources to meet operating expenses.

The rate of exchange would be modified. It was thought that the devaluation of the escudo would lead to a decline in superfluous imports and a stimulus for exports of industrial and agricultural products. At the same time, the accounting losses of the copper companies, whose revenues in escudos were lower than their cost, could be cut. Fiscal revenues from tariffs would increase. Finally, the contraband traffic to adjacent countries in those local products that included many imported components would be discouraged. Throughout 1972 smuggling to neighboring countries of pharmaceutical supplies, automobile parts, cigarettes and canned food had been growing, while scarcities in Chile were worsening. The government could not contain this flow by stiff controls on the borders, since to do so would generate political tensions, both national and international.[6]

It was clear that the new measures would be effective only if they could be brought to bear on the factors generating the fiscal deficit and the deficit in the social property area. The latter would be reduced with the new prices; the first, however, was less easy to get at. Public expenditure was extremely inflexible. It could be brought down only by cutting back on public sector salaries and wages or on spending for services, housing and construction. Both routes were politically unacceptable for the UP, since such measures would undermine income redistribution and full employment.

A tax reform was not feasible, given the hostile attitude in Congress. In its place several approaches were suggested for drawing off liquid funds from higher-income strata: new saving plans (some linked to specific durable consumer goods); a state monopoly for the sale of durable products (allowing the treasury to reap the revenues generated by higher prices); mandatory automobile and life insurance; monthly withholding for some taxes; and a campaign against tax evasion.[7] These measures had to be complemented with greater state controls on the commercialization of essential consumer goods. The government called for the strengthening of popular organizations charged with checking prices and distribution, and it proposed setting up chains of state-run supermarkets for the sale of essential goods in low-income urban areas.

The above approach was elaborated and debated over the course of July 1972. Its implementation was postponed until August, however, since the government decided to wait a few weeks until after a by-election in Coquimbo, in order to avoid the risk of the opposition making political capital of the price increases.

Implementation of the New Policy and Its Results

The first measure adopted in August 1972 was the devaluation of the escudo, by an average of 85 percent for imports and 33 percent for exports. The policy of multiple exchange rates was reinforced, differentiating among five markets: services and transfers, food and fuel, raw materials, capital goods and luxury products. Exports were also differentiated by type of product. Immediately following this move, the government authorized price increases, beginning with foodstuffs, agricultural and some industrial products. The increments varied from 30 percent to 150 percent.[8] Finally, in September, price hikes for goods and services of enterprises in the social area were approved. These included a rise in rates for public transportation, both rail and airline.

Already by September 1972, the level and number of increases had surpassed the expectations of the government. For the January to June period, the consumer price index had registered a 27.5 percent rise. After the new policy was put into effect, the soaring prices brought the increase in this index to 99.8 percent for the January to September period. The inflationary surge provoked deep concerns within the UP because it was eroding workers' real incomes while failing to reduce shortages significantly, and the opposition was seizing on these results to attack the government and mobilize its supporters.

In order to alleviate the impact of the price increases in essential goods, the Executive proposed a cash bonus in the form of a single amount paid equally to all workers. A few days later the government resolved to grant a pay adjustment beginning in October, in order to compensate for price increases registered since January. The wage-price spiral was beginning to operate openly, blunting the whole process of economic adjustment.

At the same time, overwhelming demands to hold back the price rises emerged from within the UP. These pressures became more urgent at the end of September and into October, as a reaction to ever harsher attacks from the opposition. The Right and the Christian Democrats launched a fierce offensive, calling public meetings in several provinces to protest the increases, taking up a populist stance, and pushing for wage increases for the workers. Simultaneously, new conflicts around other political problems were taking shape, conflicts that obliged the government to mobilize the workers and consolidate their organizations in factories and neighborhoods.

Under such circumstances, the consecutive price hikes provoked disquiet and confusion within the Left parties and workers' organizations. From one side, the government was asking the workers to make sacrifices in order to contain the economic imbalances; and, from the other side, the opposition was unleashing a strong institutional, ideological and mass-based offensive. It was difficult for the UP to demand sacrifices and renewed support at the same time.

The opposition offensive culminated in October with a nationwide work stoppage that achieved alarming proportions. Given this state of affairs, the government was forced to suspend the price increments and set about reaching an agreement with the striking truck drivers and store owners in order to bring the political situation under control.

Once the new price rises were reined in so abruptly, the initial intentions behind the change in economic policy came to naught, since prices of the products in the social area were not modified at all. Meanwhile the cost of local and imported raw materials and wages in the social area had grown. Instead of diminishing, therefore, the deficits in the public sector enterprises increased. The price distortions which it had been hoped to correct actually worsened, especially for the basic products manufactured in state-run enterprises.

The break with the new policy worsened economic difficulties, especially since, along with suspending the price rises, the government granted workers a 100 percent wage adjustment—pay levels were doubled. But this time the economy had already put to work all of its productive machinery and was also being victimized by a nationwide work stoppage of store owners and truck owners. Thus a suddenly increased demand was turned loose on an economy incapable of augmenting supply—an economy, in fact, which was beginning to produce less.

The fiscal deficit also mounted. The wage adjustments decided on by the government, as well as the higher cost of goods and services consumed by it, far surpassed the increase in tax revenues deriving from the price hikes. In October it was calculated that the total fiscal deficit would come to 24.4 billion escudos by the end of 1972, almost twice the amount predicted at the beginning of the year.[9]

The Allende government made various attempts to reduce this deficit. It proposed to Congress several alternatives for financing the October adjustments. Almost all of these suggestions were rejected out of hand. The government also advanced a policy of differential readjustments, according to which lower-income workers would receive an adjustment equal to the rise in the cost of living in the January to October period, while higher-income groups would receive a proportionately smaller increment. The unions and employees' associations opposed this measure, and it could not be put into effect.

Both the fiscal deficit and that of the social property area boosted the expansion in money supply. Total money grew from 36.95 billion escudos to 51.59 billion escudos between June 30 and October 31, climbing to 70.48 billion escudos by the end of 1972. In the twelve months between December 1971 and December 1972, money supply had soared by 173 percent.

Factors Frustrating the Attempted Correction

The working hypothesis of the government's economic staff was that a rapid initial increase in prices would be followed by a period of declining inflation, stabilizing after a short while at some other level. The first price increases, however, stimulated a chain reaction, one which could not be braked right away. Instead the successive feedbacks between one increase and another would have to go through several rounds before the sequence of increments could begin to die down. Deceleration would also require breaking the wage-price spiral, in order to prevent each price hike leading automatically to a wage increase. This meant that other compensatory measures would have to be adopted to stave off a deterioration in the real income of the poorest groups.

The existence of automatic readjustment mechanisms, built into the system historically over the course of a long inflationary experience and in a democratic context, impeded a sharp deceleration after the initial inflationary burst. It was inconceivable for the UP to oppose income adjustments and repress the resulting discontent.

Strong demand pressures were added to the inflationary factors on the cost side. Estimates made at that time, based on a cost-inflation model, indicated that the price level which would be produced by the variations in the principal factors (labor cost, rate of exchange, level of profitability and productivity) would be lower than that required to balance supply and demand in the money market. In other words, inflationary demand pressures were more serious than the pressures resulting from the adjustments necessary to finance production costs.

Furthermore, the announcement of the new policy and the first steps taken to implement it had created a strong inflationary expectation. Up until this point, fear of the power of the government, which exercised a rigid control over prices, had caused firms to behave cautiously. Once this barrier was broken price pressures were given free vent.

Another factor causing the inflationary surge was the sequence of implementation of government policies. This matter was discussed by the technical staff at some length, especially the question of whether to lead off with a devaluation of the escudo or with increases in commodity prices. It was decided to begin with the devaluation, but this served to boost the inflationary expectations of the private firms. Certain that higher prices would be approved and in an attempt to pressure the government to this end, private firms began to withhold their products from trade and to suspend sales while awaiting price increases. The technical staff was thus confronted with the total disappearance of some products from the market and growing scarcities on all fronts. In order to resolve this problem, immediate price adjustments were granted to the private sector. The wave of increases spread quickly; but by the time political resistance to the inflationary surge surfaced, price increments for the social property area had still not been approved. The policy was derailed just before price increases in this sector were to be granted.

Finally, the staff work behind the formulation and implementation of the new policies was weak. The various ministers could not count on stable technical support. Most of their technical assistants, too few to begin with, were absorbed with resolving specific problems arising from supply failures, strikes, seizures of private firms, and other new conflicts. While the general line of action was clear, there did not exist a coherent quantitative model capable of calibrating the various options and their effects.

Now let us consider the political context. It seems evident that the attempt at correction, even given the difficulties described above, would have enjoyed some success if the government had been able to sustain it over a longer period. This was not possible on account of the political situation which began to crystallize over the same few months. The opposition altered its line of attack radically: it began calling large meetings where the workers' loss of purchasing power was denounced and immediate compensation was demanded. The October work stoppage effectively destroyed the whole program initiated in July 1972. The government was forced to adopt emergency measures.

The experience of this attempt at adjustment convinced the Allende government that it was no longer possible to resort to fiscal and price policies in order to correct economic imbalances. Conventional policy measures simply could not work given the accumulated monetary pressures, the wage-price spiral and the intensity of political struggle. The stoppages and the virulent opposition on the part of many middle-class groups made it clear that these sectors could not be placated with mere attempts at reducing scarcities and market disarticulations. From this point on it would be a mistake to prejudice workers' incomes through price adjustments if no compensating ground could be gained among middle-class groups. In subsequent periods the government would have to sustain at all costs the living standard of the wage and salary workers who constituted its principal base of support. This overwhelming political necessity conditioned all further economic decisions. The crisis situation allowed only for more radical political choices, just at the moment when the balance of power was making such choices difficult, if not impossible, to implement.

The October Stoppage

While the government was putting into effect its new economic policies, the Right was stepping up its organizational work, and the trade associations were mobilizing. A quantum leap in this process occurred in September 1972 with the creation of a Unified Command Center for driver-owners of trucks, taxis and buses. This completed a network of *gremios*, or trade associations, among the small and medium bourgeoisie. At the same time the Right unleashed an astutely designed campaign of propaganda and psychological warfare in support of its political actions. Scarcities and economic problems were spotlighted; an image of anarchy and public disorder (which, in fact, rightist activist groups were busily stimulating) was communicated; there was a general effort to exacerbate fear and anxiety. The role of mass communications media was particularly vital here, and the opposition was dominant in this area in both quantity and quality.

Having gone on the offensive, the Right began to prepare a conflict in which its forces could be concentrated with greatest effect. In August 1972, the leaders of the various trade and business associations decreed a nationwide 24-hour work stoppage.[10] Immediate support was forthcoming from the associations of large property-owners: the Confederation for Production and Commerce, the National Agricultural Society, the Society for the Promotion of Manufacturing, and the Chilean Construction Association. This front was joined later by the Confederation of Small Businessowners. Finally, a series of incidents of public disorders was staged in Santiago, forcing the government to decree an emergency area. A few days later the Unified Command Center for Transport made public a demand for higher rates, improved supplies of spare parts and more vehicles. These demands reflected the preoccupations of all small owners in transport, who had suffered in the last few months from a growing scarcity in parts and replacements and from the freezing of their rates. At the beginning of September they threatened a stoppage if the government did not satisfy their demands. At this point the conflict still had a strictly sectoral economic basis. Slowly but surely these economic grievances were turned to fulfill the frankly seditious aims of the leaders of the protest movement, who were synchronizing their moves according to a larger plan.

The following days were marked by tension, public disorder, demonstrations and counter-demonstrations. Meanwhile the government's negotiators could not arrive at a settlement with the transporters' leadership. On September 13, the president publicly warned of the existence of a plot designed to subvert public order and overthrow the government. An attempt was being made to block all land and water transport in the country, cut supplies and paralyze the economy. A week later an Army general was discharged for complicity in an attempted coup.[11]

The offensive was deployed in full force throughout October. The Right expanded the range of conflict by initiating a campaign in favor of price increases for the monopoly paper-producing firms, presenting the question as one of defending freedom of expression. All of the trade confederations backed this demand, including the truckers, store owners, farmers and industrialists. At about the same time the Kennecott Corporation took advantage of the domestic situation to press legal suits in Europe. Kennecott requested an embargo on Chilean copper, claiming that it was the proper owner of all such shipments since it did not recognize nationalization. A French court upheld the company's position in October, after which the Chilean government ordered a temporary suspension of copper shipments to France. In the meantime the truckers' movement had received a favorable response to its petitions and things apparently had returned to normal. A new stoppage, however, was begun on October 7, this time to protest the government's attempt to set up a state-owned transit system in Aysen Province. The truck owners' stoppage went nationwide just as Kennecott was pressing its court actions abroad.

The government decided to detain the leaders of the truck owners' association and press charges against them in open court. This move proved to be the detonator in an already explosive situation. The truck owners immediately blocked the highways, and the shortages of essential products worsened. The government was forced to proclaim a state of emergency once again and delegate responsibility for maintaining public order to the armed forces. Leaders of *gremios* for bus drivers, taxi owners, fuel distributors, store owners and small industry agreed to join the stoppage. The CDP made public its total support for the movement. Simultaneously, Kennecott attempted to win an embargo of Chilean copper shipped to Sweden. On October 17, the Medical Association and the Federation of Secondary Students (controlled by the CDP) joined the stoppage, followed shortly by the Association of Lawyers. Two days later, the truck owners' leader, Leon Vilarín, announced that a "List of Demands of Chile" was being prepared. This announcement revealed that, behind the image of struggling trade guilds, a larger political operation was in motion. Also on October 17, Kennecott succeeded in embargoing Chilean copper in Holland.

On October 20, a National Command Center for Gremio Defense was created, linking together all of the confederations of large and small entrepreneurs and most of the professional associations. This National Command Center prepared a list of public demands: the government was called upon to suspend its closing down of some opposition radio stations for broadcasting seditious programs; higher prices for the single paper factory were requested; promulgation of the constitutional amendment regulating the social property area was urged; finally the petition demanded the suppression of neighborhood organizations in charge of supervising the distribution of consumer goods. This was clearly a political platform, addressing issues beyond the scope of ordinary trade guild grievances.

The pressure was increased: doctors left their emergency rooms in the hospitals, and there was a general increase in acts of violence, highway blockades and sabotage of railroad tracks and pipelines. The National Party and the Christian Democrats joined in pressing new impeachment proceedings against four cabinet ministers.

On November 1, 1972 all of the ministers turned in their resignations and on the third a new cabinet was formed, one which included several representatives of the military. Within a few days, the conflict had been resolved and the strikers had accepted the same conditions proposed by the government weeks before. The truckers' stoppage had lasted 26 days and had seriously threatened total economic paralysis.

A new political phonomenon had emerged in the larger political picture:

the opposition vanguard had been taken up by the petty bourgeois gremios. The large property owners could not paralyze the economy through lock-outs, because the state, supported by the workers, would intervene and seize the factories. The truck owners, however, constituted a large group whose activity was crucial to the economy but who were less vulnerable to intervention. The state lacked the mechanisms to replace them or to take control of their vehicles, apart from massive recourse to the armed forces. As a vanguard, the truck owners were mobile, dispersed over the length of the country, and were made up of small owners and therefore not classifiable as monopolists. The rightwing politicians and big businessmen had indeed scored a success in penetrating and mobilizing this kind of organization.

FORCES AT WORK DURING THE STOPPAGE

The government sensed from the beginning of the October stoppage that an attempt to overthrow it was underway. Nevertheless, it was thought that the action would last only for a few days, since the truckers could not survive without incomes for much longer. The government itself was eager to arrive at a settlement acceptable to the transport owners; but the leaders of the strike were putting off any agreement, expecting to be joined shortly by other gremios. Thus the government's first proposals were accepted in principle and later rejected. Week after week new demands were added until the stoppage culminated in an explicitly political challenge and key activities remained paralyzed for almost a month.

What factors finally turned back the efforts of the National Party and its allies on the extreme Right to paralyze the economy? In the industrial sector, the workers' organizations forced the owners to keep up production by threatening to seize control of all factories which were shut down. Moreover, many transport owners and professionals opposed to the stoppage stayed on the job, despite threats and sabotage. The government put the transport facilities of the state sector to work in order to maintain supply for vital activities. Students and workers formed voluntary work brigades to handle the most critical loading tasks.

The second decisive factor was the attitude of the high command of the armed forces. The latter cooperated with the government in preserving order and the institutional stability. This attitude frustrated the hopes of the Right for a coup and allowed the crisis to be overcome. The position of the constitutionalist officers was clearly reinforced by the high degree of organization demonstrated by the workers.

Seen in perspective the October stoppage was part of an overall strategy deployed at four levels by those on the Right who sought to instigate a coup. In the political-legal area, the central objective was to block legal channels and condemn the government as illegitimate. On the level of ideology and propaganda, the object was to create an impression of anarchy by spotlighting incidents of violence and disorder. Many of these incidents were in fact committed by extreme rightist groups, but the actions of the extreme Left contributed to the general atmosphere.

In the international field, the opposition plan counted on the support of the multinational corporations, particularly those whose copper assets had been nationalized, as well as of the Nixon administration, determined to shut off financing and so aggravate internal economic problems in Chile. Finally, at the level of direct action, the program of strikes, stoppages and large-scale sabotage was the first step in a series of action which would be perfected and intensified in the year to come.

The Christian Democrats were progressively drawn in to this strategy. The stated purpose of the Party, one sincerely held by most of its members, was not to overthrow the government, but to chasten it and force it to change its line. But the Christian Democrats, in order to maintain some leadership over the opposition and to avoid being isolated and overtaken by the National Party, began to adhere increasingly to the Right's tactics. Its own electoral constituency, disquieted by public disorder and economic problems, was pushing the Party toward harder opposition. Throughout the October stoppage, two attitudes were evident within the opposition ranks: some completely rejected the UP Program and sought to prevent its fulfillment at any cost, including an institutional breakdown and a coup d'état; others still honored the legitimacy of the institutional system and sought only to bring the government around to their viewpoint. Which of these positions was favored by the Center-Right alliance? While joint actions could favor both groups, the growing totality of the polarization led to the inevitable dominance of those pushing for a coup.[12]

The U.S. government was also involved in the October stoppage. CIA agents were secretly active among the groups on strike. Some truck owners admitted to the government at the time that they were receiving external aid in order to stay on strike. It should be pointed out, however, that even at this point the government lacked a clear understanding of the depth and range of U.S. involvement. Subsequent investigations by the United States Senate have thrown more light on this matter.[13]

The confrontation clearly threw the government into a very difficult dilemma. A compromising attitude, as had been exhibited in June, would only serve the hard-line opposition, since the democratic sectors in the opposition lacked the power to prevail. A hard-line position on the government's part would accelerate the confrontation. The room for maneuver was minimal, and the government's viability seemed to be slipping away. Confronted with this dilemma, the government realized that whichever option it chose, it would be essential to accumulate more force and cement firm, well-organized popular support. It was decided that the most urgent task was to consolidate the backing of the working class, adopting measures to heighten its organization and increase its share in the work of government.

We still need to know, however, why the small and medium bourgeoisie mobilized itself so overwhelmingly against the UP government. The commercial sector in Chile was grouped together into two organizations which had always been divided by differences of interest: the Central Chamber of Commerce represented large businessmen, while the National Merchants' Association embraced the smaller tradesmen. The first group had been trying since 1970 to forge an alliance with the second, a goal which was finally approximated with the help of an all-out ideological campaign. This convergence was fueled by several parallel developments: the growth of administrative controls and grassroots vigilance organizations—necessitated by scarcities, speculation, and the rise of the black market—awakened a fierce resistance on the part of smaller merchants, who saw these measures as a threat to their property. The UP behaved ineptly, failing to offer storekeepers the guarantees and favorable treatment which might have prevented this reaction. Nor was there any direct consultation with the leadership of this group of the sort that might have led to joint solutions. At the lower levels of the government, sectarianism and inconsistency were common in dealing with the storekeepers, as well as general hostility and simplistic appeals to popular organization, workers' power and spontaneity. Abrasive language and revolutionary phrase-making provoked more fear and uncertainty than did the actual measures taken by the government.

In contrast with those in trade, the truck owners did not have such coherent organizations. Because their investments were so small, usually only one or two vehicles, they had always functioned at the margins of the propertied class of industrialists, landowners and merchants. The government failed as well to grasp their strategic importance and their vital role in the day-to-day functioning of the economy. The truckers' discontent was based on real problems. Their profits had been cut by rate freezes, and the shortage of spare parts forced them to resort to the black market. Given this reality, it proved easy for the opposition to mobilize them and to use them later toward other ends. Moreover, at the ideological level they were naturally inclined to an anti-statist position because of their experience as self-made men engaged in independent activity. Despite all of these factors, many truck owners rejected the work stoppage, organized a separate union, and kept on working.

The professional associations did not have a coordinating center, and their function had traditionally been confined to fixing fees for services. The most active in the anti-Allende opposition were those in free practice rather than public functionaries. For the free practitioners, the prospect of an egalitarian social and economic order constituted a profound threat to their expectations and lifestyle. Their cultural values and consumption patterns were those of the large and medium property owners. Meanwhile the serious disturbances in the economic apparatus provoked a violent rejection of disorder and anarchy among the officeholding professionals. These developments were contrary to deeply engrained ideas of orderly procedure; they were inconsistent with notions of fixed careers, of achieved status attained over the years of deliberate conduct. The sectarianism of the UP, the abrupt shifts in personnel and in traditional promotion procedures, all provoked resistance to the ongoing changes. As for the small industrialists, they had always been at the fringes of the organized grand bourgeoisie. They were, however, quickly drawn into a common front in defense of private property by the larger owners.

The conduct of these middle groups was crucial to the viability of the UP's project. Structural change in any relatively advanced society cannot be realized without an effective political approach to the middle classes. This, in turn, demands a painstaking analysis of the factors that determine their conduct. In the crisis of October 1972, the organized workers composed a line of defense, but they could not by themselves preserve the balance of forces and go on the offensive.

CONSEQUENCES OF THE STRIKE

The October stoppage aggravated the economic imbalances. Despite the productive effort sustained by workers, salaried employees, and many professionals and technicians in the effort to counteract the strike, output was seriously affected. Partial estimates made by the government pointed to a grave situation in agriculture, commerce and transport.

Planting in the winter months (June to September) had suffered because of unfavorable climatic conditions, and it was hoped that this loss would be recouped in the spring (October to December). The stoppage, however, held up the supply of fertilizers, seeds, and other inputs, interrupting the round of farm tasks and causing a fall in the yields for the 1973 harvest. In commerce and industry, the stoppage cut sharply into inventories, already under normal operating levels. The large retail firms found themselves without the reserves needed to meet the demand that resurged once things went back to normal. Industrial production was also weakened because of the absence of primary materials, while copper production was lost as a result of the interruption in the transport of semi-refined ore to the smelting furnaces.

After this experience the government, as we have already indicated, decided that henceforth financial and pricing measures would be totally inadequate. Price increases would have to reach politically unacceptable levels if they were to have any noticeable effect. Price boosts of this order would produce a sharp drop in the real income of workers, peasants, and salaried employees, hence damaging a major objective of the UP; while such moves would not cause the middle classes to change their attitude. The social groups supporting the government would be hurt the most, while those groups interested in a coup d'état would take advantage of the new discontent to agitate for their own ends. An alternative approach began to take shape in the thinking of the UP: installing a system of direct, regulated distribution of a restricted class of essential goods to the whole population. If this kind of step was not taken and such goods were left open to market pressure, their prices would shoot up and they would become available only to upper income groups.

As for the social property area, the Executive found itself in control of 65 new enterprises after the October stoppage.[14] Many firms had shut down during this action; and the government, in concert with their workers and employees, had requisitioned them. In this sense the stoppage had an accelerating effect on the revolutionary process and fortified the workers' organizations by highlighting very clearly the profound nature of the conflict: the struggle for control of the means of production. Many of these newly requisitioned firms, however, were small or middle-sized and had not been included on the list submitted by the government at the end of 1971, nor did they conform to the criteria for socialization repeatedly enunciated by the government. This fact occasioned new problems with the opposition, which imposed as a condition for a return to normalcy the return of those firms intervened in October and a guarantee that there would be no reprisals against opposition activists. Once again the critical choice was asserting itself: whether to make new concessions to reduce the opposition pressures, thus risking the frustration of the workers who were stoutly defending the government, or to maintain an inflexible posture and thus aggravate the conflict.

At the social level the stoppage brought about a definitive alliance. On one side stood the organizations of the large owners, supported by the organized smaller businessmen, professional associations, and by some employees' unions as well. On the other side were aligned workers, peasants and the largest part of low-income salaried employees in the public and private sectors, joined as well by some professionals and small business owners. Class contradictions were overcoming the influence of party ideologies, especially in the case of the multiclass-based CDP. Thus many workers and employees originally affiliated with this party rejected the position of their national leadership and joined with their class cohorts on the Left.

The confrontation of October 1972 thus polarized the situation still more and generated a qualitative change: both sides upgraded their organizational capacity for extrainstitutional confrontation. Interpretations of events began to diverge more and more, varying according to the side in the struggle. Many foreign observers, upon listening to both interpretations, found that they seemed to pertain to two different countries, to two distinct realities.

The stoppage weakened those groups in the UP who were trying for an understanding with the Center opposition. The same occurred within the CDP, where the current favoring an arrangement capable of preserving the institutional order and avoiding the coup d'état was overwhelmed by its conservative wing. In sum the frustrated attempt at correcting economic policy weakened the supporters of a negotiated solution. It fortified the Right, which saw itself strong enough to put the government in check. At the same time it fueled the arguments of those sectors of the UP and the extreme Left who, lacking a proper grasp of the reigning balance of power, sought to accelerate the process at all costs.

From this moment on, a radical option began to seem more suitable. Within the UP, plans for gathering strength for the inevitable confrontation began to be made. The possibility of political agreements capable of overcoming the conflicts was fading fast. The entry of the military into the Cabinet meanwhile seemed to offer hope for the continuity of the process, propping up its institutional basis.

Notes

1. The Matte-Alessandri group was closely tied to *El Mercurio,* to several other economic groups and to the National Party.
2. The Right turned the case of the paper company into a *cause célèbre.* A political campaign stretching over several months was focused on this issue, in which the government was accused of trying to control the press through the supply of paper.
3. Discrepancies between the two sides persisted on this point, especially with respect to the Edwards Bank. The latter was owned by one of the most politically powerful economic groups in Chile, which also controlled *El Mercurio.* The UP insisted that the general norm should be applicable as well to this bank.
4. See E. Silva, *El tribunal constitucional de Chile (1971–1973)* (Caracas: Editorial Juridica Venezolana, 1977), pp. 181–184.
5. The Constitutional Tribunal was created through a constitutional amendment in January 1970, during the Frei government. Its principal function was to resolve constitutional conflicts between the Executive and the Congress.
6. The flow of people to and from Peru and Bolivia over the northern border had always been heavy. It was not deemed advisable to cut it off because of possible reprisals from these countries, reprisals which might affect economic activity in the border areas.
7. The UP government established a monopoly state-owned agency for the sale of automobiles. Official prices were considerably lower than open-market prices. The government decided to increase the official prices, bringing them closer to those on the open market. The state thus gained higher revenues which would otherwise have swelled the profits of foreign firms, private distributors or speculators.
8. In August prices were raised in the following proportions: cigarettes by 100 percent, agricultural products by between 36 and 110 percent, textiles by between 60 and 90 percent, coffee and tea by 100 percent, bread by 78 percent, sugar by 100 percent, milk by 105 percent. In the first few days of September, new prices were allowed for flour, window glass, detergents, shoes, clothing and other items.
9. The main cause for the swelling deficit was the failure to finance the wage adjustments approved in Congress. Thus the Wage Adjustment Law of May was approved by Congress with a deficit of 7.7 billion escudos. The new adjustment bill of October involved an unfinanced cost of 8.9 billion escudos for 1972. Thus the opposition in Congress, because it refused to approve new taxes requested by the government, was responsible for 16.6 billion escudos of the total deficit. Dirección del Presupuesto, Ministerio de Hacienda, "Sintesis presupuestria" (September 1972).
10. This was ostensibly a solidarity strike provoked by the death of a store owner in the city of Punta Arenas. The man suffered a heart attack during a confrontation between the police and a street demonstration in which he was a participant.
11. This conspiracy was called the September Plan. The discharged officer was General Canales, who was appointed to an ambassadorship by the military junta after the 1973 coup d'état.
12. For a detailed political analysis, see J. Larrain, "Orientaciones y actividad de la Confederación Democrática de Partidos durante la crisis de Octubre de 1972," *Cuadernos de la Realidad Nacional,* No. 16 (April 1973), pp. 229–249.

13. In 1975, U.S. Congressman Harrington accussed the CIA of participating in the October stoppage. He was not heard from again, and in the United States Senate hearings the CIA's role in the stoppage is touched on only superficially. Thus, for example: "In September 1972, for example, the 40 Committee authorized $24,000 in emergency support for an organization of anti-Allende business owners . . . . The 40 Committee authorized $100,000 for private organizations in October 1972. . . ." United States Senate, *Covert Action in Chile, 1963–1973*, Staff Report of the Select Committee to Study Governmental Operations with respect to Intelligence Activities (Washington, D.C.: U.S. Government Printing Office, 1975), p. 10.

14. Instituto de Economía y Planificación, *La economía chilena en 1972* (Santiago: University of Chile, 1973), pp. 99–101.

CHAPTER 7

Economic Crisis and Social Struggle

The situation confronting the government at the end of 1972 was critical: marked economic disturbances continued in the midst of a sharp political polarization. The government found itself for the first time with virtually no room for maneuver in the economic area; it simply could not contain the problems which followed one after the other in rapid succession. An adequate response would have required measures too sweeping for the government to implement, given the existing balance of forces in the country. It would be an exercise in absurdity to analyze the continuing imbalances in strictly economic terms; at this point economic phenomena were more than ever a direct manifestation of overt political and social struggle.

But how exactly did political events affect the economy? What kind of interaction was occurring between the two spheres? In order to understand this problem, we will analyze four major questions, relating economic processes at each point to the struggle for power: ownership of the means of production; income distribution; external economic relations and the conflict with the U.S.; and the parallel economy, or black market.

The Struggle for Control of the Means of Production

Once private property became subject to expropriation and incorporation into the socialized sector and workers' participation began to be implemented, political tension became acute. The shift to socialized ownership had been effected with great speed in agriculture, banking, industry and commerce. By the end of 1972, the government had practically completed the agrarian reform program originally scheduled to extend over six years. In two years almost all of the estates classified as latifundia under the existing law had been expropriated.[1] The advance had been headlong, and it stimulated a vast peasant mobilization. But at the same time the reformed estates suffered a serious setback in organization, a failure which had dire effects on production at a moment when the demand for foodstuffs was surging. The situation was further complicated by the October stoppage and the continual obstructionism of rural courts,

118

which upheld many petitions by landlords protesting the expropriation of their property. Chilean agricultural production in 1972 fell due to a decline in yields, even though the planted area had increased. Data then available showed a decline in yields of more than 8 percent with respect to 1971, while the area under cultivation had expanded by 2.5 percent.[2]

Three factors intervened to cause this decline in expropriated areas: a lack of incentive to work the collective land, decapitalization of the reformed estates, and inadequate technical assistance on the part of the state apparatus. In the matter of incentives the government established a fixed wage, one which did not vary with the time or quality of the work done. This wage became a permanent subsidy which provided no stimulus to improve production. Since the reformed estates generated no profits in 1972, there could be no distribution of surplus earnings; hence another possible stimulus to raise yields was lacking. In response the peasants began to devote their time, and some collective resources as well, to the cultivation of lands assigned to them individually. The existence of an extensive black market in foodstuffs, where peasants could sell their crops at higher than official prices, also induced them to concentrate on individual plots at the expense of collective land. Many workers conducted themselves as capitalists on their own land and as functionaries while working on other areas of the expropriated estates.

The second important factor was decapitalization. The agrarian reform law allowed former owners to keep part of their old estate; and, naturally enough, they kept control of the land which had benefited the most from capital investment. Landowners also retained machinery and livestock. The reformed lands transferred to workers and tenants came without the physical means necessary for intensive cultivation.

In the third place, technical assistance from the state, which was the only body that could take over the old functions of the landlord while the peasants organized, was inadequate. This weakness stemmed from the priority granted by the UP government to the speed of expropriation and takeover of private estates, a priority it justified on the grounds that a delay in the reform might allow the landlords to regroup and regain strength. Organizational matters were deferred, due to a dearth of suitable personnel and the general overloading of the state's administrative capacity.

The government thus had opted to accelerate the reform process, both to forestall a counteroffensive of the large owners and to prevent becoming overwhelmed by pressures from the peasants and from the MIR and some parties in the UP itself. This choice, however, caused a drop in production, which in turn had grave repercussions on the food supply. The agrarian sector had become a critical point.

From the point of view of the larger balance of political forces, the critical role of the agrarian sector did not in fact arise from the resistance of the landowners. They were already weak and isolated (with the exception of those in the southern region) and the industrial bourgeoisie itself had already abandoned them. The real political problems were occurring in the urban centers, where the irregularity of food supplies and the black market aroused general discontent. And it was in the cities, both for electoral reasons and because they were the centers of mass action, that the government's fate would be decided.

Let us examine now what had occurred in the banking sector. Just as in agriculture, the government had moved quickly in the first two years. It controlled almost the whole of the banking system, except for the Banco de Chile, the largest in the private sector, where the government had obtained only 47 percent of the stock. Banks under state control at the end of 1972 managed 90 percent of the deposits and credit placements.

Politically, the rapid expropriation of the banking system led to the displacement of large property-owning groups from a crucial power area; yet it had not aroused the same kind of stiff resistance as the expropriation of industrial firms. The government thus gained control of a vital instrument for managing financial flows, allowing it to regulate and reorient credits to the private sector. Nevertheless, this instrument was not immediately effective, as the established economic power groups won access to liquid funds from other sources. The suspension of investments and the high sales volume in the first two years of the government had the effect of supplying manufacturing firms with huge financial resources. Industrial capitalists were thus able to elude the norms that the state attempted to impose through its regulation of short-term bank credits. The liquid resources obtained directly by private firms created what was in practice a parallel financial system, one which supplied funds to keep the factories operating and also to finance the political campaign against the Allende government. The state expropriation of banking, then, did not substantively affect the economic capacity of the largest property owners. While a weakening of their power position was inevitable over the middle and long run, it did not follow immediately on the government's action.

Confrontation in Industry

The stiffest resistance to the government's attempt to constitute the social property area came from the industrial bourgeoisie. This was natural, since industry was the stronghold of the dominant groups. But the same hostile reaction occurred among owners of small and middle-sized firms, and later spread to all the middle sectors. Among other reasons, this reaction was due to the fact that the government did not define the limits of the social area until the end of 1971, a year after coming to power. The first announcement of firms to be expropriated was later replaced by narrowed-down lists, none of which the government could fulfill. The government had to intervene in firms not on these lists when the political struggle intensified, as was the case during the October stoppage.

During 1971, 167 firms had come under state control, followed by another 151 in 1972, making a total of 318. In the industrial sector, the number of state-owned firms went from 43 in 1970 to 202 by the end of 1972.[3] These 202 firms were responsible for almost 22 percent of total industrial production and close to 20 percent of sectoral employment.

Why did such an apparently minor incursion precipitate such a violent reaction? The answer is to be found in the nature of the firms involved. Those drawn into the social area were the largest; they dominated their respective markets, especially since many other enterprises depended on them for the supply of intermediate goods. Resistance spread also because many middle-sized enterprises were among the 202 expropriated industrial firms. These were not strategic enterprises, but they had passed to state control because of abandonment, strikes or shutdowns. This awakened the fear and distrust of smaller entrepreneurs, who became all the more receptive to the message of the large owners that the UP was planning to expropriate all private property. In order to counteract this argument the government handed back several smaller firms in 1972. Results were, however, unsatisfactory, since a climate of political hostility among industrialists was already an irreversible fact.[4]

The fears of government action in the industrial sector were astutely promoted in the propaganda of the Right, which harped on two main themes. First, "technical" arguments were brought up: the cry was raised that production would grind to a halt once enterprises became socialized, or even that physical risks were imminent. Second, political and ideological arguments were deployed: the public was warned that a change in property ownership would lead to the eventual loss of all liberties.

On the political-legal front, in addition to the opposition in Congress, a kind of silent obstructionism was unleashed by the controller-general's office and the Judiciary. Both of these branches of government altered their legal standards once it became evident that the balance of power was shifting to the opposition.

Traditionally the function of the controller's office was to rule on the legality of the actions of the Executive branch; it was not entitled to base its decisions on opinions as to the substance of Executive edicts. This in fact is how the office had always carried on under all governments from its foundation until 1970 and through most of 1971. But beginning in 1972, the controller's office began to perform differently by pretending to judge the substantive propriety of government decisions. In so doing it ignored historical practice and doctrine and effectively lost its claims to legitimacy.

The Judicial branch began behaving similarly at about the same time. It altered its traditional practice and arrogated to itself functions beyond its legal competence in order to obstruct Executive decisions in the social property area. The most common judicial strategy employed in favor of the property owner was the following: once the controller's office approved an Executive decree of intervention or expropriation, the proprietors of the firms in question were removed from their management positions. They then pressed suits in the lower courts which ought to have been rejected on constitutional grounds. The judges, however, resorted to a legal subterfuge: they used "precautionary resolutions" to designate auditors other than those named by the government and to retain certain of the firm's assets. But the use of "precautionary resolutions" was completely unprecedented, since this step could only be taken in the case of a civil suit and not when an administrative action was in question, as was of course the case. In resorting to this practice to obstruct the Executive's actions, the Judiciary was guilty of unconstitutionality.

The timing of this reversal in the official performance of the controller-general and the Judicial branch makes it clear that the accepted and conventional interpretation of legal norms was altered only when the larger power situation began to favor the Right. The obstacles thrown up by these two components of the state apparatus, therefore, were not inherent to the accepted institutional system; instead they were a consequence of political power relationships between government and opposition.

We should point out another factor which affected the balance of power: the performance of state-controlled enterprises began to decline seriously in 1972. A change in administration for such a large number of strategic enterprises inevitably led to a temporary deterioration in their management. These failures were accentuated in part by the influence of party politics on the choice of administrators, and in part by the absence of a new planning and control organization to take over the functions of the former owners. The government made a serious effort to organize conglomerates specialized according to production areas, but new coordination problems multiplied faster than the capacity to deal with them.

The simple fact of changing the forms of ownership of the means of production did not mean that the advantages attributed to the new economic system would appear over the short run. Neither a change in the composition of investment and production, nor a higher rate of savings could be attained without a prolonged intervening period of great organizational effort.

At the end of 1972, the management failures and deficiencies in the supply of local and imported primary materials (shortages which were worsened by the October stoppage and by international financial restrictions) damaged the production of enterprises in the social property area. This immediately affected the general supply of goods. In this sense the creation of the social area had a negative impact on the economy in the short run, a fact which strengthened the opposition's arguments blaming market scarcities on state-run enterprises. Thus the circle of ideological attack against the UP was closed: it was blamed for shortages, accused of illegality and branded as Marxist-socialist.

The Struggle for Income Distribution

The fight for income redistribution was another conflict front that conditioned economic policy. In order to consolidate achieved reforms, the economic measures adopted by the government in 1972 centered on two objectives: increasing production in order to satisfy the expanded domestic demand and maintaining the real income of workers.

By the end of this year the domestic availability of goods had reached the highest level in Chile's history. Nevertheless, the imbalance between supply and demand grew more acute. In the second half of 1972 production leveled off and growth declined; shortages spread and reached a critical point with the

October strikes. Total consumption grew by 5.7 percent in 1972, an increment added on top of the 11.3 percent growth of 1971. Total supply grew by 1.9 percent, following the 8.9 percent increase in 1971.

Growth varied from one sector to another: while industry expanded by 2.8 percent, agriculture and construction declined. The supply of manufactured goods thus reached its highest level in history, and could have gone even higher had it not been constrained by the scarcity of foreign currency necessary to buy spare parts and raw materials. Harvests of the main agricultural products brought in at the beginning of 1972 exhibited no important variations with respect to the previous year, and were supplemented by copious imports which increased internal availability of foodstuffs in 1972.[5] The availability of foodstuffs per capita grew by 27 percent in two years. Despite the difficulties, therefore, the UP government achieved its goal of steadily augmenting the internal availability of goods in 1972.

Progress in the employment area was also consolidated, thus assuring one of the pillars of the whole redistributive policy. Unemployment indices for Greater Santiago showed the lowest rates of joblessness since these records had begun in 1956. But where economic policy went out of control was in the area of wage-price spiral inflation. In order to maintain workers' real income in a phase of accelerated inflation while wielding insufficient political power, the government was forced to adopt measures which were in the end inadequate and which even aggravated inflation. As we saw in the last chapter, in order to counteract the rise in prices which followed its attempt to adjust the economy, the government agreed to grant in advance a readjustment in wages and salaries. Realizing that this would induce a bigger fiscal deficit, the Executive proposed that a uniform base pay increment be granted, followed by a differentiated readjustment with higher increases going to the poorer groups. This effort, however, was blocked by pressure from higher-income workers and by special partial arrangements obtained by the strong unions of the public sector and the large private enterprises. In the conditions prevailing at the end of 1972, virtually any strike produced immediate effects on supply levels, a fact which bolstered the bargaining power of the largest unions.

In the end the government's guidelines were overwhelmed and virtually abandoned. Thus, whereas official policies at the beginning of 1972 prescribed a 22 percent average wage increment for public sector workers, the pay hikes actually granted turned out to average 47.7 percent by the end of June the same year. Only 26 percent of public sector workers ended up with readjustments close to those originally proposed by the government.[6] Something similar occurred in the private sector. An analysis of 3088 wage agreements revealed that the average increment conceded was 34.6 percent rather than the officially recommended 22 percent—this without even considering premiums and extra benefits.

The political impossibility of obtaining congressional approval for new taxes contributed to the widening gap between expenditures and fiscal revenue. Likewise the rollback of prices for commodities of the state enterprises led to larger losses that had to be financed with fiscal appropriations or bank credits. Estimates made in March 1972 indicated that state enterprises would accumulate a deficit of on the order of 9 billion escudos for the year.[7] The outcome on December 31 was a deficit of 20 billion escudos, of which 15 billion were incurred by non-mining enterprises in the social property area. The larger copper mines ran up a deficit of 5 billion escudos.[8] This situation was due in large part to the large number of firms which the state was obliged to take over because of labor strife or the political situation, many of which had been incurring considerable losses. Moreover, as noted above, the rise in prices for products of the large state-run enterprises was much below the increase in costs. While the consumer price index went from 100 in December 1970 to 322 in December 1972, the comparable increase for prices of goods produced in the social area was from 100 to 201. Finally, employment in state enterprises increased faster than production.

The fiscal deficit and the losses in the social area opened the gates to monetary expansion. The total quantity of money grew by 172.8 percent between January and December 1972, with the increase concentrated in the public sector. Greater inflationary expectations also manifested themselves in a high marginal cash preference which grew from 0.37 in December 1971 to 0.59 in December 1972.[9]

The two largest factors behind the creation of new money were credits to the Treasury and to state enterprises. Even in this volatile context, the government managed to avoid a regression in the nominal income redistribution attained in 1971 or in the advances in consumption level gained by workers, peasants and salaried employees.

In order to measure the effect of the economic measures on consumption and nominal income redistribution, we must examine the index of real salaries and wages. From a base of 100 in October 1970, this index reached 132.8 in January 1972, dropped to 118.7 in October, and recovered shortly thereafter with the wage adjustments granted in early November.[10]

Income distribution clearly changed in two years. The percentage of families receiving less than one *sueldo vital* declined by half between June 1970 and June 1972, and the proportion of workers in the middle-income group went up.

The distribution of income was also improved through the extension of educational and health services. Primary instruction reached about 93 percent of the school-age population in 1970; in 1972 enrollments were virtually 100 percent. Secondary education attracted 40.3 percent of the population between 15 and 19 years old in 1972, compared with 30.5 percent in 1970. University enrollments went up by 51 percent in the same period.[11]

Indicators revealed rapid improvements in health services as well. Infant mortality, which had an incidence of 88 per thousand in the period from 1965 to 1970, was reduced to 71 per thousand in 1972.[12] The supply of milk to the public increased by 50 percent in 1971 over the previous year. Emergency consultations with physicians went up by 60 percent and medical consultations at the National Health Service increased by 13 percent over the 1970–72 period.[13] A great effort was also made to distribute free of charge food, school, supplies, uniforms and shoes in the schools in the poorest areas.

In sum, by the end of 1972, the UP government had fulfilled another of its central objectives: improving the well-being of the poorest people. But the struggle for a share in income and consumption intensified in the midst of an inflationary surge, and the middle and upper groups began to recoup their positions. In the absence of additional growth in supply and given the continued expansion of nominal demand, the black market emerged. The workers were not sufficiently organized on this front to claim their rights.

In order for workers to protect their positions it was necessary for them to move toward the direct control of the distribution and sale of essential goods. The success of this policy, however, required a more favorable balance of forces than the government could count on at that point.

The Balance of Payments and Problems with the United States

The third area of struggle was the international, where the antagonist was the United States. The Allende government had to deal with a contradictory situation: a surge in imports to satisfy the expansion in internal demand occurred simultaneously with a sudden reduction of international financing coming from the United States and international agencies. Both these phenomena took on dimensions unforeseen by the UP. The government had begun to reorder its international financial connections in order to replace the U.S. ties, and some favorable results were evident by the end of 1972. But even with the levels of external financing beginning to recover from the initial cut-off of credits by the United States the country's economic progress in the immediate future remained seriously affected. In order to see the extent of the problem we shall have to review the balance of payments at the end of 1972.

The trade balance showed a deficit of $438 million for 1972, an alarming jump compared to the 1971 situation when the deficit was only $88 million. What were the causes of this sudden spurt? Of the $350 million difference between the deficits for the two years, increased imports accounted for $200 million, a drop in exports for the remaining $150 million. The chief factor in the import boom was the entry of more foodstuffs: the value of food imports went from $260 million to $405 million between 1971 and 1972. In addition the industrial expansion absorbed more imported raw materials. Nevertheless, it must be remembered that half of the value of imports was accounted for by higher world market prices for food and raw materials.

About 55 percent of the total $150 million drop in exports was due to lower revenues from copper; 45 percent derived from losses in all other types of exports. Non-copper exports fell because of the expansion in internal demand, which absorbed a higher proportion of national production. The decline in copper revenues originated in the fall in price (off 1.8 percent from its 1971 level) and from a slight reduction in sales due to the embargo proceedings initiated by Kennecott in Europe. Production, in contrast, continued to increase in 1972.

The slow growth of copper production had some causes which could have been controlled by the UP and others which were beyond its control. Among the controllable factors was the deterioration of management in the mines as a result of the rapid changeover of ownership, despite efforts to retain foreign technicians. Part of the blame was due also to the incursion of political considerations in the allotment of management posts, which led to the weakening of lines of authority and a deterioration in labor relations. Absenteeism increased as did the number of partial stoppages by workers to demand higher wages.

Among the factors which the UP could not control was the fact that Kennecott and Anaconda blocked the supply of spare parts, trucks and machinery. Maintenance programs, the control of critical stocks and information on suppliers of needed goods had always been managed from the United States; knowledge or experience in handling these matters was virtually nonexistent among Chileans. In order to overcome the most urgent problems, the state firm had to make their acquisitions through third parties, paying premiums and in cash and receiving the goods only after delays. Production in the three biggest mines initially fell, and it recovered to prenationalization levels only in the second half of 1972. Total production from the larger mines rose thanks to the opening of two new sites—Exótica and Andina.

In the midst of this deficit situation, the government ran into open U.S. hostility, which provoked capital outflow. While the net flow of autonomous capital was positive in 1970, a negative balance of $74 million was registered in 1971, followed by another $181 million loss in 1972. The obstruction of capital inflow from official sources was the most important cause of this negative movement in 1972.

Let us see how private U.S. banks and the international agencies controlled by the United States blocked financing to Chile. The banks contracted their financing from $220 million in November 1970 to less than $20 million by the end of 1972. A similar contraction occurred in the case of funding from U.S. government agencies, which dropped from $59.3 million in 1970 to $13.0 million in 1972.[14] The World Bank and the Inter-American Bank, both subject to decisive U.S. pressure, also cut the flow of resources to Chile. Credits authorized by them fell from 32.3 million in 1970 to zero in 1972.

As a consequence of the financial contraction, foreign trade with the United States had to be reduced. Exports to the U.S., which represented 14.7 percent of all exports in 1970, fell to 8.8 percent of the total in 1971 and to 5.7 percent in 1972. Imports of American products went from 25.8 percent of the total in 1970 down to 17 percent in 1971 and 11.8 percent in 1972. Short-term financing from U.S. sources plummeted from 74.8 percent of the total in 1970 to 6.6 percent in the first half of 1972.[15] This kind of financial contraction and the consequent drop in trade with the United States inevitably generated serious problems in the supply of raw materials, spare parts, machinery and consumer goods. Acute dependence on immediate resources coming from the U.S. became a political weapon which, when set into motion from Washington, cost Chile dearly.

In order to get around this blockade, the government set out in two directions: renegotiation of the external debt and reordering of its financial ties. The first move paid off in the renegotiation of debts amounting to $366 million in 1972. Some success was also encountered in forging new financial ties, especially with Western Europe, Latin America and the socialist countries. Germany, Britain and France, and to a lesser extent Italy, Scandinavia and Spain, expanded their credits to Chile, thus making up in part for the loss of U.S. financing. But the most significant increases came from Latin American sources, particularly Argentina and Brazil, where financial concessions allowed the share held by imports from these countries in the total Chilean balance to expand from 25.6 percent in 1970 to 33.1 percent in 1972. Thanks to credits granted by the socialist countries, imports from this quarter grew from 1 percent of the total in 1970 to 12.0 percent in 1972.

These attainments amounted to a genuine success, and by the end of 1972, Chile had fortified its financial connections. But this reordering was bought at a high cost. First, it was not until 1972 that these new resources were captured, too late to compensate for the loss of huge sums in 1971. In the second place, the reconstitution of the financial network imposed new limitations on supply, since in many cases the help supplied took the form of bilateral or restricted credits. This meant an obligation to acquire many products from new suppliers who were not previously active in the Chilean market. These products had different specifications than those to which users in Chile had been accustomed, and adapting to them would cost time and money. This kind of adjustment was not simple and could not be effected quickly. It demanded a farflung network of information with outposts in many different countries. In the third place, some key spare parts would still have to be obtained somehow from the United States, especially those destined for the copper and petroleum industries. All of the American-made industrial complex and automotive fleet had to be supplied from the United States.

These considerations lead us to conclude that while the U.S.-planned financial blockade was partially compensated, it had a critical affect on the final phases of the Allende period. Another general conclusion also emerges: once a process of transformation is undertaken, it is necessary both strategically and tactically to have access to international reserves sufficient to dampen the negative impact of a sudden contraction of accustomed economic and financial relationships with the United States. Such a reordering requires a long time; hence an accumulation of international reserves serves as a necessary defensive bulwark. If such an accumulation does not exist, then the process must be regulated so as not to cause sudden damage on this front. This kind of security is vital, given that a profound change in any Latin American country must necessarily confront the entrenched economic and political interests of extremely influential power groups in the United States.

Economic Relations with the Soviet Union

The Soviet Union headed the list of socialist countries supplying financial support to the Chilean government. This support, however, involved limitations which prevented it from being put to use quickly and effectively. Many of the credits were bilateral, linked to the purchase of specific commodities or capital goods. The great necessity for the UP at the end of 1972 was to obtain freely disposable funds which could be used in any country to acquire whatever goods were most urgently required. But here Chilean expectations were to remain disappointed.

During the second half of the year, the government forecasted a growing deterioration in the balance of payments and warned that if considerable international support was not obtained it would be impossible to maintain the level of supply and of industrial activity. Moreover, predictions for 1973 indicated a deficit of about $500 million. Confronted with this emergency, the government decided on two steps. First, it began to establish its priorities in order to restrict economically nonvital imports. Second, it began to accelerate its negotiations with the U.S.S.R. and the other socialist countries in order to obtain immediate liquid resources.

During 1971 and 1972, Chile had received about $80 million in short-term credits from financial outlets controlled by the Soviets. In November 1972, President Allende decided to travel to Moscow to speed up negotiations, hoping to obtain a significant volume of funds with which to handle the critical situation. The results, however, were very modest: the $80 million debt was refinanced; $20 million in freely disposable funds were conceded; and $27 million was obtained in credits toward the import of raw materials and foodstuffs from the Soviet Union.

This situation caused consternation within the UP, since backing from the socialist countries was thought to be assured by many political leaders, who were counting on as much support as was necessary to deal with whatever emergency might arise. Too late they were forced to come to the conclusion that all the country could count on to sustain itself was its internal effort.

What was the reason for this unsatisfactory outcome? Two hypotheses are suggested. In the first place, it is possible that the Soviets, who had sent several technical teams to Chile to evaluate its economic situation, decided that credits would be used up rapidly without resolving any of the basic problems. Perhaps the economic cost of their financial collaboration with the Cuban revolution encouraged them to take a more cautions position in the Chilean case.

This reasoning suggests that the Soviet Union was waiting until the political situation in Chile showed some signs of consolidation. Its appraisal of the national scene had led to the conclusion that, in the absence of a wider political accord, conditions did not allow for stabilizing the process and making new progress. This hypothesis is confirmed in part by statements made in the U.S.S.R. to high political leaders in the Allende government at the end of 1972.

Their message was that it was a matter of high priority to consolidate the process politically by cementing an understanding with some of the opposition forces. The same comments were offered to Chilean functionaries in other socialist countries. A second hypothesis, advanced by American and British sources, is that the Soviet interpretation of the international situation led to restraint in their collaboration with the UP government.[16]

Recollections of high officials who accompanied President Allende during his visit to the Soviet Union offer support for both hypotheses or for a combination of them. In the first place, Chile did not constitute a high priority in the international view of the Soviet Union. Thus, at the first meeting in the Kremlin, Mr. Brezhnev offered an analysis of the world situation. The most important problems, in his view, were Vietnam, Egypt and Cuba; next came five or six other countries; and finally Chile. Brezhnev also emphasized that the Soviets saw no stability, that the UP government seemed to be fighting the center and was not accumulating any forces.

It is certain that these results disappointed President Allende, who felt that they amounted to an important defeat—an opinion which prevailed among his collaborators. Their gloomy appraisal was perhaps provoked not so much by the scantiness of Soviet aid—it had been much increased compared to the past—as by the excessive expectations which had been entertained by some UP leaders on simplistic and idealistic grounds.

Aside from these political considerations, the limited use made of Soviet resources can be explained by the diminished Chilean capacity to absorb bilateral credits. These could not be put to use right away due to unfamiliarity with the new suppliers and the quality of their products. This was the case with machinery, spare parts, medicines and foodstuffs.

At the same time, the negotiating procedures of the socialist countries hindered utilization of the credits. Negotiations were effected in two stages, first the political and later the technical. Results were rapid in the first area because of the general desire to collaborate politically. But then the negotiating apparatus of the socialist enterprises went into operation, an apparatus trained to conduct tough bargaining. These discussions were frequently broken off, causing suspicion on the part of the Chileans, only to be reopened because of political maneuvering. The situation was worsened by the fact that the socialist countries did not have organizations specialized in disbursing emergency economic aid; there was nothing like the many U.S. agencies, including AID and EXIM, devoted to this purpose.

In sum the Chilean experience demonstrated that no process of profound transformations can survive without its external flank protected, especially when there is a high degree of dependency on the United States. It is also clear that the process was weakened by the contradiction between the accelerated pace of change in agriculture, copper mining and the expansion of internal demand on the one hand, and the fragility of external financing on the other. The government did not correctly forecast the magnitude of pressures on the balance of payments stemming from internal policies; nor was it sufficiently agile in its responses to effect corrective moves en route. Finally, the simplistic notion of unlimited support from the socialist countries was all too widespread. In reality no transformational process can hope for success if hard sacrifices are not imposed in order to draw the maximum sustenance from within.

The Emergence of a Parallel Economy

The parallel economy or black market had already appeared in 1972, and it expanded appreciably in 1973. The economic disequilibria grew faster than the new control mechanisms; a gap opened between the variety of new situations and the policy instruments available to regulate them. This gap created the conditions for the emergence and development of the black market. In fact, when the structures of a complex system are subject to deliberate attempts at change, some aspects of the old system are always perpetuated, surviving by adopting new modes of functioning designed to neutralize the corrective measures being applied to them. Thus efforts to modify the bases of income distribution and property ownership were counteracted by high inflation, speculation, and the suspension of investments. The attempts by government to channel the distribution of essential goods were offset by the appearance of parallel merchandising circuits, supplied not only by the private sector, but also by the reformed agricultural and state-owned industrial enterprises.

If we are to learn from this experience, we must observe how the black market grew and spread. The excess demand and the consequent monetary expansion intensified during the first half of 1972, surging markedly after the attempted correction of economic policy and the October stoppage. Excess liquidity continued to accumulate chiefly in the hands of the larger business owners, merchants and financiers. Thereafter, with the heightening of inflationary expections, the pent-up liquidity was released in a wave of consumption and speculation.

On the other hand, even though supply increased through 1972, it reached a stable level by the end of the year. With a static supply, it became more difficult to maintain the consumption levels of the poorest groups. Higher income groups, in contrast, could protect themselves more effectively. Confronted with the prospects of shortages, the subject of continual scare campaigns in the press, they accumulated large stocks of basic consumer goods. This hoarding, encouraged by the low prices of these products, led in turn to an artificial increase in the normal demand.

In order to alleviate the impact of shortages and the black market on the poor, the government decided to exert more control on the distribution and sale of goods. In this way the flow of a large volume of consumer goods was diverted toward poorer neighborhoods—goods which, in the absence of such intervention, would have been channeled to high-income areas for sale at higher prices. These measures, however, also had negative effects. A new species of speculator emerged, men who specialized in acquiring goods at controlled prices in low-income neighborhoods and reselling them in middle-class areas for much higher prices. This phenomenon spread to the agricultural sector where parallel private circuits for the purchase and distribution of food-stuffs began to compete with the official state-supervised network. One very profitable speculative operation consisted in advancing money to peasants to finance planting, harvesting, fertilizer and seed, in exchange for the delivery of the crops at an agreed-upon price. These products were then sold to consumers at prices above those set officially.

This kind of speculation was limited to some extent by the creation of a set of state enterprises for the distribution of meat, cereals, fruit, sugar and dairy products. By the end of 1972 the government had come to control almost 30 percent of the sale of finished food products, but no more than 14 percent of the total agricultural production.[17]

Relative price distortion also encouraged the parallel economy. The prices of finished goods produced by private firms, which were more difficult to control, climbed rapidly. At the same time, prices for intermediate goods produced by state-owned firms were held down in order to limit the inflationary advance. Those private firms which were getting intermediate goods at controlled prices and selling final products at uncontrolled prices obtained enormous profits. Such cases were especially common in the textile and construction industries. While fabric was selling at relatively low prices, finished clothing was being distributed at high prices. In construction the scarcity of cement and iron gave rise to a fast-spreading black market.

A kind of economic psychosis swept the nation's bourgeoisie and also reached other strata of the population. Distorted expectations so dominated the economy that it came to be said, correctly, that a speculative capitalism had taken root. The political uncertainty surrounding its future in the country led the national bourgeoisie to look for new means of retaining its economic power. Suitable activities had to fulfill two requirements: high returns and liquidity. The most attractive area was black market dealing in dollars. This market was supplied by a variety of sources: those receiving their incomes in dollars, firms or speculators who were selling off currency specially brought in from outside the country in order to finance speculative and contraband operations, and increasingly by foreign funds used to finance the opposition's political operations. The speculative wave extended later to include those goods which were relatively more scarce and less controlled by the state. Trade in automobiles was an especially prominent component of the parallel economy, followed later by other consumer durables and culminating in consumer necessities.

The black market also involved workers. Many unions demanded a part of their wage payments in kind, in order to protect their members from inflation and permit them to profit from the scarcity value that the goods which their factories made were rapidly acquiring in the marketplace. These payments in kind were used to fuel a growing trade between unions; much was also sold directly on the black market. This situation was clearly perilous for the larger economy. It was combated by the CUT, whose leaders recognized in this phenomenon something with potentially fatal political and moral consequences.

Those in the opposition interested in fomenting a coup saw in the black market a weapon to weaken the Allende government, and they staged a series of operations to extend and deepen the distortions. They initiated several scare campaigns warning of future shortages and price rises. They also urged members of business associations to obstruct sales and disturb distribution. Furthermore, they introduced dollars into the country to finance stoppages, strikes, sabotage and press campaigns. Finally, they called for the rejection of state administrative and grassroots control and inspection activities, hoping thus to eliminate the last forces retaining the wave of speculation. Another economic consequence of the black market was the decline in fiscal receipts. Merchandise routed through the parallel market escaped the control of the Treasury. Receipts from taxes on sales and profits were reduced, thus explaining in part the decline in real revenues of the Treasury in 1972 and the concomitant increment in the deficit.

From a systemic viewpoint, the parallel economy was a new mode of functioning of the Chilean capitalist system, a way of evading the transformations and reproducing the old income structure. The market had been the main economic mechanism for repelling changes in income distribution; once these changes had been imposed by the government, the market could be adapted to undoing the reforms and forcing a return to the original situation. The interests of the minority groups, owners of the means of production or high-income earners, were overwhelmingly favored by the parallel economy. Their supply of goods was assured at the expense of access by lower income groups, while at the same time they reaped enormous profits.

These considerations suggest that the black market arose from the deliberate actions of the economic elite. Therefore, in order to eliminate it, it would be necessary to exercise political control over the sector that was behind its emergence and spread. The main task would consist in taking control of the large distribution firms, extending grassroots organizations, and reestablishing control over market mechanisms by resorting to direct distribution of goods. However, from a strictly economic point of view, the parallel market was an inevitable consequence of the financial imbalances. As business owners and consumers sought to maximize their profits or satisfactions, they would automatically turn toward speculative activity. From this perspective, one can argue that the black market could have been fought by correcting the financial disturbances and price distortions. Neither approach can by itself explain the whole reality. Objective economic conditions existed which made the appearance of a parallel economy possible. But the parallel economy had political origins as well: it was fomented by the Right opposition to undermine the government.

Interaction Between Economic and Political Variables

It is necessary at this point to emphasize three political-economic features that emerge from the analysis of this period.

1. The UP project demanded a short-term normality in order to deal successfully with continuing elections and an opposition which could conduct itself freely within the established rules of the game. The economic disturbances threatened the fulfillment of this criterion. Once the process had advanced considerably, it became much more difficult to attempt a correction of the economy. The power conditions necessary to effect such a maneuver were obviated by the balance of political forces which the same economic disturbance had helped to create.

2. The opposition's strategy of frontal attack forced the UP government to defend itself from day to day and to orient its economic policy toward preserving stability. It would be a serious methodological error, therefore, to interpret the economic policy of this period from a strictly economic viewpoint, assuming its autonomy from the political sphere. On the contrary, economic policy has to be interpreted in the framework of a conflict between two adversaries and hence permanently circumscribed by the actions of the opposition.

3. The extent and scope of the transformations and of the political conflict changed the way the economy functioned and modified the traditional economic behavior of the various social groups. The usual working hypotheses used in designing economic policy lost their validity, and, as a consequence, the outcomes were very difficult to foresee. The corrective attempt of August showed the weakness of these assumptions. The pace of inflation exceeded the forecasts; the October stoppage changed the picture; the investment behavior expected from the middle bourgeoisie did not return to normal even with guarantees and higher profits. The traditional causal relationships no longer applied, since all of the variables of the system were interacting and changing simultaneously.

From the end of 1971 to the end of 1972, the situation had evolved as follows:

1. By the end of 1971, the Allende government began to worry about the direction economic developments were taking, and at this point the political conditions necessary to get the financial imbalances under control still existed. By the end of 1972, the sheer magnitude of the disturbances made a financial correction practically impossible; only an advance toward tighter administrative and popular controls over the economy could suffice. This approach, however, required a balance of power which was difficult to attain. The main problem for the government from this point on, therefore, came to be a matter of politics. While what was really needed was a course of action which would respond to the interests of a

broad social bloc and avoid polarization, the actual social and political dynamic pushed the process in the opposite direction.

2. By the end of 1971, certain traces of the tripolar balance of forces still existed. The CDP was maintaining its autonomy with respect to the National Party and the extreme Right. By the end of 1972, the Christian Democrats had lost this autonomy and were moving in tandem with the Right, although this did not mean that they necessarily shared the final objective of overthrowing the government and breaking with the estab- lished institutional order. Rather this was a tactical alliance. The Christian Democrats still thought they could return to power through democratic means, something the National Party did not count on. The Christian Democrats wanted to force the government to yield and retreat, hence they thought it necessary to align themselves with the National Party. The latter, on the other hand, wanted to overthrow the government outright; a goal which required a working agreement with the CDP. The tactical area of cooperation in fact favored the Right, which succeeded in subduing the Center.

3. By the end of 1971, the Right had found a mass political base and mode of organization with which it could fight the government: the professional and trade guilds, or *gremios*. By the end of 1972 this apparatus was in full operation and had won significant support from the CIA and other U.S. government agencies. The forces supporting the UP had also attained a high degree of organization and morale, and election statistics demon- strated that the coalition had consolidated behind it about 50 percent of the population. The popular response to the events of the October stop- page revealed an advanced capacity for organization and work on the part of the grassroots groups. It was clear thereafter that it would be impos- sible to overthrow the government through purely civilian action. Orga- nized popular support was the strategic factor which protected the government from collapse during the October events. It served to dis- suade coup-prone groups and gave backing to those middle-class groups which opposed the paralysis of the economy. Surveys carried out during and after the stoppage revealed that a high proportion of the middle classes recognized the political nature of this campaign. Among those middle-class persons surveyed, only 34 percent stated that they would be willing to back another stoppage of this sort; the rest said they would withhold their support from any such action. But while the Right could not hope to bring down the government, the UP's popular support was not sufficient to allow it to govern.

4. The popular backing fortified the constitutionalist officers within the armed forces. They maintained control of the military and managed to return the country to normality. Within the military, however, a right- wing tendency was growing, inclined to a resort to fascism in order to deter the change process. At the end of 1972, the constitutionalist posi- tion still prevailed even though its strength had begun to diminish. In any

event, the predominance of the constitutionalists within the military at this point permitted the formation of a new cabinet in November 1972 and provided some additional leeway in the effort to uphold the institutional order.

Notes

1. Between 1971 and 1972, 3570 estates were expropriated, and the total area subject to the reform approached 35 percent of the cultivable land in the country. S. Allende, *Tercer Mensaje del presidente de la Republica ante el Congreso Nacional* (May 1973).
2. The figures released afterwards by the IMF and the World Bank indicated that agricultural production fell 1.7 percent in the farm year 1971–72 with respect to 1970–71; while the decline was 16 percent in 1972–73 with respect to 1971–72. The farm year runs from May to April. International Monetary Fund (March 1975), p. 82.
3. Instituto de Economía y Planificación, *La economía chilena en 1972* (Santiago: University of Chile, 1973), pp. 95–99.
4. In 1971, 167 firms had been taken over, 27 of which were later returned to private hands; 38 of the 151 firms intervened in 1972 were returned. In these two years the government took control of more than 150 firms not originally included on the list that it had formulated and publicized. Instituto de Economía y Planificación, *La economía chilena en 1972*, pp. 95–99.
5. The index for agricultural production for the farm year 1971–72 (May 1971 to April 1972, with the main harvests occurring between December and March) was 106.0, up slightly from the previous farm year (1970–71) when the index was 105.5. International Monetary Fund (May 1976), p. 60.
6. Data from the Comisión de Remuneraciones del Sector Público, Ministerio de Hacienda, June 1972. Cited in Instituto de Economía y Planificación, *La economía chilena en 1972*, p. 254.
7. Dirección del Presupuesto, Ministerio de Hacienda, "Sintesis presupuestaria" (September 1972).
8. Internal documents from the Departmento de Empresas, Ministerio de Hacienda.
9. Data from the Banco Central de Chile.
10. Instituto de Economía y Planificación, *La economía chilena en 1972*, pp. 264–265.
11. *La economía chilena en 1972*, p. 271.
12. Data from the Servicio Nacional de Salud. See M. Livingstone and J. D. Raczynski, "Analisis cuantitativo de la evolución de algunas variables de salud durante el periodo 1964–1972," CEPLAN (Santiago: Catholic University of Chile, July 1974), p. 55.
13. *La economía chilena en 1972*, p. 272.
14. The flow of credits from AID, P.L. 480, EXIM and CCC—all U.S. government agencies—evolved as follows: $80.3 million in 1969, $59.3 million in 1970, $21.6 million in 1971, $13.0 million in 1972, and $9.8 million in 1973. See Center of International Policy, *International Policy Report* (Washington, D.C.: September 1976 and June 1977).
15. Ministerio de Hacienda, "Exposición sobre el estado de la Hacienda Pública," ante la Comisión Mixta de Presupuesto del Congreso Nacional, en Banco Central, *Boletín Mensual* (November–December 1972); and Dirección de Créditos Externos de la Secretaría de Relaciones Económicas Externos (SEREX).
16. There is some evidence, stemming from the U.S. government itself, that supports the hypothesis that the Soviet Union had already decided on its position with

respect to Chile. In his testimony before the U.S. House of Representatives, Charles Meyer, then Undersecretary of State for Latin American Affairs, stated on October 15, 1971: "The Soviets have been very hesitant to move into Chile on a leadership basis . . . I think they would not, at least present indications are that they would not, particularly welcome the thought of taking on the total support." U.S. House of Representatives, *United States and Chile during the Allende Years, 1970–1973*, Hearings before the Subcommittee on Interamerican Affairs of the Committee on Foreign Affairs (Washington, D.C.: U.S. Government Printing Office, 1975), p. 59. Similar conclusions are advanced by R. Edwards, *Soviet Foreign Policy, 1962–1973* (London: Oxford University Press, 1975), p. 122

17.   *La economía chilena en 1972*, pp. 238–239.

CHAPTER 8

The Military in the Cabinet

After the events of October 1972, a political accord with the Center became impracticable given the advanced state of polarization. Confronted with the antagonism of the Christian Democrats, the government was no longer able to pursue its former strategy. The entrance of the military into the Cabinet temporarily fulfilled the functions of a UP-CDP accord.

An understanding with the Center would have moderated or overcome the conflict between the Executive and Congress; it would have provided the force necessary to turn back the rightist assault; and it would have conferred more legitimacy on the government's actions in the eyes of the middle classes. Faced with the breakup of the Center, however, it was essential to tap another source of power to overcome the crisis. The armed forces seemed capable of supplying crucial support in the struggle to reestablish normality. The military appeared as an autonomous force, one which, for many middle-class groups and some sectors of the opposition, guaranteed the continuity of the institutional order. This was the reasoning that led President Allende to his crucial decision: naming representatives of each of the three branches of the armed forces and the Corps of Carabineros as Cabinet ministers.

If the role of the military in this conjunction was so conceived, all that could be hoped for was that its participation in the government would permit the restoration of public order and generate conditions favoring an agreement between the majority political forces, the UP and CDP. No more favorable outcome could be seriously anticipated. Because of their essential character the Chilean armed forces were not inclined to favor the UP; if they were to oppose the government openly, its downfall would be certain. If the political forces in favor of institutional continuity had correctly grasped the role of the military in this conjuncture, they might have taken advantage of this period to seek out the basis for an agreement that would have allowed them later to dispense with such a decisive participation by the military in the government. Its role could at the very least have been limited to that of an arbitrator. But events did not develop in this direction.

Within the political parties, those sectors that seemed best to understand the situation did not formulate a clear line of action; nor could they muster the force to impose such a position. Thus hardly had the new government been formed, when new controversies emerged. Within the UP debates arose as to whether military participation really constituted a support or instead a freezing of the change process. There was a divided reaction within the CDP: The progressives saw that possibilities for a Center-Left accord would open up so long as the military could provide a guarantee. The more conservative groups argued that there was a risk that the UP would trap the armed forces, or the high command, into a commitment to the government program.

The period analyzed in this chapter was critical in that within a matter of a few months the chances for reducing the marked political polarization first seemed to open up and then disappeared altogether. It is essential to observe in detail some of the circumstances that led later to the departure of the military from the Cabinet and to explain the incapability of the Chilean political system to generate a satisfactory solution to the crisis.

The new Cabinet lasted only five months, from November 1972 to March 1973. Together with the military, it included, for the first time, the top leaders of the CUT, the largest labor federation in the country.[1] The most important figure in the Cabinet was General Carlos Prats, Commander-in-Chief of the Army, who was designated Minister of the Interior.

In the economic sphere, the new Cabinet—in what was hardly the first such effort—attempted to resolve the political-legal crisis stemming from the creation of the social property area. It also made another unsuccessful attempt to correct the most serious economic disequilibria. On the political front, General Prats was determined, even in the absence of a formal declaration on the part of the military Cabinet officers, that a general agreement be arrived at before the armed forces became involved in partisan political conflict. As far as the parties were concerned, all of their energies were devoted to preparations for the congressional elections in March. They neglected the daily business of government, hoping that the electoral outcome would break the deadlock and open up new options.

Taking Up Positions

General Prats' first effort was devoted to returning the country to normal after the October stoppage. This task was not an easy one, and it took almost the whole month of November 1972. During this period the UP manifested its solidarity with the military ministers; but once the consequences of the stoppage had been overcome, two positions emerged. Some in the coalition sought to consolidate the transformations with military support, while others thought that the continued presence of the armed forces would freeze the process and cost the government popular support.

This disagreement hindered the action of the new Cabinet considerably, weakening the chances of a more permanent relationship between the UP and the armed forces. The differences paralyzed, or impeded at any rate, adherence to an unambiguous line. A mistaken perception of the balance of forces led the most radical sectors in the UP once again to propose offensive actions. This time, however, their thinking was even more muddled, as it was based on an inconsistent analysis of the armed forces. Given the isolation of the UP from the political center and its acceptance of military support, it made no sense, on the one hand, to share the functions of government with the military and, at the same time, to obstruct the constitutionalist officers. This would only weaken their position and risk antagonizing the armed forces.

But what was the attitude of the constitutionalist officers in the armed forces? The chief explicit purpose of General Prats, as stated above, was to repair the damage of the October events and to reduce the level of political conflict. In Prats' thinking, the maintenance of the institutional order assumed an understanding between the UP and a segment of the opposition, even at the risk of provoking splits in both groups.

In the first few months as minister, Prats undertook conversations with the different political parties in order to estimate how viable his goals were. In meetings with the president of the CDP, he stated his conviction that unless a compromise with the UP was reached there could be no resolution of the crisis, and the whole Chilean institutional system might collapse. This kind of accord, he argued, was a necessary condition if military intervention was to be avoided.

The internal situation of the armed forces did not allow General Prats much room for maneuver. The number of officers inclined toward a coup was growing, and the chance that the constitutionalists might prevail depended on the success of the new Cabinet. This success would be measured by the degree of autonomy maintained by the military representatives with respect to the political parties and by their capacity to produce a more normal political and economic situation. But as events impeded these tasks, General Prats lost ground and was forced to justify his presence at the head of the Cabinet as simply a guarantee that congressional elections would be carried out as scheduled. He had to abandon his original goal of creating the conditions for a larger political accord.

The Christian Democrats had initially reacted favorably to the entry of the military into the Cabinet, in the belief that the preservation of constitutional order would be guaranteed. After a short time, however, they changed their position. For the more progressive sector of the CDP, the military presence appeared to assure institutional continuity and could also exert a moderating influence on the UP program. The conservative wing of the Party, on the other hand, saw in this development the possibility of a growing understanding between President Allende and the constitutionalist officers. For the coup-inclined groups among the Christian Democrats, such an outcome had to be avoided; hence it was essential to drive a wedge between the government and the military and between General Prats and the rest of his fellow officers.

The Right proceeded very cautiously. First, it was decided to halt the stoppage and seek an accommodation in order to avoid a confrontation with the military. Second, they strove to isolate General Prats by putting out the argument that he was committing the armed forces to the support of the UP. In the midst of this tangle of forces the new Cabinet began to function. Its chances for success were clearly limited. This, however, was a critical juncture; failure would lead once more to an open confrontation between the UP and the opposition. A new political impasse would cast the armed forces once more as arbitrators, but with the possibility that they would turn to another, less congenial position later on.

From the beginning of December 1972, all political energies were focused on the upcoming elections. The struggle between the opposition and the government intensified. The election campaign released the accumulated tensions, and the competition for votes hardened the adversary positions even more, making any negotiations practically impossible. Polarization heightened to a point where it led, for the first time, to a shift in the configuration on the formal electoral blocs. Two new supercoalitions appeared: the Democratic Confederation, which included the National Party, the CDP and other smaller groups, and the Federated Party, the united electoral front of the UP parties.[2]

The electoral front of the opposition parties effectively suppressed the programmatic differences between the CDP and the National Party, with the former moving ever closer to the latter's positions. The Nationalists set out to win an electoral triumph that supply the opposition with a two-thirds control of Congress. With this legally required margin of support the president would be impeached, thus eliminating his government by constitutional means. The Nationalists' election propaganda proclaimed that not just a new Congress, but a new government as well was at stake. This approach was the last resort of the Right in the effort to replace the government by institutional means. The Christian Democrats adopted a more realistic line. They argued that the elections would constitute a kind of plebiscite, that with a majority vote the opposition would be able to demand a total change in the government's policy.

The UP had to carry out a mighty electoral effort to repulse these attacks. Its principal worry was the economic situation; the focus of the opposition's offensive. This concern forced the government to commit all of its spare resources in order to reduce the shortages and prevent a deterioration in real incomes through inflation. As a result the austerity measures necessary to contain the economic maladjustments were ruled out.

Consolidating the Social Area

In the areas of agrarian reform, banking and copper, the chief goals of the UP had already been fulfilled; and the pace of change began to slow down a bit. In the industrial area, however, the situation was far from resolved. The government had succeeded in taking control of only a fraction of the 90 large firms included on its public list at the end of 1971. On the other hand it had intervened in almost 200 small and middle-sized firms which had been seized by their workers at the height of the struggle.

On the initiative of General Prats, the Cabinet Economic Committee set out to design a new law which would consolidate the principal advances in the formation of the social area and set aside the secondary problems. The proposed law included the following points:

1. Those firms which appeared on the public list of the 90 largest enterprises, already requisitioned but whose ownership had not been transferred to the state, would be promptly expropriated. The status of the other firms on the list, which continued under private control, would remain unaltered.
2. Another group of firms, not on the original list but already requisitioned, would be expropriated as well because of their strategic character.
3. A management commission made up of representatives of the owners, workers and the state would be set up for enterprises covered under the points above in those cases where the owner was inclined to negotiate. The commission would be transitory in character.
4. Smaller firms which were not considered strategic would be returned to their owners once an ad hoc commission determined the time and manner of doing so. The same action would be taken with those agricultural estates not originally subject to expropriation which had been intervened in because of labor conflicts.
5. Finally, a commission was proposed to resolve those problems pending as a result of intervention in foreign-owned enterprises.

The ideas had been discussed by Prats with several groups and parties, in an attempt to arrive at a minimal range of agreements necessary to calm the crisis. It was generally thought that the new proposal would be acceptable to the Christian Democrats. Success on this front would reinforce the constitutionalist officers in the armed forces. With these considerations in mind, General Prats made the proposed law public.

Within a few days a serious split within the UP became publicly known. The president and the Communist Party supported the Prats initiative. The Socialist Party, however, opposed it, rejecting any return of enterprises to private ownership. The president responded to these objections by pointing out that the proposed actions were sanctioned by the UP program. This split weakened the UP and left it paralyzed once more. On the one hand, the participation of the military was actively sought; but on the other hand, the conditions for gaining from this conjuncture were not being created. This incoherence was the reflection of the essential duality in the coalition's political line, a contradiction which could not be overcome. Among those groups which favored a continued advance at all cost there prevailed a devotion to "principles" devoid of all tactical sense. Theory took the place of reality in their analyses, and a simple assertion of will outweighed a consideration of objective conditions.

Had the UP conducted itself in a unified manner, the chances of consolidating the process under General Prats' auspices would have been good. In any event it has to be kept in mind that the success of this effort was by no means assured, since the opposition was making no concessions as the nation moved into a general congressional election. The previous experiences of the government suggested that the Christian Democrats might not be disposed to negotiate after the elections either. This information reinforced the line set down by the Socialist Party: any concessions would serve only to demobilize workers' organizations and provoke conflicts with unions which had seized control of their factories, and the hoped-for compensation of an accord with the CDP would not be forthcoming in any event.

Thus the political impasse toward which Chile had been heading appeared in all its force. It was not possible to articulate a policy of consolidation within the UP, while the alternative presented by the Socialists left no room for legal solutions to the crisis. Instead the latter position would lead directly to a break with the institutional order, which was the principal objective as well of the opposition exponents of a coup d'état. Thus one more effort to find a larger agreement collapsed. The possibilities for consolidating the structural changes within a generally accepted institutional framework became even more remote.

Defensive Economic Measures

Given this political situation, the two criteria guiding economic decisions were purely defensive: to prevent an acceleration of inflation and to avoid a deterioration in wages. Along with these objectives there was a pressing need to obtain freely disposable external resources in order to maintain levels of production and employment. Containment of inflation was to be effected through a rigid control of prices and, secondarily, through a new effort to reduce the deficits in the Treasury and the social area. In order to attack the second deficit, some price increases were authorized for state enterprises, while stiff controls were maintained on the prices of products manufactured in the private sector. Nevertheless, these price adjustments were minimal; they were effected so cautiously and slowly that losses in the state enterprises were not significantly reduced. Nominal wages continued to grow through bonuses and special compensatory payments, granted to offset the mounting inflation. The costs of intermediate goods manufactured by the private sector also rose.

At this point the effectiveness of price controls was severely damaged by the enormous pressures coming from all of the enterprises. The administrative apparatus was hopelessly overloaded. There existed neither the personnel nor the organizational capacity necessary to supervise the whole economy. The problem was compounded by the rise of the black market, which obliged the administrators to concern themselves with hoarding as well as keeping vigil over prices. Once a certain limit of financial maladjustment had been surpassed, the number of products, firms and consumers that had to be controlled began to grow so rapidly that the state apparatus was simply incapable of keeping up with the job. Worse still, as the power of the control system decayed, more people chose to elude its rulings. A self-reinforcing vicious circle was set in motion.

The mechanisms for consolidating the UP's income redistribution also weakened. This objective was unattainable through market mechanisms and price controls. The government resorted therefore to two additional methods: it scheduled another wage adjustment for the beginning of 1973, and it began to plan direct distribution of essential goods to the populace. Let us examine now how such measures were conceived and why the results were so disappointing.

Wage Policy under Hyperinflation

Freezing wages and salaries to combat inflation was incompatible with the maintenance of workers' income levels. If the wage-price spiral were allowed to operate unchecked, however, inflation would accelerate even more. Government policy on wages and salaries was trapped between two opposed, equally unviable options. This situation offered one more proof of the proposition that a substantial income distribution cannot be sustained in a market economy with limited government power.

How did this impasse come about in practice? At the end of December 1972, the Cabinet Economic Committee began to study a new wage adjustment. Given the magnitude of the inflation and the consequent diminution in real wages, it was suggested that an adjustment should be granted in advance. In order to avoid aggravating the fiscal deficit, two ideas were considered. First, increases would be granted every four months, instead of in a single annual increment. Second, the adjustment in pay would be variable, according to the level of wages earned. For low-income groups, the percentage increase in wages would equal the percentage increase in the cost of living index from the date of the last adjustment up until the moment of each advance payment: for the remainder of the wage and salary earners the advance payments would be constant. Once the year was completed, a readjustment equal to the increase in the cost of living would be granted to all, discounting the sums already paid in advance.

As a first step the government proposed that "low income" workers be defined as those receiving pay equal to less than two *sueldos vitales* (a monthly salary or wage equal to two times the legally fixed minimum). Later, after discussions with the CUT, whose support was crucial if the policy was raised to three *sueldos vitales*. About half of all public sector employees fell into the low-income group according to this definition.

The second step was to request congressional authorization for financing the readjustment. Care had to be taken to avoid the passage of a law which allowed the spending without authorizing the requisite fiscal revenues, as had occurred before. The opposition-dominated Congress had always rejected new taxes proposed by the Executive with the excuse that they would damage the middle class. This time the UP government proposed procedures which withheld payment of wage adjustments so long as Congress had not allowed for new fiscal income. Thus the opposition parties would be made to accept the responsibility for their own parliamentary obstructionism. The proposal consisted specifically in setting up a Wage Fund which would be filled with new resources approved by Congress. The new taxes studied by the government were intended to reduce the liquidity of middle and upper groups. They included increases in the capital gains tax, a stockholding tax, real estate taxes (to be progressive) and taxes on private sector credits.

The potential coherence of this approach suffered a grave setback at the hands of Congress. In February 1973, the Chamber of Deputies rejected most of the proposed taxes, the Wage Fund and the provision for graduated pay increases. Proposed in their place was a readjustment equal to the increase in the cost of living for all of those who received wages or salaries up to *20 sueldos vitales*. The Chamber of Deputies also suggested that a monetary devaluation or its equivalent in higher taxes on imports should be adopted as an alternative source of supplementary revenues. Furthermore, the benefits of the readjustment were extended as well to other sectors not originally considered by the Executive. Taking advantage of its control of both houses of Congress, the opposition passed a bill completely different from that originally introduced by the UP. In this way an enormous deficit was created. With these moves Congress infringed on the Constitution, since it lacked the legal power to establish new levels of expenditure.

The Executive was quick to level these charges, and a new conflict between the two branches was opened up. The government appealed to the Constitutional Tribunal to resolve its new dispute with Congress. The Tribunal ruled in favor of the Executive, holding that Congress did not have the power to establish new levels of spending. However, it supported the right of Congress to veto the provision for the Wage Fund.

This debate took place in the middle of the election campaign. The government argued that Congress was withholding the resources to finance the pay adjustment for workers and employees, protecting the most powerful groups, and contributing to inflation. The opposition responded by pointing out that the government was discriminating among workers, to the disfavor of the largest group who earned middling incomes. According to the opposition, this was nothing less than an attack on the middle class. Moreover, organizations of employees in some government agencies began to demand that the government eliminate the provision for scaled increases. The CDP mobilized its militants and sympathizers to oppose the government's initiative.

As a consequence of this struggle the government agreed to modify its proposal at the beginning of March 1973. A six-month delay between adjustments, rather than a four-month period, was proposed; and the lower wage limit for a complete readjustment was advanced from three to five *sueldos vitales*. Thus considerably more workers would receive wage hikes equal to the rise in the cost of living.[3] The new proposal was submitted to Congress, which once more rejected most of the taxes and the idea of the Wage Fund. The outcome was that the new readjustment was severely underfinanced and, as a result, the fiscal deficit foreseen for 1973 grew even larger.

These events made it clear that it was impossible to implement a firm economic policy in an unstable electoral context, with a polarized party system and high inflation. These limitations forced the government to search for new openings. The most significant of these was the direct distribution of goods to assure their supply to the poorest groups.

Direct Distribution of Essential Goods

The idea of setting up a program of planned distribution of essential consumer goods was at first resisted from within the UP. Two arguments were advanced against it. In the first place an intense reaction from the opposition was feared. The government would be blamed for shortages and accused of attempting to set up a rationing system to underwrite its total political predominance. Second, placing in operation a nationwide planned distribution was a complex task and it would take time. A premature announcement, one made before an adequate organization had been assembled, would make this job even more difficult.

Despite these objections, plans for direct distribution continued to be studied and began to attract more adherents. Confronted with the failure of all other measures, this radical approach seemed the only possibility. But operational progress was very slow; it was still not clear how much of the nation would be reached by the new system of distribution, nor how many products would be involved.

In the middle of these discussions and before the required rulings had been adopted, the minister of finance announced new distribution policies in January 1973, two months before the elections. The measures announced were as follows:

1. Creation of a National Office of Distribution, responsible for formulating and implementing the programs under study.
2. Channeling all of the production of state-owned enterprises through state-run commercial operations.
3. Establishing purchasing contracts with private firms.
4. Suspension of direct sales to the public in producing firms, elimination of barter trade between enterprises, and a halt to payment in kind to workers.
5. Rationing of the distribution of 30 products, according to the needs of the population.
6. Development and expansion of the Price and Supply Councils (Juntas de Abastecimiento y Precios, or JAPs) as popular support organizations.[4]

In the midst of an election campaign that had accentuated a climate of total confrontation, these measures excited an intense reaction. The military members of the Cabinet were the first to indicate their disapproval of the general tone of the finance minister's speech. The Navy's representative resigned from the Cabinet and had to be replaced by another admiral.[5] The speech also produced disquiet within the UP. Those objecting to the new line argued that it contradicted the attempts of the new Cabinet to reduce the areas of conflict.

Technically, it was very difficult to implement the announced measures right away. An apparatus capable of administering the direct distribution of even two or three products had never been assembled, to say nothing of one that could manage 30. The economic effect was the opposite of what had been wished for, since the public, anticipating the rationing, rushed to accumulate merchandise purchased at private outlets. The failure to announce exactly which products would be among the 30 to be rationed encouraged an indiscriminate rush on all merchandise.

The public announcement of the new measures turned out to be a bad move in every respect. Politically, it supplied the opposition with a weapon to use against the UP and government; and the measures were technically impossible to implement. While the essential orientation was correct, given the impossibility of other approaches, the timing and form of presentation of the new policy were poorly chosen.

In sum, the efforts to correct economic imbalances were unsuccessful. Constrained by events and immobilized by unyielding political rigidities, economic policy was at the mercy of everyday conflicts. Working with limited power, given the political isolation of the UP and its internal divisions, it was impossible to sustain a consistent economic policy.

Factors Determining the Economic Outcome

The dominant tendencies in the economy could not be reversed during the rule of the civilian-military Cabinet. In the first trimester of 1973 industrial production declined with respect to the same period in 1972. The fiscal deficit and the deficit in the social area continued to grow. The rate of inflation hit 22 percent between January and March, and the supply of money in the private sector grew by 43.3 percent in the same period.[6] The remunerations policy proposed by the government could not be implemented; there were no advance payments and workers' real incomes began to deteriorate. The rate of exchange remained fixed and had already lost all economic meaning.[7] The balance of payments presented even more difficulties than at the end of 1972. Despite the hopes for this Cabinet, it had proved impossible to implement an economic policy capable of reducing the maladjustments—instead they became even more serious.

Many factors contributed to this outcome. In the first place, the inflationary surge stemming from the corrective policy attempted in August 1972, together with the October crisis, took the government by surprise and led to a very cautious attitude. In the absence of a coherent alternative economic policy, it was decided to introduce as few changes as possible in order to avoid agitating the system even more.

In the second place, the number of political tasks to be attended to—all in the midst of a generalized confrontation—overwhelmed the capacity of the economic staff. Events compelled the government to devote all its resources to coping with daily problems; new courses of action were effectively ruled out.

In the third place, the economic staff lacked a single source of authority. The dual power structure, divided between the government and the parties of the coalition, granted to each minister and high executive a degree of autonomy that effectively obscured the lines of authority. The ministers' technical support staffs were unstable; they tended to form and split along party lines.

A fourth important element was the particular approach employed by each of the principal political parties in its thinking on economic policy. The Communist Party and its representatives in the economic directory attached great importance to the solution of the financial problems, emphasizing their negative effect on strategic objectives. The Party's channels of information functioned well and fed directly into internal leadership levels. The Communists were concerned with the financial imbalances, and they emphasized that production had to be increased and management improved in the social area. That Party, however, could not supply a coherent alternative approach. It offered useful solutions to specific problems, but these did not come together in a globally coherent policy. One example of this failing was the enormous emphasis placed on increasing production when this factor was largely secondary in importance to the expansion in demand as a cause of market disequilibria. Another example was the method the Communists proposed to reduce the deficit in the enterprises of the social area. Here as well, increased production was recommended to reduce the growing deficits, despite the fact that these deficits stemmed mainly from the relative decline of prices and the growth in wage payments.

The Socialist Party, on the other hand, did have many technical people who exercised considerable policymaking power and who were equipped analytically to formulate coherent overall programs. But the linkage of the technical staff with the political hierarchy of the Party was weak; the technicians wielded relatively little influence on the inner workings. The Party leadership was ineffectual and poorly organized. Different groups competed for influence within it, and their policy positions, many of which reflected ideologically simplistic economic thinking, were in continual conflict. One characteristic element was the emphasis placed on "the masses" as a factor presumably capable of overcoming the insufficiency of savings, generating foreign currency reserves, raising production and eliminating shortages. Basically, popular mobilization was viewed as a cure-all spontaneous organizing device. Finally, the electoral process itself acted like a straitjacket on economic policy. It proved impossible to demand sacrifices of the workers when the stability of the government depended to such a great extent on the March 1973 congressional elections.

One single factor, however, was at the basis of all these circumstances, a factor whose influence was felt at every level: the government simply did not possess sufficient political power at this point to design and implement a coherent economic policy, whatever this might be, to deal with the maladjustments accumulated in two years of uninterrupted expansion of demand. Thus the basic political-economic problem of the UP appeared once more: the essential incongruence of a program of structural transformation with an economic policy that was, in the end, excessively expansive and redistributive.

A More Radical Option

The picture just described was seen clearly by the government. Given the impossibility of action on the eve of the election, an analysis was begun of the steps that should be taken afterwards. In February and March 1973, the Cabinet Economic Committee held a series of meetings. The reports and debates pinpointed the gravity of the situation in unsparing terms. The two critical areas upon which the analysis focused were the balance of payments and the internal financial disequilibria.

In order to appreciate the magnitude of the economic effects that would be generated by the diminishing availability of foreign currency reserves, the government drew up a budget in foreign currency for each sector and quantified the recessive impact of this scarcity. The results demonstrated that if the 1972 levels of supply, employment and overall activity were to be maintained, a balance of payments deficit of some $400 million would have to be faced in 1973. In the calculations of income, the new resources obtained during the president's trip to the Soviet Union and the other socialist bloc countries had been counted into the balance. In addition a slight improvement in copper prices, the influx of credits from Western Europe and Latin America, and the renegotiation of the external debt had all been taken into consideration. The only remaining source of aid was a standby loan from the IMF, which would doubtless have aroused political resistance from within the UP.

The review of this data revealed that there was no choice but to limit the level of imports. The basic question was whether the restrictions should fall mainly on raw materials or on foodstuffs. The first option would lead to a reduction in production levels and a rise in unemployment; the second would produce a sharp contraction in the per capita availability of food. In the Economic Committee it was agreed to restrict raw material imports for industry by 25 percent. Food imports would be kept under tight controls; the ingress of less essential goods would be cut back while additional resources were sought which might avoid the worsening of shortages.

The examination of external finances revealed, in summary, that the government would have to face a drop in production and a tighter food situation in 1973. The intensity of this situation would depend on the level of agricultural production and the success of the efforts to obtain additional resources in foreign currency or in products.

In the studies of the fiscal situation carried out in March 1973, the projections for the fiscal budget and the accounts in the social area indicated that the overall deficit would keep on increasing. At the end of 1972, it had been estimated that the 1973 fiscal deficit would come to some 50 billion escudos. In February 1973, the new calculations yielded a deficit of 100 billion escudos for the same year; the projected deficit had doubled within two months.

The estimated annual deficit in the social area as calculated in February also turned out to be greater than the figure projected in December. According to the Economic Committee the deficit would reach a sum of 100 billion escudos. It was determined as well, however, that if prices on the products of state enterprises remained controlled, the deficit might turn out to be even greater. Later, in the light of these calculations, the minister of finance estimated that inflation could expand prices by 300 percent in 1973. If corrective measures were not adopted, he warned, this figure might be even higher.[8] This diagnosis suggested that the situation was out of control, with demand continuing to grow while available supply was diminishing.

Only drastic measures would suffice, and these could take one of two basic approaches. The first option was an orthodox policy that would involve raising prices drastically, freezing wages, devaluing the escudo, and granting guarantees and exemptions to the private sector, foreign and national. The second option was a policy that would assure direct distribution of goods, advance and consolidate control over the large enterprises, impose controls on wages and public spending, and extract all possible resources from middle- and upper-income groups.

The first option was rejected on principle. Its weight would have to be borne by the workers; it would lead to an economic contraction; and it would favor the owners of medium and large firms in commerce and industry. This meant a retreat with respect to the gains of 1971 and 1972. For the UP the second option was the only possible choice. This option was itself a difficult one: its technical design would have to be very complex; it would require strong popular backing, superior in fact to that which the government had heretofore enjoyed; and it demanded an apparatus of leadership and direction more solid and well-organized than anything that existed at the time. The viability of this plan was, in short, extremely precarious; but there was no other approach that could be taken. The underlying situation of social, economic and political tension forced the government to turn to very radical policies which it had originally neither anticipated nor advocated. What was at issue was a clearly revolutionary approach, one which would have to be implemented just when the balance of power was becoming unfavorable. As is always the case historically, when a desperate situation is confronted, the recourse to extreme actions becomes more likely.

The Electoral Outcome and the New Political Picture

The UP won a surprise victory in the congressional elections of March 1973. It was generally believed both by the political leadership and by the public at large that the progressive economic deterioration had undermined the government's popular base of support considerably. Despite these expectations, the UP won 44 percent of the vote, a proportion even higher than that attained in the presidential elections.[9]

According to the prevailing belief in political circles, there was a direct relation between the economic situation of the moment and electoral results. It was assumed that low rates of inflation and unemployment in the economy, combined with medium to high growth rates, would help shore up the government. Moreover, it was felt that the election results depended on the manner in which these rates varied. If the prevailing tendency in the economy was towards higher levels of production, electoral conditions ought to favor the government. Inversely, if recession, inflation or a reversal in income redistribution were manifested, electoral support would fade. The first set of conditions was in effect in April 1971, and accordingly the government improved its vote. In March 1973, the opposing circumstances prevailed, but the election results were also favorable. How can such a high vote in the middle of an economic crisis be explained?

Over the course of two and a half years of the UP government, important advances in the level of organization and political consciousness of the workers had been produced. The struggle over the ownership of the means of production and the distribution of income, as well as the hostility of the United States, served to emphasize and clarify the underlying conflict of interests. The number of popular organizations expanded rapidly: in the factories (Production Committees, Vigilance Committees, participation in management), in the countryside (Peasant Councils, cooperatives, collective forms of farm administration, seizures of estates), in the urban squatter settlements (Price and Supply Councils, community health organizations, the continuing and expanded work of the Mothers' Centers and Neighborhood Councils), and in the CUT (an increase in the number of unions and unionized workers, organization by economic sector and by geographic area). It was this heightened political consciousness of the workers, developed in the conflict itself, that led them to see short-run problems in the wider perspective of structural change. The clash of interests with the dominant groups became obvious.[10] But the same qualitative change occurred as well among the social groups represented by the opposition. The manifest result was rigid polarization, a situation of minimal flexibility, and a progressive tendency toward global confrontation.

The election results stood out as a fundamental political fact. The outcome of the voting set off a new debate within the UP on the subsequent political course and, especially, on the role of the armed forces. President Allende and the greater part of the UP held that, while the electoral support indeed strengthened the government, it was still important that the military continue to serve in the Cabinet. The government had already conferred on the military a crucial political role as a force for mediation. Their exit, therefore, would be interpreted as proof that the UP had used their presence simply to further its own immediate partisan interests. The basic civil and institutional conflict had not changed; conditions similar to those that had allowed the Right, with help from the United States, to stage the October stoppage might easily arise again. This time the armed forces might adopt a less helpful attitude to the mortal detriment of the government.

This analysis was rejected by the Socialist Party. Its leaders believed that the continued presence of the armed forces in the Cabinet was holding back the whole process and alienating the workers from the government. There was a growing risk that the government would shift toward the Center, looking only for opportunities to negotiate and making more concessions. In this case it would end up merely as the administrator of the advances achieved in the first phase.

But this paralyzing debate had already been rendered irrelevant because the situation within the armed forces had changed significantly. The Minister of the Interior, General Prats, soon discovered how difficult it was to arrange a political agreement and introduce significant corrective measures. His relationship with the Christian Democrats, which seemed to be promising at first, was soon frozen by the latter in order to avoid strengthening the government. The aborted attempts at a solution for the problems of the social area and the general deterioration of the economic situation hurt Prats' position within the armed forces. In the meantime the Right was making steady inroads among the military, with the aim of fencing in and weakening that group of officers still determined to support the institutional regime. These considerations led General Prats to decide to leave the Cabinet; his presence was more important, he felt, in the army.

Nonetheless, a new attempt was made on April 5, 1973 to assure the continued presence of the military in the government. The panel of generals involved met with the president and stated their willingness to continue in the Cabinet as long as the following conditions were fulfilled:

1. A resolution of the institutional crisis by means of an accord with the Christian Democrats on the organization of the economy.
2. Disarming of the paramilitary groups of the Right and the Left.
3. Guarantees for public order, meaning specifically an end to the disorders erupting daily.
4. Restoration of orderly public services and prompt carrying out of the government's decisions by its functionaries.
5. Improvement in relations with the United States.

Dissension within the UP, however, limited President Allende's room for maneuver. He tried to adapt himself to the possibilities of the moment, but without success. As a result the constitutionalist officers were forced to withdraw from the government and return to their military duties in order to contain the growing support for a coup that was developing within officers' circles. The government had lost one of its decisive supports, and the notion of taking power directly began to attract more attention within the armed forces.

The vote won by the UP in March caused the National Party and the conservative wing of the CDP to discard the possibility of putting an end to the government through electoral politics. The Executive was already aware before the elections that the Right would actively foment a coup d'état if the UP won more than 40 percent of the vote. If these efforts were to succeed, General Prats would have to be induced to leave the government, and the Right would have to drive a wedge between him and the rest of the officer corps.

By the end of March, President Allende was forced to name a new Cabinet made up entirely of civilians. The political confrontation re-emerged once the remote possibility of a consolidation managed with the support of the armed forces had disappeared altogether. The generals had entered and departed from the government without altering the essential balance of social and political forces. In order to overcome the impasse, the military would have to throw its weight entirely behind one group or another.

The UP alone remained completely blocked. It had committed a double error. First, it had not come out clearly for an understanding with part of the opposition. Second, it had failed to take account of the limitations on the support that the constitutionalist officers could extend to the government. The most important change caused by the incorporation of the generals in the Cabinet occurred within the military itself: from this point on the impulse to fill the power vacuum with their own might would build inexorably within the armed forces.

Notes

1. The new Cabinet included three representatives of the armed forces and two from the CUT, its president and vice-president. Allende's purpose was to include new forces, drawn from outside the UP parties, which would lend more stability to the government.
2. At the end of 1971 two new political groups had been created: the Christian Left, a splinter group from the CDP that joined the UP; and the Left Radical Party, a split from the Radical Party which, after remaining for awhile in the UP, left it in 1972 to join the opposition. Both divisions revealed the intense polarization and the vanishing middle ground between the two largest forces, the UP and the CDP.
3. It was estimated within the Cabinet Economic Committee that 70 percent of public employees received a salary less than five *sueldo vitales.*
4. The JAPs were grassroots organizations, elected directly by people in each neighborhood, which had the power to aid the government in the supervision of prices and the fight against hoarding.
5. The departing officer was a certain Admiral Huerta, who had been Minister of Transport. After the coup d'état in September 1973 he was named Minister of Foreign Relations by the military junta.
6. Data from Banco Central de Chile.
7. Comparing the average 1969 index with that of the first trimester of 1973, the consumer price index had shot up by 430 percent, while the exchange rate had varied by 180 percent. Banco Central de Chile.
8. On the basis of a simple cost model, which took account of the effects of a program of price increases for intermediate goods manufactured in the social area, an inflation rate of 300 percent was projected. A model based on supply and demand equilibrium in the money market predicted inflationary pressures of be-

tween 300 and 500 percent for 1973. Direccion de Presupuesto, Ministerio de Hacienda, "Perspectivas del APS y el resto de la economía en 1973" (March 1973).

9. The Left vote came to 36 percent in 1970 and 50 percent in the 1971 municipal elections. Between the elections in April 1971 and those of March 1973 the number of voters grew from 3,660,000 to 4,542,000 in part due to the reduction of the minimum voting age from 21 to 18.

10. A story that became popular in Left circles illustrates this qualitative change. During a popular demonstration directed at President Allende himself, a worker was seen carrying a big placard with the following inscription: "This government is full of shit, but it's *my* government." The first clause reflected common opinion concerning the conjunctural situation, its failures and imbalances. The second clause affirmed a strategic commitment to the government.

CHAPTER 9

The Institutional Collapse

In the tense final months of the UP government the fissures in the institutional system widened until it finally collapsed entirely. Only a political accord could have held the scaffolding in place, but the chances for reaching such an agreement were practically nil. Between March and September 1973, President Allende sought to forge a basic consensus which might ward off the collapse, but his efforts were in vain. The possibilities for re-enlisting the armed forces as a temporary bulwark for the political-legal system, in a role subordinate to the UP government, had faded. The permanent state of conflict stemming from the political and social polarization effectively alienated the support of the armed forces, even of the constitutionalist officers. Instead the political vacuum became a force of attraction for the military; more and more they came to think of themselves as filling the gap alone.

At the same time, as so often happens in periods of generalized crisis, embryonic manifestations of "people's power" began to appear. These popular initiatives did not have a chance to develop; but had the experience been more prolonged, they might have become a supporting element in the creation of a new institutional order. The political consciousness of large sectors of the working class and its growing organization constituted an ascendant force, a source of growing support for the government. This fact was duly noted by those pressing for a coup. Once the prospects for effective political-legal opposition faded, they began pressing for a complete break with the democratic order.

In the economic sphere decisions fluctuated with the struggle for political survival, and the financial imbalances worsened. But certain positive elements emerged as well, even though they did not have a chance to develop fully. The changes in property relations in copper, banking, the large manufacturing firms, and in the countryside fundamentally altered the structure of decision and control in the economy; a new, more egalitarian economic model began to take shape. The state could thus count on new forces with which to confront the economic difficulties. Other positive indicators also appeared: the price of copper began to recover, and the planting season promised a good agricultural year in 1973. Both developments would alleviate the delicate balance of payments situation.[1] But these budding positive features were stymied by the opposition offensive, a reversal also caused in part by the inadequacies of the government and the UP.

The flux of events was determined essentially by the preparations for a coup, and all of the actions and reactions that occurred have to be placed in this context. A climate of undeclared war prevailed. The attack was directed from the parties of the Right and extreme Right, their house organ *El Mercurio,* and the U.S. intelligence services. Considerable sectors of the CDP and the *gremios* of the middle and large bourgeoisie provided supporting forces. The coup itself was to be executed by a group of high-ranking officers in the armed forces. But the fundamental factor was the political struggle; political defeat preceded and was a necessary condition for the military intervention.

Between April and September 1973, President Allende made several Cabinet changes in an attempt to find a way out of the growing crisis. The first Cabinet, formed just after the congressional elections, did not include any military representatives. It lasted only three months, until the end of June, when an armored regiment rebelled, sending a shock wave through the country. At this point the president turned again to the military, seeking to enlist the participation of those loyal generals who had suppressed the uprising. General Prats entered the Cabinet for the second time, as minister of defense. He lasted only a few short weeks in this position. Submitted to strong pressures on the part of the army officer corps, he resigned his ministry and a few days later withdrew as commander-in-chief. The officers who continued in the Cabinet were no longer the commanders of the various branches of the armed forces. Prats' departure from the army left the door open for the coup which was finally unleashed on September 11.

The Design of the Last Economic Program

In the middle of this crisis it was impossible to focus energies to implement a new economic program. Nevertheless, the initial breath of life infused by the favorable election results of March 1973 inspired the entering Cabinet to consider new measures. The objectives were purely defensive: (1) avoid accelerated inflation; (2) maintain as far as possible the level of consumption of essential goods already achieved by low-income families; and (3) minimize the decline in production due to the shortage of foreign currency. In order to approximate these objectives, an economic policy was outlined which included the following principal elements:

1. *Prices:* Gradual increases, beginning with products of the enterprises in the social area, in order to reduce the deficit. The escudo would be devalued immediately. Finally, price increases in the private sector would be authorized, but with the provision that they be less than the increases

allowed in the social area. The intention in enforcing this sequence of price adjustments was to avoid a repetition of the failed attempt of August 1972. Another idea that took shape was to discriminate among consumer goods according to their relative necessity. A small group of essential goods would remain under strict control, while higher prices would be authorized for nonessential goods. Thus the market would be segmented into two areas: the first, for a small number of essential goods in excess demand, would be "rationed by quantity"; in the second, goods would be "rationed by price." In order to implement this idea the goods manufactured in the social area would be divided into three groups: essential consumer goods, intermediate products, and nonessential consumer goods. Prices for the first group would be adjusted slightly, while they would be raised significantly for the other two groups, especially the last. The adjustment of August 1972 had accelerated inflation and taken the political leadership by surprise. This time advance warning was given: the same initial inflationary surge could be expected. The full cycle of adjustment would be a long one; but, once adopted, the policy should be pursued without interruption. The warning was certainly necessary, but the possibilities for sustaining this kind of policy in a period of total confrontation seemed highly doubtful.

2. *Wage policy:* If some restraint on the galloping inflation was to be achieved, it was essential that public spending increase less than the consumer price index. In other words, the wage-price spiral would have to be broken. Several approaches were considered to accomplish this goal. First a revision was suggested in the price index used as a basis for calculating wage adjustments. This index, which reflected a median or average consumption pattern, did not accurately represent the situation of any specific income stratum. What was needed was an index reflecting the consumption of low-income groups, those whose situation the incomes policy was intended to effect. Without such a new definition, price increases for nonessential and luxury goods would inflate the index, which served as the basis of negotiation for all pay increases. In the second place, it was decided that wage hikes should be tied to improvements in production and productivity. This criterion would shortly be put to the test when the government was confronted with a strike of copper miners at El Teniente. Finally, the idea of granting differential increases in income was put forth again, either in the form of proportionately higher increases for low-income people or, what amounted to the same thing, an equal amount in escudos to be granted to all.

3. *Deficits:* The system of taxation had been shown to be totally unable to capture new revenues, while spending proved very difficult to restrain. Some new measures were suggested, such as proposing new tax rates to Congress and a crackdown on evasion, but with the foreknowledge that the result would be meager. As for the social area, it was estimated that the new prices would diminish somewhat the operating deficit. Finally,

some consideration was given to a monetary reform. This measure was finally abandoned, since its approval depended on Congress and its effectiveness would be stunted if the cause that generated the excessive liquidity—namely, the deficit in the public sector—was not first dealt with.

4. *Internal production:* Attention was focused on three critical areas: agriculture, copper and transport. In the agrarian sector, it was decided to clear up once and for all the confusion concerning forms of ownership. In addition production-linked incentives would be implemented in place of a fixed salary paid to farmworkers. The organization and operation of the reformed units would be upgraded in order to raise production and thus alleviate pressures for food imports. It was essential to reduce the gap which had opened up between the change in property ownership and the installation of a new organization of production. In copper, as well, labor discipline would have to be restored promptly and the technical managerial apparatus consolidated. During 1972 and the first months of 1973 the incidence of partial work stoppages and labor conflicts in the mines, and particularly at Chuquicamata, had worsened. There would have to be a turn towards effective management of the social area. Surprisingly, transport had become a severe obstacle and a powerful weapon in the hands of the opposition. Facilities in truck and rail transport were inadequate to supply inputs to the agricultural sector, to move copper to the ports, or to deliver fuels. Port capacity was overtaxed and there were serious problems in unloading imported foodstuffs. Provisioning of the large cities, suffering from high levels of demand and a lack of stocks, was help up further by delays in the arrival of boats and by problems in unloading them. Labor productivity in this sector had also declined. It was essential to tighten labor discipline and to make investments that could improve the capacity to move goods.

5. *Distribution of consumer goods:* It was considered that throughout 1973 the policies on prices, wages and taxes would have only a marginal effect on the magnitude of the gap between supply and demand. In order to protect the consumption levels of the poor, it was decided to implement a direct distribution scheme. This assumed that the state distribution apparatus would be strengthened and its organization upgraded. In addition popular participation would be extended, in order to consolidate grass-roots organization and carry out massive campaigns against hoarding and speculation.

6. *Foreign trade:* The necessity of adjusting the exchange rate was emphasized once again, as well as the importance of negotiating with intervened or requisitioned foreign-owned firms. The latter was necessary in order to reduce pending problems with European governments which were obstructing additional financing. Moreover, it was decided to develop an administrative system for the control of imports and to promote a change in the production lines of state enterprises so as to reduce the use of imported products.

These central ideas encompassed minimal objectives; but given the prevailing situation, the chances of fulfilling these objectives seemed slight.

The Nonviability of the Proposed Program

Quantitative analysis revealed the weakness of the measures outlined above; and, shortly thereafter developments rendered most of the proposals impracticable. Doubts first centered on the anti-inflation aspects of the program. Given an underlying inflation rate of 10 percent per month, a substantial adjustment in prices in the social area could generate an uncontrollable situation. The relative weakness of the price control machinery, together with the extent of the black market, allowed the private sector to raise prices without fear of reprisals. A devaluation would be similarly frustrated. The inflation propagating mechanisms would operate with even more force than during the August 1972 experience.

The magnitude of the black market was illustrated to the Cabinet Economic Committee by two examples. First, it was estimated that the surplus of money supply, multiplied by the velocity of circulation in April 1973, yielded a value equal to 80 percent of the 1972 GNP. This figure was an indicator of the excess in aggregate demand. Second, in order to compare official prices and real prices for retail commerce, a sample study of 100 products revealed an average difference of 60 percent, and for foodstuffs 100 percent. These facts suggested clearly that an anti-inflationary policy that did not attack the root causes would be futile.

As for the policy of differentiated pay raises, this had only barely been sustained in April 1973. The prospects for reviving it were even more precarious; already in April and May 1973 the number of strikes mounted considerably, culminating with the prolonged conflict in the El Teniente copper mine.

In this context, the measures proposed to bring down the fiscal deficit were not effective. Even when they were implemented, they produced infinitesimal results: the deficit was reduced from 50 percent to 44 percent as a percentage of total fiscal revenues. As for the deficit in the social area, it was calculated that an increase of 70 percent in the prices of its products would cause a 40 to 50 percent jump in the consumer price index, even assuming effective price controls. Costs would rise immediately, diminishing the initial impact of the price increases.

The deficits were no more than a consequence of an overambitious redistributive policy which had been implemented so brusquely as to exceed the capacity of the Chilean economic system. With a very different balance of forces, it would have been possible to extract more revenues from the middle and upper strata; but even in this case the short-run economic effects would have been very serious. Furthermore, such a favorable balance of power never existed, except perhaps in the first few months of the government. Here lay the central contradiction of the whole economic policy: the surplus actually disposable, given the existing balance of forces, was incompatible with the redistributive expectations that were encouraged first by the government, and later exacerbated by the opposition.

The new economic program encountered other obstacles, as well. The measures designed to boost production in copper and agriculture could not yield immediate returns. The new investment and the administrative and technical reorganization would show dividends starting in 1974, with only a minimal impact being felt in 1973. The same would be true for the efforts to implement a system of direct distribution of essential goods.

The right-wing media unleashed an intense and effective campaign harping on all of the technical problems mentioned above. From April 1973 on, there were regular announcements concerning shortages in key areas, particularly bread, fuel, cooking oil and sugar. These news reports generated widespread panic, sending people rushing to stores in order to stock up on these goods. In the case of gasoline, for example, rumors concerning shortages, transport failures and strikes among gas-station workers excited an alarmist response on several occasions. Car owners exhausted gas station supplies in a matter of hours, leaving most vehicles without fuel.

The intentions of the new economic program were lost in the day-to-day struggle. The Allende government had to steer its way under harassment by a violent opposition, pushed on all sides by organized social forces, and weakened by differences among the very parties that supported it.

The Copper Strike at El Teniente

An excellent illustration of the prevailing political torment was the strike at the El Teniente copper mine.[2] This was the most serious labor conflict ever confronted by the UP government. What started as just one more strike soon became a grave national problem, culminating in the military uprising of June 29.

The strike began in April 1973 and went on for 70 days. Its origin was apparently economic in nature. The problem arose from a disagreement between the nationalized enterprise and union leaders concerning the interpretation of the national law that granted the wage adjustments of October 1972. On that occasion Congress accepted the Executive's proposal that the payment of the wage increase originally scheduled for January 1973 be moved up to October 1972 in order to alleviate the effects of the inflationary outburst. In the law it was established that those unions with contracts already in effect could either keep them unchanged or opt for the government formula and thus obtain a proportionate increase to cover the rise in prices since the date of the last contract. The El Teniente workers opted for the government formula. They would receive a percentage increase in their incomes equal to the rise in prices between April 4, 1972, the date of the last labor contract, and September 20, 1972, the date the new adjustment went into effect.

Unlike others in the labor force, the El Teniente workers benefited from an automatic escalator clause in their union contract. Whenever inflation exceeded 5 percent, their wages were to go up by half of the percentage increase in inflation. Accordingly, between April 4 and September 30, 1972, their wages had already been raised, while the rest of the wage workers and salaried employees in Chile continued to receive the same amounts specified in the original contracts.

The unions at El Teniente demanded that the new adjustment be calculated on a base figure which would include the automatic increment, as reflected in the wages already being received. The management of El Teniente argued that the readjustment law specified that the wages in effect when the collective contract was signed should be taken as the base for increments. In their view the workers were entitled to a net increment equal to the difference between the percentage rise in prices for the April to September period and the percentage increase in wages already obtained. Otherwise the workers would be benefiting from what would amount to a double adjustment.

This difference remained latent during the electoral campaign and did not re-emerge until after the March 1973 elections. During the campaign all of the political parties supported the workers' demands—a fact which raised their expectations. Once the balloting was over, the workers pressed their claims. When no agreement could be reached, the matter was taken on appeal before the ministers of mines and labor. The hearing took the form of an arbitration commission between the enterprise and the workers. When the mine was under foreign control, the arbitration commission exercised considerable independence; but since the nationalization of the firm, the government had become more identified with the enterprise. It was also clear that the government would attempt to enforce respect for the national wage policy. The ministers, in fact, did find in favor of management. The workers in turn refused to recognize the decision and went on strike.

In order to restrain the conflict, the government and the UP parties appealed to the workers to go back to their posts. They promised to work for a solution in the meantime, and warned that the strike would play into the hands of the opposition. According to the government's wage guidelines, wage increases exceeding the cost of living would only be granted if production was improved. Several different compromise agreements were proposed on this basis, and negotiations were begun. The loss of foreign currency revenue was so great and the moment so critical that any effort to hold back the strike would be important in keeping the economy going and maintaining institutional stability.

The government's proposals were accepted by most of the wage workers' unions in the mines, in the main under the predominant influence of the UP. While the workers agreed to go back on the job, however, the salaried employees' unions, whose leadership was mostly Christian Democratic, refused. This was a new development, because blue-collar and white-collar workers had always acted together. This shift in behavior could only be attributed to political factors, both the direct influence of the political parties on the two groups and the difference between them in the degree of overall identification with the UP program. The strike also demonstrated to the UP that, even in the full exercise of all its political powers, it could not contain labor demands. Grass-roots social pressures had their own dynamic, and they had been encouraged historically by the Left parties. The Left was thus caught in a trap of its own making. It was also evident that labor policy could not be changed abruptly. It was the first time in two and a half years that the government had a struck a firm posture.

But events had moved too far for this position to be successful. Once workers began to return to the job, an unprecedented wave of violence and terrorism was unleashed. Roads leading to the mines were blockaded; attacks were staged on buses transporting workers; and street demonstrations with accompanying disorders were held in Rancagua, where the administrative offices of the mining company were located. In response the government declared the area an emergency zone and put it under military control in order to guarantee public order and the right to work.

Meanwhile direct negotiations continued. Several labor organizations tried to mediate, presenting a compromise proposal to the leadership of the El Teniente workers. This proposal won the acceptance of most of the union leaders, but a minority withdrew from the meeting. In doing so they flouted the accepted respect for majority decisions and decided to prolong the conflict at any cost.

The use of violence and the dilatory, intransigent attitude of the strikers convinced the government that the initial bread and butter issues were now no longer primary. The strike was now being supported and fomented as part of a nationwide plan to re-enact the general stoppage of October 1972. Events soon confirmed this hypothesis. The first phase of straightforward union action had given way to a second phase of violence and delaying tactics; now a third stage, one of nationwide political agitation, was inaugurated. All of the opposition forces converged on the strike, using it as a catalyst and rallying point. An overall plan of action was formulated which included the following elements:

1. Fomenting a general economic crisis: A nationwide stoppage in all of the copper mines was attempted, along with strike agitation in other enterprises. According to the plan, the stoppage would enlist the support of those *gremios* that had gone out in October; but this time workers and employees, rather than transit owners, would be the spearhead. The opposition had to rally more mass participation than it could count on in October, and the copper workers constituted a politically and economically critical sector.

2. Exacerbating the political conflict and the political-legal impasse: An avalanche of indictments was set off in Congress against ministers and other high government officials. The minister of mines and the minister of labor were impeached and removed from office, on the grounds that their "improper" interpretation of the law had impelled the strike. As has been

noted before, this kind of impeachment procedure was a legal abuse, since it was not provided for in the Chilean Constitution.

3. Creating a climate of chaos and violence: Political violence and street demonstrations soon spread to Santiago, where the striking workers received the support of business owners, *gremios* and white-collar labor groups under Christian Democratic political control. The groups which now posed as activists "in defense of the workers" had, of course, never before exhibited solidarity with labor.

The tense situation came to a climax on June 29, 1973 with a military uprising. The nascent coup was put down by the loyal armed forces. Once the failure of the putsch was known, the strike leaders hastily accepted the government's proposal and gave up on their walkout. The leaders of *Patria y Libertad* sought asylum the same day in the Ecuadorian Embassy in Santiago, revealing their complicity in the coup attempt. Among the documents found by the police in the possession of the head of this group was the rough draft of a declaration, released a few days earlier in the name of the strike leaders, threatening to prolong the stoppage indefinitely.

The El Teniente episode taught several lessons. In the first place, a sudden reverse in wage policy was very difficulty to support at this point in the process. In the second place, the blue-collar workers' conduct had undergone significant changes; for the first time they agreed to postpone their wage claims in order to support the government's policy. Wage workers had followed this line from the beginning of the strike, but not salaried employees. The conflict had gone to the heart of the labor alliance, destroying the unity between white- and blue-collar workers. In the third place, the opposition had resorted once again to a tactic that would finally lead to the government's downfall. Individual conflicts which could be isolated and regulated under normal conditions were being made to function as parts of an overall scheme, each one being used to accentuate the general crisis. Just as in the October events, the internal opposition received financial, logistic and technical support from U.S. intelligence agencies.

The Government's Recurrent Dilemma

The intensification of the social and political struggle placed the government between two opposed forces. On one side, Congress, the controller-general and the courts were frustrating any chance of altering the political-legal system in order to accommodate the new transformations in the economy. On the other side, workers' organizations and the UP parties radicalized their approach in anticipation of an eventual coup d'état, urging the seizure of those firms whose owners sympathized with the opposition's subversive intent. The confrontation of these forces left little leeway for legal action. The government was firmly trapped in what had become its central political dilemma: an ever more rigid political-legal situation in conjunction with a deployment of social forces increasingly too massive to control.

This situation was particularly evident in the social area. In April 1973 the government exercised its constitutional right to overrule the controller-general in an attempt to normalize the requisition and intervention of 45 firms. This decision was made a few weeks after the congressional elections; and the government, under pressure from the most intransigent sectors of the UP, took advantage of the favorable conjuncture in order to legalize what was already de facto state control of these enterprises.

The opposition counterattacked immediately by reopening the debate on the Executive's vetos of the constitutional amendment governing the social area. The Christian Democrats declared that the Executive's overruling of the Controller revealed its intention to bypass legislative authority, a move Congress was obliged to prevent. All of the Executive's vetos were overridden, and the opposition majority passed its own constitutional amendment on the social area wholesale, without any effort to compromise with the government. The amendment was a step backwards, since it required the government to return to private ownership most of the firms under state control.

As already observed above, the overriding of the vetos was accomplished with a simple majority vote, and not with the two-thirds required by the Constitution. The Executive responded by appealing to the Constitutional Tribunal, on the grounds that the issue was one of conflict between two branches of government. In order to create a constitutional impasse and power vacuum, the opposition insisted that the Constitutional Tribunal lacked jurisdiction to rule on this matter. In May 1973, the Tribunal declared itself incompetent.

The institutional log jam had ended in the paralysis of the state in a crucial policy area. At this point there existed no organ of government capable of resolving the conflict between the Executive and Legislative branches. President Allende, in a final effort, sought a global political solution: a call for a plebiscite. The UP, however, could not agree on this proposal, and the matter was postponed. As an intermediate step to avoid institutional paralysis, the president announced in June that he would promulgate only those parts of the amendment on the social area upon which both Congress and the Executive agreed. This time the controller objected, arguing that the Constitution permitted only promulgation of measures passed by Congress or the call to a plebiscite. With this decision the government's proposal collapsed, but the situation in the social area had picked up new momentum. The military uprising of June 29 gave rise to a new phase. The CUT had instructed its member unions to seize control of the factories in case of a coup attempt. On the 29th, after news had spread of a tank attack on the presidential palace, the workers occupied several thousand factories. Once the military threat had dissolved, more than a hundred of these firms remained under workers' control, not for reasons of economic strategy, but as a strictly defensive measure. The matter was not in the hands of the government; rather it was a political action on the part of the workers' organizations that were the government's major base of support. In July and August 1973, hoping to cool tensions and prove its determination to stick by the guidelines of its announced program, the government proceeded to hand back some of these enterprises. But such measures could change nothing at this point. Politically, only one way out remained—a plebiscite.

Conjunctural Crisis vs. Structural Transformation

Never before had Chile experienced a situation in which reality was perceived in such a totally distinct manner by the two principal social classes at loggerheads. The same facts were interpreted from completely different viewpoints. In the economic sphere, the bourgeoisie could only see a profound conjunctural crisis provoked by what it saw as the technical incompetence of the government and by a devious, destructive design aimed at the subsequent seizure of total power. The working class and the UP parties saw the unfolding of a revolutionary process that was transforming the economic base and power structure of the country. On this view the economic crisis was a reflection of the underlying power struggle, and it was being aggravated by the premeditated actions of the Right.

The structural interpretation of the crisis became compelling only with the intervention of theorical and ideological analysis; it was a product, therefore, of more advanced political consciousness. This interpretation was widespread by wage workers, salaried employees and peasants. In the period of most intense social struggle, the structural contradictions were quite evident; they appeared without mediations: the underlying structure was rendered transparent in everyday reality. In the last few months, however, sizable sectors of the middle class perceived social reality through daily events that suggested only a devastating conjunctural crisis. They were unable to appreciate the quite impressive alteration in the structure of the socioeconomic system that was going on behind the daily stream of events.

All of the conventional indicators did point to a deterioration. Inflation surged by 114 percent between January and July 1973; and in 12 months (July 1972 to July 1973) the price level climbed 323 percent.[3] Total money supply grew by 126.2 percent between January and July, while the rate of increase for the twelve-month period was 287.6 percent.[4] Domestic production declined over the same period in 1972; the contraction was felt in industry, agriculture, construction and copper.[5] The initial income redistribution suffered a setback, even though real wage and salary levels remained favorable compared to those of 1970.

Despite this setback, the government managed to defend its strategic achievements. Consumption, production and income distribution held steady at levels higher than those of 1970, even when the 1973 recession was counted in. We must emphasize the importance of this assertion, since the enemies of the UP government have portrayed its economic performance strictly in terms of the temporary, transitory maladjustments; they have concealed the positive results in production, income distribution and reforms in property ownership.

Table 9-1 shows the notable increase in total supply for the period 1971–73 and in particular the substantial increment (over 13 percent) in personal consumption. Production also exceeded 1970 levels, even though the figures here include the months of September through December 1973, a period of growing repression and near paralysis in the country. Considered only through August 1973, production levels were even higher. As for income distribution, real gains were made in favor of the poorest half of the population. The poorest 20 percent of the population increased its share of total income by 50 percent over what it received in 1970. The poorest 50 percent moved from a 14.1 percent share of income in 1970 to 17.2 percent in 1973 (see Table 9-2).

If production and consumption, as well as income distribution, advanced with respect to 1970, then the negative political repercussions of the economic process cannot be attributed to the absolute levels attained, but instead to the characteristic change in these levels: a rapid advance followed by an abrupt fall. From this point of view the central problem was discontinuity, the sudden alteration in the workings of the economy. A smoother course of change would presumably have had different political consequences.

The State's Paralysis as a Prelude to the Coup

The fierce social and political combat in the context of political-legal obstruction led to the paralysis of the state and a fatal immobility among the political leadership. Once the alliance between the CDP and the Right had been sealed, events unfolded quickly. It is clear upon analysis that a simultaneous three-

TABLE 9-1. Aggregate Supply and Demand, 1970 and 1973
(in billions of 1965 escudos)

	1970	1973	% increase 1970–1973
Aggregate Domestic Demand	23.23	25.44	9.5
Government consumption	2.59	3.15	21.6
Personal consumption	16.77	19.00	13.3
Fixed Capital investment	3.41	2.95	−13.6
Variation in stocks	0.46	0.34	−26.1
Supply	23.23	25.44	9.5
Gross Domestic Product	22.70	23.54	3.7
Imports of goods and services	3.65	4.21	15.3
Exports of goods and services	3.12	2.31	−26.0

Source: IMF, May 25, 1976, p. 32, Table 11.

TABLE 9-2. Personal Income Distribution in Greater Santiago, 1970–1973*
(Figures for June of each year)

Percentiles of Income-earners	1970	1971	1972	1973
Poorest 50%	14.1	15.8	17.8	17.2
Poorest 20%	(2.4)	(3.1)	(3.8)	(3.6)
Next 30% below the median	(11.7)	(12.7)	(14.0)	(13.6)
30% above the median	24.9	27.2	28.6	27.1
Next 15%	29.9	31.3	31.2	30.5
Highest 5%	31.1	25.7	22.4	25.2
Highest 1%	(11.3)	(8.1)	(6.6)	(8.7)
	100.0	100.0	100.0	100.0
Gini coefficient	0.563	0.520	0.481	0.501

*Includes inactive income recipients and unemployed persons.

pronged offensive was implemented: (1) political-legal obstructionism and paralysis of the state; (2) aggravation of the economic crisis; and (3) anarchy, public disorder and violence. Let us review the tactics employed on each front:

1. *Institutional obstructionism:* The sustained, deliberate effort to paralyze the political-legal system continued, with Congress characterizing government actions as illegal. Among the most evident maneuvers contributing to this end were the following: (A) An attempt to repudiate the March 1973 election results and the whole electoral system through a campaign intended to prove voting fraud and irregularities in registration. This slander was also designed to discredit recourse to a plebiscite as a way out of the political impasse. (B) Constitutional indictments against ministers and high government officials and a threat to impeach the whole Cabinet in order to create an impression of total governmental instability. (C) Provocation of conflicts between the Executive and the Judiciary. The courts stated in several rulings that the Executive was refusing to respect judicial authority, ignoring its decisions, and violating the law. (D) Setting the controller against government decisions. The controller overturned the intervention decrees and the partial promulgation of the constitutional amendment on the social property area. (E) An unceasing propaganda attack against new popular organizations, such as the Industrial Cordons and Community Commandos. (F) The joint action of the opposition majority in the Chamber of Deputies in a vote condemning the government for violating the constitutional and legal order. This vote provided the legal cover for the overthrow of the government.

2. *Aggravation of the economic crisis:* The opposition, aided by the U.S. government, persisted in its efforts to paralyze the economy. This campaign included the copper strike that culminated in the aborted coup attempt of June 29 and a second stoppage of truck owners, beginning in August and continuing through September 11.

3. *Violence and public disorder:* In the last phase of the government, especially after the June 29 coup attempt, a series of terrorist incidents was staged. Attacks were mounted on the homes of political leaders, against railway lines, fuel transport and electric lines. The most serious incident was the assassination of the president's naval adjutant in July 1973. These acts were accompanied by the diffusion of alarmist stories concerning the presumed existence of armed workers' groups. Thus the climate for subsequent repression was prepared beforehand.[6]

The Nixon administration was intimately involved in the design and implementation of the opposition campaign, although the emphasis was from the first placed on a military coup. The plan was to aggravate economic difficulties by supporting strikes and propaganda campaigns in the press, as well as through the international financial blockade. The major difference in emphasis between the efforts of the foreign and domestic opposition was that the U.S.

government exerted its influence primarily through the armed forces, where it was indeed effective.

Internal Differences within the UP

As the options for the government began to diminish, the fissures within the UP grew more serious. As restrictions on the government's ability to act became insurmountable, the radical option began to attract more support. The radicals urged a continued advance in the socializing process, organization and mobilization of the workers to confront the opposition, and preparation for a decisive confrontation. The extreme Left was clearly strengthened within the coalition by the growing attractiveness of the radical option.

With respect to the armed forces, the radicals made recommendations for action based on two contradictory assumptions: that the military was still constitutionalist so that the conflict would be restricted to civilian circles, and that a possible coup d'état could be neutralized by appealing to soldiers and junior officers to disobey their coup-inclined commanders and refuse to move against the government. This approach drew on the widely held notion that the Chilean armed forces were somehow "special," unlike the military in other Latin American countries. At the same time optimism was justified by a rudimentary class analysis of the armed forces: the social composition of the military would supposedly encourage a breakdown in discipline. The growing influence of this simplistic approach demonstrates a grave failure within the UP: the absence of a single-minded resolve to pursue one principal strategy, combating those deviations which never took into account the actual balance of forces.

Final Options

From July 1973 on, President Allende searched resolutely for a political solution to the crisis. He was constrained in his efforts by one fundamental restriction: the unity of the Left had to be preserved. Aware that the chances of a coup were increasing daily, Allende tried to enlist armed forces representation in the Cabinet once more. Once it became evident that this was impossible, the president was faced with three options which he put to discussion among the leaders of the UP: confrontation, negotiation or plebiscite.

The first option was discarded at the outset, since no one in his right mind could fail to see what the outcome would be. This option had been articulated to bring out the urgency of a political solution. Nevertheless, during all of July and August the UP could not arrive at an agreement on one of the two remaining options. Negotiation was rejected by the Socialist Party, and a plebiscite was considered premature. Faced with these internal disagreements, the president made two new initiatives during July and August: he called for a dialogue with the Christian Democrats and moved to draw the armed forces into the Cabinet.

At the end of July the government appealed to the CDP, taking note of an urgent call by the bishops of the Catholic Church to the political parties to find a solution that would lessen the imminent threat of a military coup. Two meetings were held, in which the positions below were taken.

The UP argued that the authority of the government had to be upheld; that it could not be subordinated to the will of the armed forces; that the UP program was not and would not become insurrectionist. The Christian Democrats responded that the government had to offer guarantees that it would honor these commitments, and that the only acceptable guarantee was the inclusion of the military in key government positions.

The Christian Democrats urged a general disarmament of paramilitary groups. The UP agreed to reject the option of arming the populace, asserting that grassroots support organizations had to be subordinated to the CUT and the government in order to avoid clashes with institutional authority. The UP wanted to clarify once and for all the different spheres of property ownership and to adopt an economic program to combat inflation and shortages. The Christian Democrats insisted on the return to private ownership of those enterprises intervened by the state in the wake of the June 29 events and the promulgation of the constitutional amendment which they had sponsored and Congress had passed.

The president proposed to the CDP chief, Senator Patricio Alwyn, a package of agreements and the setting up of mixed working groups to study possible solutions. This suggestion was promptly labeled by the Christian Democrats as a delaying tactic, and the conversations were cut off. Isolated, Allende put together a new Cabinet with military participation in order to meet the Christian Democrats' demands, but the latter shirked its commitment once more. The Christian Democrats, in an act of cunning with tragic consequences, had only feigned participation in the dialogue in order to save their reputation for responsibility in the light of approaching events.

It was already too late; the opposition was now determined to overthrow the government. The National Party and the rightwing *gremios* staged a new transport strike and began planning the last nationwide stoppage. Meanwhile the advocates of a coup had gained practically total predominance within the armed forces. At the end of August the three commanders-in-chief of the armed forces resigned from the Cabinet and were replaced by generals of lesser rank. At the beginning of September the UP decided to resort to a plebiscite. The president announced to the UP and to his Cabinet that he would speak to the nation on September 11 and make this decision public. Two days beforehand, he informed the commander-in-chief, General Pinochet, of his decision—a communication that doubtless served to hasten the coup.[7]

The Armed Forces and the Coup

When the military entered the Allende Cabinet for the first time, the process of politicization of the armed forces was accelerated to the detriment of the constitutionalist position. The withdrawal of the generals from the Cabinet in March 1973 and the incessant deterioration in the political and economic situation strengthened those sectors ideologically opposed to the government. In order to carry out its plans, the anti-government faction had to eliminate those high officers who upheld the constitutionalist line. This goal was fulfilled in August when General Prats, the commander-in-chief, was compelled to resign his commission, along with several other generals and admirals who shared his position. Immediately after these resignations at the top, constitutionalists in the lower ranks were forced out or pushed to the margins of command in order to cement control by the conspirators and prevent possible dissention.[8]

Several factors coincided to allow the consolidation of the coup-inclined officers' position. In the first place, there was their anti-leftist ideological background, expressed as "anti-communism" and devotion to an ideology of "national security." According to this ideology, the principal conflict is internal and the main enemy is the Left and the popular organizations that support it. In the second place, the location of the military in the social structure made it susceptible to rightwing thinking. The social origin of professional officers and their connections with the upper and middle classes meant that the conservative political parties exercised great influence in military circles. The officer corps took as its primary reference groups the middle-class urban sector and, when stationed in the provinces, the owners of large and medium agrarian estates.[9] Finally, the economic difficulties and the social and political turmoil natural to a transformative process violated notions of order and discipline, fundamental values for the military.

Among the factors that delayed military intervention, two were especially important. First, the coup proponents were initially inhibited by the magnitude of the repression that would have to be exerted in order to crush the popular movement and suppress the democratic culture of the country. Second, the continuing loyalty of an important sector of high officers to the prevailing institutional system made it difficult to secure the internal unity necessary for a successful coup d'état.

The role of the United States in shaping the "national security" ideology was essential. Traditionally, the thinking of the Latin American armed forces on security problems had a territorial bias and was focused on international phenomena. From the end of the World War, a new conception was formulated, one tending to widen the role of the armed forces in society beyond strictly tactical-military problems. Geopolitical concerns were linked more closely with concepts of internal development. This way of thinking favored the interests of the United States in the hemisphere, as it linked the security of each Latin American country directly with that of the United States. The armed forces would provide the guarantee for such security within each Latin American country. After the Cuban Revolution, the Pentagon encouraged Latin American armies to confront an elusive internal enemy; the emphasis switched to training in the struggle against subversion. The guerrilla movements in the region reinforced the tendency of the military to move from a territorial notion of security to an emphasis on internal security.[10]

This ideology was widespread among the Chilean officer class, many of whom had participated in training courses offered by the U.S. armed forces in the School of the Americas in the Panama Canal Zone. The number of graduates from this program rose rapidly after 1968 and reached its maximum in 1973. The content of these training courses covered such subjects as economic development and internal security, popular mobilization, disorder, subversion and guerrilla warfare.

Surprisingly, the Chilean Left did not take this reality into account. The Left remained perhaps the most captivated by the myth of the "professionalism" of the Chilean armed forces. In the last analysis, the viability of the process sponsored by the UP depended on the attitude of the armed forces. But there was almost no support in military circles for a socialist program; instead, openly anti-socialist tendencies were quite pronounced. The only factor constraining sentiment in favor of a coup was lingering loyalty to the established political-legal system. Once this premise was accepted, as it was in the UP program, it was essential to understand the factors that effected the balance of power between constitutionalists and anti-socialists in the military. The UP, however, lacked both a realistic analysis and a coherent policy approach toward the armed forces.

The Unidad Popular government was ended by bloody military intervention. The causes of this collapse lie ultimately in the internal conflict which tore apart Chilean society. As noted from the start, it was the political defeat of the UP that led the way to military overthrow.

Notes

1. The price of copper rose from an average of 48.6 cents a pound in 1972 to 80.8 cents in 1973. International Monetary Fund (May 1976), p. 84. The 1973–74 farm year (crops sown in 1973) showed a major comeback: the index of agricultural production went from 91.1 to 100 between the farm years 1972 to 1973 and 1973 to 1974. International Monetary Fund (May 1976), p. 60.
2. El Teniente is the second largest copper mine, after Chuquicamata, in Chile. Eleven thousand white- and blue-collar employees worked in it; and the yield in 1972 (190,000 tons) constituted 32 percent of the production of the larger mines. The firm was nationalized in 1971.
3. Consumer price index, Instituto Nacional de Estadísticas. These figures do not take the black market into account, a sector that was attracting a growing number of consumers.
4. Data from Banco Central de Chile.
5. In the January–July 1973 period, industrial production declined 9.4 percent and the supply of intermediate goods 9 percent with respect to the same period in 1972. Data from the Sociedad de Fomento Fabril.
6. With respect to the CIA's activities it has been pointed out that: "The most extensive covert action in Chile was propaganda. By far the largest was the money provided to *El Mercurio* . . . The 40 Committee authorized $700,000 for *El*

Mercurio on September 9, 1971 and added another $965,000 to that authorization on April 11, 1972 . . . According to CIA documents, these efforts played a significant role setting the stage for the military coup." United States Senate, *Covert Action in Chile, 1963-1973*, Staff Report of the Select Committee to Study Governmental Operations with respect to Intelligence Activities (Washington, D.C.: U.S. Government Printing Office, 1975), p. 8. In addition to the U.S. Senate hearings, see A. Uribe, *El libro negro de la intervención norteamericana en Chile* (Mexico: Siglo XXI, 1974); and P. Vuskovic, *Acusación al imperialismo* (Mexico: Siglo XXI, 1975).

7. See J. Garcés, *Allende y la experiencia chilena* (Barcelona: Ediciones Ariel, 1976), pp. 351–353, for a detailed account of the events of September 9–11.

8. The importance of eliminating the constitutionalists was such that, even after the junta had established itself, General Prats was assassinated together with his wife in 1974 while living in exile in Buenos Aires.

9. See J. Rojas and A. Viera Gallo, "La doctrina de la seguridad nacional y la militarización de la política en América Latina," *Revista Chile America*, Nos. 28–30 (April 1977).

10. "But there was another component in U.S. policy toward Latin America. Counterinsurgency techniques were developed to combat urban or rural guerrilla insurgencies often encouraged or supported by Castro's regime. Development could not cure overnight the social ills which were seen as the breeding ground of communism." United States Senate, *Covert Action in Chile*, p. 4. In the case of Chile it is important to point out the almost simultaneous implementation of two tactics: (a) the Alliance for Progress, which attempted to eliminate the causes of discontent through a program of social and economic development; and (b) the counterinsurgency programs designed to suppress by force any radical political changes.

CHAPTER 10

Transition and Economic Disequilibrium

Those who promote structural changes in order to attain democratic and social-ist ideals judge the results of their actions by the consequences anticipated in the middle and long run. They tend, however, to underestimate a crucial aspect of the process: the viability of such changes depends on short-run effects and on the political capacity to control them. Our conclusion is that the Chilean Left concerned itself principally with the structural aspects of the situation and did not pay sufficient attention to the conjunctural phenomena of a transitional stage.

One critical inadequacy in the analytical framework employed by the UP parties consisted in the failure to relate structural transformations and financial problems. Put more generally, the role of the market in a transitional phase was not understood. This failure is not unique to the Chilean experience: it has been repeated in other recent attempts at structural change, and it is a weakness of programs advanced by many Left or Center-Left political coalitions.[1] This issue is, therefore, of central theoretical and practical interest for all attempts to transform relatively complex economies within a democratic framework. The case of revolutionary processes where the question of power has been resolved in the first stages is distinct in this respect.

What was peculiar in the Chilean case was the extent of the disequilibria. An analysis of events in Chile can provide specific lessons on the nature of economic policy in a period of abrupt change. Economic policy in Chile was designed to prepare the way for structural transformations by creating favor-able political conditions. The outcome demonstrates the strategic incompatibil-ity between an abruptly and intensively expansionist policy and a process of deeper changes when both are attempted in a short period. This inconsistency provoked a deterioration in the political situation, weakening the underlying social alliance and strengthening the opposition.

It is not enough, in hindsight, to make general statements. If we are to evaluate the economic policy suitable to a transitional strategy, it is necessary to analyze how much surplus was available to redistribute, how it could be extracted, and what effects on economic functioning would be generated by changes in property ownership and the implementation of popular control.

The Planned Strategy and the Actual Trajectory

As was noted in previous chapters, other options existed which could have altered the direction of events, expanding the margin of viability. The trajectory actually followed was influenced by the government's economic strategy, but not determined by it. There was not a direct, causal relationship between the decisions adopted by the UP government and the actual outcome. Events depended on a number of factors, including the strategy and tactics of the government, the reactions of the opposition, and the autonomous dynamic of the social forces in action. Thus an approach capable of explaining the real trajectory would have to embrace these three elements simultaneously. Nevertheless, granting the limitations involved, the following analysis will be centered principally on the actions of the government.

Examining the causal factors stemming from the government's initiatives does not mean ignoring the crucial importance of the opposition in the collapse of the Chilean experiment with socialism. Rather this focus is justified because we must identify the theoretical failures of the UP leadership and their effect on subsequent decisions, especially as these failures derived from an inadequate understanding of the transition period.[2] In order to evaluate the policies which were actually implemented, we must keep in mind the economic thinking that underpinned the government's efforts to manage the transition from the initial situation to the target situation. It was thought that the economic model prevailing in 1970 would be transformed through a rapid change in the distribution of income, which would in turn cause the pattern of production and investment to shift and adapt itself to satisfying the basic needs of the general population. For its part the state would directly or indirectly assure the production of capital and intermediate goods.

The dynamic would be set in motion by a modification in the composition of demand. In its first phase, this change would lead to the full employment of installed capacity, and would immediately thereafter generate a new pattern of investment and supply. Moreover, the production of essential goods would be less capital-intensive, absorbing more manpower. This fact would allow for accelerated growth without an increase in the historical rate of savings. At the same time it would mean a more intensive use of local resources and a more balanced geographical distribution of economic activity.[3]

In order to put this model into effect, two steps would have to be taken at the same time: a change in the ownership of the basic means of production and a rapid redistribution of income. These two measures constituted the very pith and marrow of the economic strategy guiding the government's program. As described here, the UP strategy is vulnerable to a number of direct criticisms. In the first place this approach was highly qualitative; the probable effect of the policy actions was not subject to measurement. In contrast, quantitative studies carried out by university researchers in 1970 indicated that the effect of a change in income distribution on growth and employment would be slight and in any event less than what was promised by the UP program.[4] In the second place, the program did not specify the intensity of the speed of the redistributive process; nor did it discuss the extent to which such a sudden redistribution was compatible with actual political restrictions. In the third place, the changes in property ownership were formulated simply as objectives, without specifying the sequence or intensity which such changes should follow. This is a serious failure in any strategy. Finally, the simultaneous impact of redistribution and property changes had not been taken into account. The economic strategy of the UP, in summary, was global, qualitative, and—in many respects—imprecise.

The Redistribution and the Economy's Response

The goals of the redistribution were set out in 1970 by the National Planning Office (Odeplán). These goals, to be sure, were surpassed quickly; even if this had not occurred, fulfilling them would have been very difficult. The assumptions on which these calculations were based were very weak, as we shall see below. For 1976, the end year of Salvador Allende's constitutional period, Odeplán foresaw a large shift in income in favor of wage-earners and independently employed workers. They would increase their share of total income from 51.0 to 60.7 percent at the expense of property owners, businessmen and foreign interests, whose income would diminish because of state expropriation and nationalization of firms and tax reform. The "margin of redistribution" or "surplus available for redistribution" would be made up from the 10.3 percent of income extracted from proprietors and entrepreneurs (whose share would decline from 18.6 to 8.3 percent) and from 1.8 percent of total income to be diverted from foreign interests. Together these sources would provide a 12.1 percent share of total income available for redistribution. Of this proportion 9.7 percent would go to increase the incomes of wage earners (whose share would go from 51.0 to 60.7 percent), and 2.3 would go to boost the savings and investment funds of public and private enterprises (this amount would rise from 11 to 13.3 percent).

What was to occur with savings in the initial schema of the Planning Office? Total savings would grow from 16.6 to 18.2 percent but it would be drawn from different sources in 1976. On the one hand, entrepreneurs and owners would reduce their level of savings, a reduction which would be compensated by an increase in workers' rates of savings. In effect families would move from a negative savings rate (−0.1 percent) to a positive one (1.0 percent). The other major source of savings and investment would be the social property area. But were these Odeplán figures in accord with the policy instruments actually available? Did the government have sufficient power to effect such a massive transfer? Subsequent events demonstrated that these estimates were based on assumptions that did not hold true. Let us review each of these assumptions separately.

In order to attain the proposed objectives, wage-earning families would have to increase their average savings rate substantially, in order to offset the drop in savings by owners.[5] But was this first assumption justifiable? It seems plainly inconsistent to attempt, over a short period, to increase savings in the midst of an accelerated redistributive process with all of the uncertainty that would grip the private sector. The propensity to consume of the lower income strata was very high, and it was to be expected that they would immediately satisfy their most pressing needs for food, clothing and other necessities.

The assumption concerning savings by high-income groups was also unfounded. On the contrary, it was more likely that their consumption would not immediately be cut back. A reduction in their incomes, therefore, would first effect their savings and only later, over the longer run, their consumption habits. Moreover, the impact of the change in ownership of the means of production would be felt mostly among a limited number of large owners, given the high property concentration. The remainder of the entrepreneurial sector would at first maintain their income sources, which would only begin to dry up later, as state control stabilized and was extended. The initial tendency of the lower-income strata was to devote their new funds to consumption, while at the same time the high-income sectors maintained their spending levels. The immediate consequence was a rise in aggregate consumption and a drop in domestic savings.

The third assumption was that the social area enterprises would boost their savings rates. The validity of this assumption over the middle run was not so questionable, but in the short run this objective was incompatible with the other redistributive measures imposed on the state enterprises: wage increases, expansion of employment and price controls. The end result was a surge in operating deficits. As for private firms, the political conflict occasioned by the change in property ownership led the smaller owners to reduce their level of investment considerably. This reaction was inevitable, even though its intensity could have been moderated. The tendency for short-run investment to fall was a characteristic, but under-appreciated, feature of the transition period in Chile.

The failure of these assumptions explains the expansion in overall consumption and the reduction in the rate of savings. The drop in the level of investment was not, in our judgment, determinant in the evolution of political events. The very brevity of the UP experience argues against the relevance of a higher investment level, the fruits of which would only have come to maturity late in 1973, after the coup. The crucial problem in Chile during the UP experience was the rapid and intensive expansion of demand for consumer goods.

The increase in demand by far exceeded the government's goals. The workers' share of total income in 1971 was 61.7 percent, and 62.9 percent in

1972.[6] That is, the goal set by Odeplán for 1976 had already been surpassed by 1971. Such a rapid change bore with it the germ of subsequent disequilibria; this was because, in addition to the shift effected in percentage shares of total income, the manner in which this change is attained is also crucial. If the increase in the incomes of the poorest strata is offset by a contraction in the wealthiest groups, then redistribution can be effected with only a moderate increase in nominal demand. If, on the other hand, resources are not extracted from the high-income groups and the incomes of the poorer strata are simply boosted generously, then total demand will grow disproportionately. In this case the economy will have to face the consequences of an abrupt shift in the level and composition of demand for consumer goods.

Once wages and public spending (of a redistributive character) had been increased so excessively, only two options remained: (1) this expansion could be financed by extracting large amounts from middle- and upper-income sectors—a course of action which implied a high level of political domination over the second group and would very likely endanger the social alliance being sought with the first; or (2) a set of market disequilibria (inflation, shortages, etc.) would be provoked, the control of which would also require the consolidation of great power in the hands of the state and the workers.

The second possibility was the one that was finally realized in Chile, and the disequilibria were so intense that they could not be contained with the tools available to the government and its working-class constituency. In sum the crux of the redistributive problem rested in the limited amount of "redistributable surplus" given the existing conditions of power and the type of social alliance upon which the government was based.

Insufficiencies in the Mechanisms of Redistribution

Another lesson of the Chilean experience is that the mechanisms employed to redistribute income rapidly and irreversibly were ineffective. The almost exclusive use of wage policy exhibited two weaknesses: wage increases could not be targeted specifically enough so as to relieve the poorest people, and wage policy by itself was incapable of causing changes in the structure of demand to be translated through market mechanisms into changes in the structure of supply and investment. Thus two conclusions can be inferred: In the first place it is necessary to use more precise instruments to reach the poorest groups, policies that take into account their mode of insertion into the productive structure. In the second place, direct state action on the productive structure is required in order to modify the level and composition of supply.

Concerning the problem of policy precision, previous experiences in Chile had demonstrated that attempts to improve the level of living of unfavored groups based on the use of wage policy produced only temporary results, the situation returning to its initial state shortly afterwards. The typical cycle produced by these policy efforts was as follows: wage increases were effected at the cost of reducing the profits of private firms and led to an increase in public spending. In the first phase, two factors compensated for the rise in wages: the existence of unutilized productive capacity and an increase in tax revenues. The first factor allowed firms to maintain aggregate profits, even when profit per unit declined. The second allowed for the financing of part of the wage increases in the public sector and of new expenditures on services in education and health. One requirement for the initial success of these measures was the political capacity to impose controls on prices. Once this authority had been exhausted, a new and retrogressive phase of income redistribution began.

The first effects of this type of wage policy were always positive. But once installed industrial capacity had been put to work and wage demands began to intensify, the country would find itself in a situation of slow growth with accelerating inflation, regression in income redistribution, and increasing social tensions.

The cyclical phenomenon described here recurred in the 1970–72 period, but in a much sharper form. In 1971 the UP granted proportionately larger wage adjustments to the lowest income groups. Nevertheless, the close correlation between the organizational capacity of groups of workers and the size of the adjustment obtained ultimately frustrated the purpose of the policy: workers in strong unions (located in modern oligopolistic firms and in the large public institutions) ended up with wage increases that were equal to or greater than the adjustments received by poorer, less well-organized workers.

The figures in Table 10-1 confirm what has been asserted above. They show that 80 percent of employed workers received a similar increase in income; that is, the needier workers did not benefit from a relatively larger adjustment. While the poorest 20 percent obtained a 58.4 percent increase, wage earners in the 30 percentile group above the median won a 59.6 percent adjustment.

On the other hand, for 95 percent of those surveyed, the wage adjustment was higher than the 22 percent originally proposed by the government. Government policy, in other words, was simply overwhelmed, its guidelines swept away. In the following period (1972–73), the wage-price spiral was already in motion, and hardest hit by the inflationary tide were the poorest strata, who lost most of their initial gains because of their lower degree of organization.

In order to explain the inadequacy of wage policy as a redistributive mechanism it is necessary to analyze the occupational structure. It can then be understood why these policy initiatives barely affected the truly dispossessed. The poorest stratum of the population is composed essentially of wage workers and, to a lesser extent, of the self-employed. Almost half of this group belongs to the agricultural sector. The next largest group within the poorest stratum consists of workers in the service sector; and, in the third place, come low-paid industrial workers. The majority of this needy half of the work force (in 1967, 45.7 percent of the country's workers received less than one *sueldo vital*, the official minimum wage) were employed in the agricultural sector. Workers in this sector were effectively beyond the reach of wage policy: self-employed workers were by definition unaffected by it; while many wage-earners in agriculture were part-time workers or had unstable jobs and hence were not subject to the norms applied in the case of urban-industrial workers.

Self-employed service workers (including street peddlers, plumbers, artisans and domestic servants) were the second largest group among the poorest half of the population. These are workers the nature of whose jobs leads to atomization, inhibiting the emergence of organizations which could unite them to defend their interests. Most are urban dwellers, living in the "marginal areas," or squatter settlements, of the large cities. Since they lack employers, wage policy does not affect them directly, but only indirectly, through a general reactivation of the economy. In periods marked by regression in income distribution and low rates of growth, they suffer the most.

The third component of the poorest group consisted of industrial workers in small firms or artisan shops. These enterprises belong to the "traditional sector" of industry; they are under-capitalized and operate at low levels of productivity. Even though these workers are generally more poorly organized than those in larger firms, wage policy benefits them more than it does agricultural and service workers; but serious structural limitations inhibit its effectiveness. The use of antiquated technologies and the low productivity of this sector make it impossible to approach the wage levels enjoyed by workers in modern, oligopolistic firms. Once wages in these smaller firms exceed a certain point, they can no longer compete in the market. The UP government took note of these deficiencies and implemented new measures to benefit the needy who subsisted at the margins of the market. These policy initiatives, however, went into effect only at the end of 1972 and into 1973, when market distortions were already excessive and the political opposition had become very active.

A strategy that attempts to effect irreversible changes in the distribution of income cannot attach excessive importance to mere increases in wages; rather it must press into use other instrumentalities, beyond the market. In the case of

TABLE 10-1. Income Variation by Percentile Group, 1970–71
(Greater Santiago)

Percentile Group	Average in Income Variation 1970–71 (percent change)
Poorest 20%	58.4
Next 30%	56.1
30% superior to the median	59.6
Next 15%	48.9
Next 4 %	25.5
Richest 1%	2.1
Total: 100%	Average: 43.4

the rural poor, it must bring about changes in land ownership, help to create cooperatives among small landholders, increase the productivity of labor and promote agro-industrial activity. For the urban marginal stratum, the state must act to strengthen local community action, encouraging forms of collective consumption. In general direct actions should be aimed at extending education and health services, and at implementing such measures as free nutritional programs for children, dispensing breakfasts, and essential school clothing and supplies. Finally, the state must consider establishing a system for the rationed distribution of certain basic foodstuffs. These actions, however, require a relatively extended period to be organized, and they presuppose a readjustment in the supply of goods. To attempt a far-reaching redistribution by means of short-run changes in wage levels is a simplistic approach whose effects are reversible and which creates severe political and economic problems.

Two lessons emerge for any strategy intended to raise the degree of equality: first the necessity to assign part of the "redistributable surplus" to selective policy areas, working outside the marketplace; second the need to moderate the expansion of wages and salaries while new redistributive mechanisms are becoming consolidated, supported by a change in the composition of supply.

The Composition of Supply and the Redistribution of Income

The appropriate magnitude of a redistribution is determined by the existing capacity to modify the level and composition of internal supply. When this linkage is not recognized, the phenomena we have observed in the Chilean case soon emerge.

Wage increases (and, in general, all redistributive mechanisms that act on demand) are easy to apply and yield immediate results; while changes in the productive structure require a period of several years to manifest themselves. At the same time, the political and social pressures to which governments are most sensitive are exerted in favor of quick-response policy instruments—wages and public spending. Adjustments in production and investment have a more delayed and less spectacular effect; they are easily relegated to second place.

The conventional measures operate only on demand, and they are effective when only slight modifications, which do not alter the pattern of consumption, are at stake. A transformative strategy, on the other hand, must contain elements that act simultaneously and jointly on two fronts: the composition of demand and the structure of production.

In the 1971–72 period, the alterations in demand reached a level incompatible with the capacity of the productive apparatus to respond. The harnessing of unutilized productive potential partially offset this imbalance, as did an increase in imports. However, existing unutilized capacity did not have a sectoral composition corresponding to the new composition of demand; so that the latter had to adapt itself to the former.

Even more problematic, some of the government's investment programs were incompatible with the kind of income distribution that was being attempted. The most striking example of this kind of inconsistency occurred in the case of the automobile industry. The production guidelines fixed initially by the government would have required a concentration of income comparable to that existing in 1969 in order to create the appropriate demand. Likewise the sharp rise in consumption of foodstuffs could not be satisfied without a programmed distribution unless unlimited imported resources could be counted on.

The adaptation of supply to the new pattern of demand was the object of renewed efforts in 1972. Standardization of the production of mass consumer goods was undertaken, and an attempt was made to concentrate production of collective consumer goods. Production contracts were signed with the private sector to manufacture current consumption items and the supply of state services was extended. But the structure of supply and the capacity to design and carry out new investment projects could not keep up with the abruptly changing pattern of demand.

The lack of correspondence between the changes in consumption and production constituted a central problem in the transition and produced a serious impact on economic functioning. Paradoxically, while the UP's objectives arose from a structural analysis with long-run projections, the government's decisions had a markedly short-run orientation. What was missing was a middle-range view capable of linking the two opposed perspectives.

The Structural Transformations and the Functioning of the Economy

While the reactivation and redistribution schemes gave rise to an increase in demand, the structural transformations had an impact on supply. The former were the principal cause of the economic problems, but it is essential as well to point out the fundamental weaknesses in the program of structural changes.

The study of the short-run consequences of structural reforms presents serious difficulties. Conventional economic theory is applicable in situations of political and institutional stability, when the behavior of the different social groups and the efficacy of the various policy instruments can be assumed to be constant. In transition periods, however, the outcomes depend on an almost unlimited number of factors that are varying simultaneously, and it is more difficult to establish causal relationships. In the Chilean case, transformations occurred simultaneously on all fronts, producing interacting effects. Hence the outcomes cannot be explained by isolating individual variables. Deepening the analysis, we can distinguish three aspects: (1) the speed of the transformations on each front (agrarian reform, copper, the socialized sector in industry, banks, workers' participation); (2) the sequence of these transformations (whether occurring jointly or consecutively); and (3) the quality of management by the state in its new functions.

The UP strategy did not clearly specify either the speed or the sequence of the changes it proposed. It established only a set of objectives which, according to its estimates, ought to be fulfilled by 1976. There was no general debate concerning how to coordinate the different transformations as the balance of power changed from moment to moment. This failure was clearly a basic inadequacy; it was fundamentally important and entirely possible to lay down a coherent initial strategy.

Our first conclusion here is that it was not the speed of the changes, but their sequence, that had the greatest effect on the functioning of the economy. The quality of management by the state, although of increasing importance, was in our view a secondary factor. Later we conclude that no single transformation taken by itself had a determining effect. Instead, it was the simultaneous imposition of all the changes that was the main cause of the disequilibrating effects. In order to support these conclusions, each area of change will be discussed separately.

Agrarian Reform and Agricultural Production

What relationship existed between the rapidity of the agrarian reform and the level of production? From available evidence we can conclude that, despite the abruptness of the expropriation process, production was not seriously affected until 1973.

The actual pace of the reform exceeded government plans. The elimination of the latifundios was scheduled to be attained after six years of UP government; instead it was an accomplished fact within two years.[7] In order to appreciate the velocity of change in the rate of change, it is instructive to contrast the 1971–72 period with the Frei administration (1965–70). During the Frei period, an average of 230 estates a year were expropriated; in the first two years of the Allende regime, the annual average was 2200.[8] During the Frei period, the pace of expropriation was moderate, and production held steady during the first three years of his government. In 1969 there was a sharp drop, but this was largely due to a drought. It is somewhat difficult, therefore, to distinguish the quantitative effect of these two variables (speed of the reform and weather conditions) on production. It is clear, however, that, because of the relatively slower rate of expropriation, the state apparatus could devote itself to organizing land already subject to reform; it did not have to exhaust itself in attending to the actual change in ownership, as was the case in the first few years of the Allende government.

In 1971 and 1972 the number of expropriations increased spectacularly. Production, meanwhile, increased in 1971, held steady in 1972, and declined significantly in 1973. Thus there was a clear relationship between the rapidity of the expropriations and the level of production. Because harvests depend on sowing the year before, the effects of the changes in property ownership are only manifested after a year's delay.

Even granted this relationship between the speed of the reform and the level of agricultural production, it is still not possible to establish its importance because many factors beyond the government's control also impinged on the situation. During the winter sowing period (June to July) of 1972 unfavorable climatic conditions prevailed. The spring planting season (September to October) of the same year was marked by the October stoppage which cut off the supply of inputs. Both developments hurt production in 1973. Winter planting in 1973 increased, however, which explains the subsequent jump in production in 1974.[9]

But was the agrarian reform as executed by the Allende government a decisive factor in causing the maladjustments in the market for foodstuffs? While we have certainly established that the reform affected the level of production, it does not seem to have been determinant in producing the market imbalances. These are primarily attributable to the expansion in demand and only secondarily to the decline in supply occasioned by the reform.

In sum, when exogenous factors like the weather and stoppages are excluded, the agrarian reform was not the determining cause of shortages of foodstuffs in the market, despite the headlong pace of expropriations in the 1971–72 period. This is not to suggest that the reform had no short-run consequences; but the explanatory importance of these temporary disruptions has to be seen in perspective. There is no doubt that the management of the reformed area was seriously set back by the speed of expropriation. But the administrative capacity that existed in 1970 was a favorable element that maintained a certain coherence in the process. This capacity derived from the 1965–70 period when the Chilean government had created ad hoc agencies equipped with administrative resources and technicians. This fund of bureaucratic experience cushioned somewhat the impact of the sharp acceleration in the reform. Had the whole process begun in 1970 without being able to count on this available administrative capacity, the results would have been much less favorable.

In order to complete the analysis of the speed of the agrarian reform it is necessary to observe its political repercussions. Those favoring an even more rapid pace of expropriation argued that the landowners might be able to reorganize and put together a tougher political opposition if they were given a respite. Besides, they argued, a gradualist approach would not favor production: once the landlords saw that expropriation was inevitable, they would reduce production and investments.

This argument seems incorrect, since a generalized fear among landowners could have been avoided if those estates subject to expropriation had been plainly identified in advance. Furthermore, even though imminent expropriation was on the horizon, private landowners would not stop tyring to maximize their short-run incomes through increased production. This had occurred in fact under the former government. As for new investments, they would doubtless have fallen off in any event. Finally, it was essential to evaluate the state's capacity to expropriate and administer simultaneously. If this capacity was in fact limited, it would be preferable to regulate the speed of the reform and keep some resources in reserve for administration.

The argument that resistance would grow if the pace of reform was slowed

TABLE 10-2. Copper Production, Projected and Actual, 1970-73
(in thousands of tons)

	1970	1971		1972		1973	
		projected	real	projected	real	projected	real
Larger mines	541	787	571	872	593	883	615
Chuquicamata	263	300	250	354	234	354	265
El Salvador	93	90	85	90	83	90	84
El Teniente	177	260	147	274	191	274	171
Exótica	2	77	35	90	31	102	39
Andina	6	60	54	63	54	63	56
Smaller mines	151	165	137	200	124	202	120
Total	692	952	708	1.071	717	1.085	735

Source: Projected figures obtaines from CODELCO, "Proyección de Cobre y Molibdeno, años 1971, 72 y 73." Santiago, December 1970. Values for actual production obtained from CODELCO "Indicadores del Cobre." several issues. Figures for the smaller mines from ENAMI.

has more validity. Nevertheless, it must be remembered that the landlords were a politically weakened sector and that the agrarian reform was widely accepted as legitimate. Given these conditions it was not necessary to attain the goals in only two years. In any event the advantage of a less frenzied pace can only be judged in the light of the overall conflict. Let us examine, then, the other fronts.

The Nationalization of Copper

In what way did the nationalization of copper influence the larger economic outcome and hence the viability of the whole process? The answer to this query will be considered in the light of three variables: the speed of the transformation, its place in the sequence of other changes, and the quality of management in the nationalized mines.

With respect to production levels, it is essential to point out that these increased in the 1970–73 period (see Table 10-2). Nationalization did not induce a drop in total production. As a consequence it may be affirmed that had the nationalization of copper been an isolated, unique transformation, it would not have disturbed the short-run functioning of the economy.

But while production did indeed increase, it was still below the goals that had been scheduled as necessary to offset the effects of the other transformations. In 1970 it was estimated that copper production could reach 900,000 tons within the first few years of the government. This projection was based on two assumptions: that the expansion goals announced by the Frei government would be fulfilled, and that nationalization would not have a significant impact on production in the short run.

These assumptions, however, were not vindicated. This was due to three major causes: (1) failures in the investment plan carried out by the foreign firms during the 1966–70 period; (2) obstacles interposed by the multinational corporations to the normal supply of spare parts and machinery; and (3) deficiencies in the administration of the enterprises.

The exact weight of each of these causes is difficult to assess. On the basis of reports submitted by foreign evaluation missions, and considering the serious lack of spare parts and machinery, we can conclude that the first two causes were determinant during 1971 and part of 1972. However, the weaknesses in the management of the nationalized enterprises and labor indiscipline became more and more important in the course of 1972 and in 1973.

Here we must specify those factors over which the Allende government could have exercised a certain control; only then can we see if the copper situation might have been handled so as to provide more room for maneuver in alleviating the overall economic situation. First we will consider the manner in which nationalization was effected: its timeliness, speed, the manner in which it was justified internationally, and its sequential order with respect to other transformations.

Nationalization was effected with great speed. From an economic point of view, this was advantageous. The foreign firms were anticipating expropriation. The Anaconda Copper Company undertook at Chuquicamata an exploitation strategy designed to maximize the immediate extraction of high-grade ores, putting off the development of the mine and the disposal of slag. This strategy damaged later production possibilities seriously. Had nationalization been delayed, the consequences would have been even more severe. On the other hand, the state in Chile already commanded the infrastructure necessary to control production and sales and could count on the loyalty of most of the technicians in the mines. The risk of an interruption in administrative continuity was not great. Politically, internal conditions were also favorable for a quick decision. Thus, with respect to the timeliness and speed of the nationalization, the government proceeded correctly, minimizing the possible negative consequences.

The main question concerns the amount of compensation paid. The decision to refuse indemnity to the two largest U.S. firms—Kennecott and Anaconda—aggravated the interference in the provision of spare parts and in the placement of copper in the European market. Moreover, it hardened the attitudes of the international agencies and of the U.S. government, providing them with a handy excuse to justify the financial blockade.

If the cutting off of spare parts, in addition to the other forms of financial, technical and commercial blockade, did indeed depend on the amount of compensation paid, then the government's decision to refuse any indemnity is certainly open to question. Copper exports and the availability of hard currency were vital elements for the viability of the UP program, a fact which was amply demonstrated in 1972 and 1973. The role which copper had to play in the transition stage was to increase as much as possible the availability of hard currency in order to reduce the country's external vulnerability. But how important was the decision to discount excess profits in provoking the stubborn opposition of the United States? Was this opposition in fact inherent to any socialist transition process undertaken in Chile?

To attribute the subsequent reaction on the U.S. corporations and the financial agencies to the compensation question is no doubt inconsistent with the rest of the facts already analyzed on U.S. intervention. This interference was already in evidence prior to the presidential elections, continued after the elections, and persisted following Allende's inauguration—and all of these events preceded the decision on the amount of compensation. Nevertheless, we would argue that a different indemnification policy would have provided more room for negotiation, hence diminishing the harmful effects both of the embargo on machinery and spare parts and of the financial blockade. And in such tight situations any additional leeway is crucial.

Let us consider now the quality of management in the nationalized enterprises. State intervention was not exercised with the efficiency that was actually possible. Relations with the workers suffered from the fallout of the political struggle that was shaking the country. Thus, in the first few months following nationalization, several conflicts with technicians and supervisors occurred which led to some of them quitting their positions. The constant stimulus to union struggles and the policy of rapid changes in the relationship between the new executives and the workers caused a rupture in the lines of authority and a deterioration in the fulfillment of work norms.

The lower output of labor in the large copper mines during the UP period is apparent when we observe the increases in production attained during the month following the coup d'état. In October 1973, Chuquicamata produced 24,500 tons, while the monthly average during 1972 was 19,500 tons. In El Teniente production increased to 20,100 tons in October 1973 and 21,300 in November, while the monthly average in 1972 was only 15,800 tons.

These same figures, however, lead us to another conclusion: that the productive capacity in the mines remained intact. The widespread criticism that the economy was "destroyed" under the UP was therefore false. If such had been the case, it would have been impossible to raise production within a month's time. The reduction in activity was a temporary phenomenon, stemming inevitably from changes in management and from the intensity of the political and social conflict that marked the last year of the Allende government.

The nationalization of copper suffered from the same inadequacies as the agrarian reform: overemphasis on the changes in ownership and insufficient regard for subsequent management. The lesson of the Chilean experience is that a clear distinction ought to have been established between the change in ownership and an alteration in the internal authority relationships of the nationalized enterprises. In the case of copper, it was essential to maintain efficient management in order to provide the cash funds that the redistributive process would siphon off, funds which would become scarce once the credit lines from the United States were cut. To expropriate without immediately ensuring the efficient management of the expropriated enterprises is to open the gates to failure.[10]

The speed of the nationalization therefore did not have an unfavorable effect in the short run. The loss of efficiency in the management of the mines would not have been crucial, either, if the Chilean economy had not been undergoing other transformations at the same time. It was the simultaneous superimposition of several fundamental changes that brought about the failures in internal supply. A strategy that admitted a rapid increase in the demand for foodstuffs at the same time as an accelerated agrarian reform was already open to criticism. But if we grant that this conflict in goals was inevitable, then it was surely inadmissible to allow copper production to fall off. The lack of a temporal sequence synchronizing the different transformative measures was a major inconsistency in the UP strategy for change.

The Socialized Industrial Sector and Its Impact on Economic Functioning

Clearly, the social property area was at the heart of the UP's strategy of change. It is important, therefore, to understand what effect it had on the viability of the overall process. Particularly, we want to know: (1) What was the impact of the creation of the social area on the economic outcomes? and (2) What general lessons can be drawn concerning the establishment of a socialized industrial sector?

As to the first question, it appears that the impact was not significant. As in the case of the other transformations, however, a different speed and sequence of change might have reduced the amplitude of the subsequent distortions in the economy. The assertion that the state-run industrial enterprises did not suffer significant short-run damage is supported by the fact that their production levels followed the same cycle as the rest of the industrial sector: rapid growth up to mid-1972, followed by a negative tendency thereafter. The fall-off in production in 1973 is attributable to overall economic problems, such as the restriction of hard cash funds, which were exogenous to the functioning of the industrial enterprises themselves. Thus we can affirm that the change in property ownership in industry was not a significant factor in explaining the overall economic disturbances. Its impact was of secondary importance, manifested in a drop in supply in the last stage of the government.

Nevertheless, production could have been higher (and the decline in 1973 less precipitous) if the management of the enterprises had been more efficient. As in the agrarian reform and the nationalization of copper, there was also a delay here between state takeover and organization. This lapse was a consequence of the secondary importance attached to organization per se in the UP strategy. It was argued, of course, that the change in form of property ownership would allow the introduction of a new economic rationality, but how this rationality was to be attained was never specified.

Would the extension of the state apparatus bring about a change in the allocation of resources and permit the establishment of new regulatory instruments in the short run? How would the predominance of the social area over the private sector be attained? On the basis of the initial decisions adopted by the economic staff, it appears that a central assumption was taken for granted: that the functioning norms of the economy would change in a quasi-automatic fashion following changes in property ownership.

This assumption was not vindicated because it was poorly founded. Even if management problems were resolved quickly, the new pattern of allocating resources and the new production programs would require different policy instruments, whose installation demanded longer periods of transition. Centralized planning or the imposition of physical production goals demanded a more well-integrated apparatus of control than that which existed. In addition the coexistence of the social area with an extensive private area obliged the former to operate through the mechanisms of the marketplace. Thus two problems emerged, the solutions to which would require an extended period of transition after the change in property ownership: (1) the reorganization of state-run enterprises on the basis of new management criteria, and (2) rendering this organization and these criteria compatible with the existence of a vast private sector.

In order to appreciate the magnitude of the task, it is enough to note the size that the social area was to have attained had the government's plans been fulfilled. It would have included 70 percent of the assets in the industrial sector, almost 44 percent of the gross value of production, and 22 percent of sectoral employment. By mid-1973, the state had come close to fulfilling these goals, having absorbed at least 173 large industrial enterprises. These enterprises were very diversified and their management constituted a complex administrative problem. On the other hand, the number of enterprises that were to remain in the private sector would by very high, including almost all of those employing less than 100 people.

All of the enterprises in the social and mixed areas employed 100 or more persons. In order to coordinate the activities of 200 to 300 state enterprises with 35,000 private firms, the market would have to play a fundamental role. In the initial phases centralization based on administrative criteria and physical production goals was not viable. Unfortunately, problems were accentuated by a predominant tendency to centralize, in an attempt to supersede the market as a regulatory mechanism before establishing and consolidating instruments to replace it.

The market serves a dual function. It is the mechanism through which income is divided between capital and labor, following the shares allotted to wages, prices, profits, and interest. It is also the mechanism through which productive resources are allotted and consumption decisions are arrived at according to relative prices. In a transition phase, what must be sought is to alter the distributive function of the market without at the same time destroying its allocative function. When this latter is ruptured by a hasty attempt to redistribute income, then the most likely sequel is inflation, recession in income distribution. The creation of the social area in Chile ought to have been undertaken so as to preserve the equilibrium between both functions; the speed of expropriation should have been adjusted so as to maintain market mechanisms as regulators as long as the new control organs were not yet in place.

The speed with which the UP program was implemented ought to have been adjusted to take into account some other variables as well. If the number of firms subject to expropriation was limited and the list of firms affected publicized, then it was clearly advantageous to move with dispatch. From the economic viewpoint, gradualism could induce the firms in question to reduce investments, neglect the maintenance of machinery, and sell off some assets in order to obtain greater liquidity in the short run. This is in fact what happened. The small and medium-sized firms reacted negatively to the slow advance of the social area, fearing that their turn, too, would soon arrive. State control should have been imposed rapidly and its extent limited thereafter. The political stakes were high: the large firms were the base of the dominant economic power groups, and the gradualist approach allowed these sectors to regroup and block the whole process.

The manner in which the social area was installed suggests two further critical observations. In the first place it would have been advantageous to specify right from the start a list of firms to be expropriated, but this was not done. In the second place, once this list was formulated, the expropriations should have been carried out right away; and the limits of the list should have been strictly respected.[11] The list of firms to be expropriated should have been formulated so that the enterprises involved could be placed under state control quickly, but without dislocating the market. These limitations meant that the government would have been obliged to direct its efforts at a selected number of large firms, rather than in a scattershot fashion.

Lessons from the Creation of the Social Area

Even though general rules cannot be deduced from the Chilean experience, valid conclusions can be drawn applicable to transitions effected in relatively complex economic systems under conditions of limited power.

CRITERIA FOR SELECTING FIRMS TO BE EXPROPRIATED

Power conditions in Chile did not permit a vast socialization process, a fact which made it essential that objectives be defined rigorously. Two central criteria for forming the social area were derivable from the economic strategy as a whole: (1) the basic nature of the enterprise, the extent to which it was important for the new model of development, particularly its involvement in intermediate goods, capital goods, or the control of foreign trade; and (2) the monopolistic nature of the firm. In practice two other criteria were imposed: the number of workers employed (since unions, stronger in firms with more workers, exerted powerful pressures in favor of socialization) and the size of profits. Simultaneous adherence to these criteria does not permit a definitive list of firms to be formulated; rather they have to be understood as guidelines. Ultimately, the relevant criterion is political. The central idea should be to concentrate available forces on the key economic-political groups in industry, finance and basic resources—those groups, in short, that control the economic system and wield decisive power.

EXTENDING THE PROGRAM OF SOCIALIZATION

The application of these criteria should lead to the formulation of a list of clearly identified firms. Indefinition creates serious problems, inasmuch as the number of firms potentially affected is very large, and a much wider political and economic crisis may therefore be touched off. Once the list is formulated it must be respected absolutely. Only in this way can a chain reaction involving the whole of the private sector be avoided. Those firms not subject to socialization must be supported and shielded without hesitation or wavering. Such a policy cannot be understood as a merely tactical question. It is a strategic decision, one that is valid in the whole period of the transition government and even beyond, in the historical stage of which the government forms a part. The extent of the socialized area as initially foreseen can be altered in the course of the process by unforeseen events. One such event, very important in the Chilean case, was the necessity to control the distribution of essential consumer goods, a necessity arising from the intense dislocation in the market. This area involves serious complications, since the organization of distribution is technically more complex and politically more explosive than the socialization of industrial enterprises and banks. It is essential, then, to avoid a runaway expansion of demand capable of throwing the whole program out of control. Finally, state takeover of the strategic enterprises can be complemented by the creation of smaller worker-managed enterprises with cooperative or other forms of ownership. Thus expropriation by the state of medium-sized firms can be avoided in some critical cases that might threaten the credibility of the government's program.

THE SPEED OF THE SOCIALIZATION PROCESS

Assuming the existence of a list drawn up and publicized in advance, the basic question is whether or not enterprises should be socialized step by step or rapidly. Significant limiting factors may exist, such as legal criteria that must be lived up to or a lack of qualified personnel to take over the management of the enterprises. Even keeping these restrictions in mind, it is preferable to proceed speedily and consolidate the advances later. The step-by-step policy is more tenuous and wastes valuable time, a lapse which may lead to economic deterioration in these firms and to political regrouping on the part of the owners. Subsidiary agreements stabilizing the tenure of the technical staff in expropriated firms should be concluded with dispatch; it is better to reach rapid agreement on compensation rather than postpone decisions. It is essential, in any case, to disturb the functioning of the economy as little as possible.

MANAGEMENT OF SOCIALIZED ENTERPRISES

The enterprises of the social area do not constitute a closed subsystem. On the contrary, they are in open interaction with private firms. Hence the market continues to play a central role as a mechanism of regulation and coordination. Planning becomes more effective and more extensive with the existence of a larger number of state-run enterprises, but it is still not possible to impose physical production guidelines or establish generalized administrative criteria. The private sector will continue to function with profit maximization as the guiding principle of behavior. Within this framework the problem consists in introducing planned production and investment while utilizing the market as well. The predominance of the social area over the private area is a dynamic question, one that has to be resolved through a more rapid expansion of the former.

The Superimposition of Structural Transformations and Redistributive Policy

The accumulation of the effects of a strongly expansive and redistributive economic policy along with the effects generated by property changes and the extension of popular participation were not compatible with the conditions of power in Chile. The economic process was driven by two fundamental tensions: (1) an expansion in demand much greater than the growth of internal supply, and (2) limitations on the expansion of supply stemming from a set of structural transformations.

As a consequence of the first tension a critical lag developed between the shift in the level and composition of demand and change in the level and composition of production and investment.[12] Because of the simultaneous and immediate introduction of several extensive structural transformations, another lag emerged, this time between the change in ownership and the new organization of the state apparatus. The two lags superimposed and converged, producing a level of disequilibrium difficult to control. The disturbances thus generated by the transformations exceeded the regulatory power of the control devices that were created during the process. The latter required a longer period to become solidified and established. As a result the principal deficiency of the strategy was the lack of orderly sequence in the transformations. More attention should have been devoted to considering the amplitude of the effects of the structural changes and to their unfolding in time.

The abrupt increase in demand was the dominant effect. Hence it can be concluded that the redistributive and structural change components should have been coordinated, especially with respect to their intensity and their timing. Given the deeper and more irreversible nature of the changes in property ownership and popular participation, these should have enjoyed first priority, while the redistributive and expansive policy should have been more moderate. This assertion is supported by two arguments. In the first place, the redistributive measures depended ultimately on the capacity to extract resources from middle- and upper-income groups. Only thus could the government avoid a serious gap between supply and demand, a fall-off in savings, or a drastic increase in imports. This "extractive capacity" depended in turn on the government's political power, which would be consolidated as the changes in property ownership were effected. It follows, therefore, that popular participation and property reform should have been consolidated before the redistributive policy was implemented at full strength. Second, income redistribution required a supply compatible with the new demand. This compatibility could have been achieved over the short run by a resort to imports and marginal adjustments in the production of some commodities (especially standardization and simplification). In the longer run more radical changes in investment and the type of technology and products would have to be effected. These longer-run adjustments would require a dominant state-run sector and planning based on real power.

A rapid advance on all fronts at once was not at all the best approach. Keeping in mind the fact that the core of economic power in Chile was located in the industrial-financial complex and in copper, it is clear that the process of state expropriation and nationalization ought to have enjoyed first priority; the rest of the transformations ought to have been adapted to accommodate this central objective. Besides the internal financial disequilibria, the balance of payments deficits were another critical area. It was clear that the greater the scarcity of hard currency in Chile, the more effective U.S. opposition would be. Hence, in order to diminish the external vulnerability of the process, it was essential to coordinate the increase in imported foodstuffs with the speed of the agrarian reform and the efficiency of management in the copper mines. But the rates of change occurring on these three fronts were incompatible. The idea that a more equal income distribution would permit growth with fewer imports (the new economic strategy) may have been valid for the longer run, but in the short run exactly the opposite occurred.

The conclusions above derive from an economic analysis of the transition. They are therefore partial in nature, since they do not take into account the impinging political factors, national and international. Nevertheless, the systematization of these economic considerations clarifies the central question: whether a democratic transition to socialism is indeed viable.

Viability is Control

We will conclude this chapter with some methological reflections which, despite their abstractness, illustrate the interaction of the essential components in the Chilean case. All systems are capable of assuming a large number of possible states; this number is referred to as system "variety" in cybernetics. In order to assure the viability, or survival, of the system this variety must be controlled. Hence the number of control elements that can be deployed (the variety of control) must be at least as great as the number of states the system can adopt.[13] When a system attains a level of variety superior to the variety of control elements which can be counterposed as regulators, it ceases to be viable. An economic system possesses internal regulatory mechanisms and a control center (the government) that operate to maintain viability. Once structural changes are introduced, systemic variety increases enormously. This growth can be confronted in one of two ways. Either the variety of control can be increased (more instruments of action can be granted to the government), or the variety in the system can be reduced drastically (more rigid norms can be imposed and certain behaviors prohibited).

In the present case, systemic variety grew because of structural alterations and disturbance of the existing self-regulatory mechanisms (principally those of the market). But the directing center (the government) did not expand its variety of controls with the necessary speed; nor could it replace the existing self-regulatory mechanism with new ones.

When a complex system is subject to transformation it is essential to master systemic variety at every moment. To this end three kinds of action have to be combined: broadening the variety controls (government), establishing new self-regulatory mechanisms (automatic), and reducing the variety of the system (restrictive norms) when power conditions allow.

Notes

1. See, for example, the analysis of the Chilean and Portuguese experiences and of the French Left in S. Kolm, *La transition socialiste* (Paris: Les Editions du Cerf, 1977), Chapters 1 and 2.

2. The concept of the transition to socialism is subject to several different interpretations; varying with respect to such questions as the point at which the transition can be said to have begun and the point at which it has become irreversible. Concerning the Chilean experience, Paul Sweezy has been one of the most emphatic writers. He locates the beginning of such a transition at the point "when a preliminary condition has been satisfied: State power must first be transferred from the bourgeoisie to the working classes." With respect to the UP government, he asserted in 1971: "I do not think that it is possible at this point to speak of Chile as a society in transition . . . Chile has still not overcome the first barrier blocking the entrance to the road to socialism." P. Sweezy, "Hacia un programa de estudio de la transición al socialismo," in P. Sweezy et al., *Teoria del proceso de transición* (Buenos Aires: Ediciones Pasado y Presente, 1973), pp. 2, 12. In our analysis, the term "transition" is taken in a restricted sense. It does not refer to the general notion of the passage from one mode of production to another, from capitalism to socialism; nor does it depend on whether or not we decide such a period begins before or after the resolution of the question of power. The term is limited here to problems of discontinuity, maladjustment or disequilibrium that arise in periods of accelerated change.

3. A detailed discussion can be found in P. Vuskovic, "Distribución del ingreso y opciones de desarrollo," in M.A. Garretón, ed., *Economia política en la Unidad Popular* (Barcelona: Editorial Fontanella, 1976); and in Odeplán, *Resumen del Plan de la Economía Nacional, 1971–1976* (Santiago, 1971).

4. See A. Foxley, "Redistribución del Consumo: efectos sobre la produción y el empleo," in CEPLAN, ed., *Bienestar y Pobreza* (Santiago: Ediciones Neuva Universidad, 1973). This quantitative study indicated that the rate of growth in production would not increase, but that the rate of employment would rise. See also E. Silva, *Efecto de distintas estructuras de consumo sobre el dinamismo del sector industrial,* graduate thesis (University of Chile, 1971). In the industrial sector, redistribution would lead to a slight rise in the rates of growth and employment.

5. See S. Bitar, A. Foxley, R. Ffrench-Davis, and O. Munoz, "Hacia un desarrollo igualitario" (Santiago: CEPLAN, Catholic University of Chile, 1973); and A. Foxley and O. Munoz, "Redistribución del ingreso, crecimiento y estructura social," in A. Foxley, ed., *Distributión del Ingreso* (Mexico: Fondo de Cultura Económica, 1974), pp. 361–364. In the works cited it was estimated that the marginal rate of savings of wage-earners should have come to 18 percent, working with the assumption that the owners would reduce their savings before consumption.

6. International Monetary Fund (May 1976), p. 58.

7. Originally, a six-year period had been planned for the expropriation of 3800 estates, benefiting 70,000 peasant families. Odeplán, *Plan Anual, 1971* (Santiago, 1972). In actuality, some 4395 estates were taken over in 1971 and 1972.

8. The number of estates expropriated per year was as follows: 99 in 1965, 264 in

1966, 217 in 1967, 220 in 1968, 315 in 1969, 293 in 1970, 1378 in 1971, and 3017 in 1972 and the first few months of 1973. Data from the Corporación de la Reforma Agraria; and S. Barraclough and J. Fernandez, *Diagnóstico de la Reforma Agraria Chilena* (Mexico: Siglo XXI, 1974), p. 75.

9. The increased production in 1974 under the military junta's administration, was due to planting carried out during the UP government—clear evidence that agricultural production had been recuperating in the last phase of the Allende regime.

10. In his "Immediate Tasks of Soviet Power," written in April 1918, Lenin argues as follows: "If we were to continue expropriating today at the same pace as before, we would doubtless suffer failure, since our work in the area of proletarian organization, accounting, and control has been inadequate by any standard. . . ."

11. Our analysis of the Chilean experience is here in agreement with the general observations by Lange concerning transition periods. See O. Lange and F. Taylor, *On the Economic Theory of Socialism* (New York: McGraw-Hill, 1956).

12. Quantitative studies completed later (in 1976) support the conclusion that a more controlled economic policy would have yielded better results in the longer run. It has been concluded from the study of a simulation model that "(T)he maintenance of profit levels (of private and state-run enterprises), together with policies limiting public spending and increases in the money supply would have yielded better results than a sharp acceleration in the process of income redistribution." A. Varela, "El comportamiento de la inversión en Chile," (Mexico: Universidad Nacional Autónoma de México, 1977), pp. 48–49.

13. This formulation is known as the "law of requisite variety," as proposed by R. Ashby. His dictum reads: "only variety can destroy variety." See R. Ashby, *An Introduction to Cybernetics*, (London: Chapman & Hall, 1971), p. 207; and S. Beer, *Decision and Control* (London: John Wiley, 1974), p. 279.

CHAPTER 11

Economic Program and Social Alliance

The strategy of the Unidad Popular assumed that a broad social alliance could be assembled that would allow the dominant groups to be isolated. Were the government's economic measures consistent with the sought-after alliance? Our basic conclusion is that they were not, that the Chilean experience was marked by an absence of coherence between this overriding political necessity and the actual economic program pursued by the government.

In order to draw useful lessons from the experience, it is necessary to examine analytically the social structure of Chile and observe how the different economic measures affected each group. The political attitude of the middle sectors turned out to be crucial; hence we are obliged to specify the factors that conditioned the behavior of each component in this large middle group. Above all we believe that it is essential to move beyond the global categories of peasantry, proletariat and bourgeoisie. These simplistic notions help in concocting sweeping formulas, but they conceal distinctions and nuances that are fundamental for the design of an overall strategy.

How did economic factors impinge on the political behavior of the major social groups? Current economic analysis does not consider modifications in collective behavior, which is assumed to remain constant. The interaction between economic policy measures and their political consequences is submerged by the division among the disciplines of economics, sociology and political science. This separation means that a purely economic approach yields partial or erroneous conclusions.

Economic theory deals with economic conduct explicitly through the so-called behavioral functions which allow a causal relationship to be established between a policy measure and its outcomes. Such functions, however, presume political stability or unimportant marginal changes; but intense social conflict provokes more substantial modifications in underlying behavior. In this case lineal causality ceases to be valid, and the interplay between economic measures and political conduct must be observed. Otherwise the economist may fall prey to absurd simplifications, such as judging the results as a question of technical competence or incompetence in policy design and execution, thus taking no account of the social and political conditions in which specific measures are immersed.[1]

Changes of Behavior in a Transitional Phase

In order to insert behavioral changes into the analysis, we can distinguish three levels. At the first level, which has been outlined in Chapter 10, we observed the relationship between specific policies and results (or action on the system and changes in its functioning). There we attended exclusively to the economic variables without considerirng changes in basic conduct. An example is the effect of income redistribution on demand and imports. According to this conceptualization the government's economic team implements specific policies, evaluates the results and corrects the measures.

At the second level we have to render assumptions about economic behavior explicit and consider how it was modified in the course of the larger process. For example, the redistribution of income created new expectations among low-income groups and generated pressures in favor of yet more equality. At the same time, among upper-income groups, the redistribution stimulated a fall-off in savings and investment, while consumption levels were maintained.

The alterations in behavioral functions were brought about both by the government's actions and by the reactions of the opposition. In both cases it is essential to distinguish between the impact of actual outcomes and the effect of a simple announcement of policy measures, due to the manner in which they were perceived. Individual "rationality" changes substantially due to a series of subjective factors, such as the perception of a threat or the awakening of new expectations. Thus, for example, when the Allende government began to set up the social area by concentrating on the largest companies, many middle-level owners feared that they too would be expropriated later on, even when no such measure was adopted. Likewise, when the government implemented its redistributive policy and the first disequilibria arose, the opposition mounted massive press campaigns accusing the UP of attempting to impose "total rationing." This campaign modified the conduct of a large part of the population, stimulating hoarding, a higher propensity to consume, and faster circulation of money. The a priori assumption, no matter how well-founded, that a policy measure has larger or ulterior intentions is a determining factor in the course of a process of abrupt transformations.

It is useful now to relocate some of the economic facts examined in previous chapters within this new model. A striking example was what occurred immediately following Allende's victory in the 1970 elections. Within hours after the electoral outcome was known, and before the government then in office could adopt any policy measures in response, a bank run of alarming proportions was touched off. A few weeks later private investment in construction contracted, sales of durable consumer goods fell off, and people in high-income groups were rapidly increasing their liquidity. These reactions were the result of the perception of a transformation, of the threat and insecurity that this implied. The intensity of this reaction obliged the Frei government to modify its policies. It was not, then, a specific governmental policy initiative that produced a change in behavior; to the contrary, the change in behavior forced the adoption of new policies by the government.

Another interesting example can be seen in the magnitude of the subsequent wage push. The inauguration of the new government stimulated high expectations among workers and employees. The victories for which they had been struggling for many years now seemed imminent. A popular mobilization was unleashed that caused the already ambitious redistributive goals of the Allende government to be overwhelmed. Despite the attempts to contain this push, the government was forced to give in. The changes in property ownership reinforced this tendency and encouraged spontaneous actions, seizures of land and housing sites.

False Premises in Building the Social Alliance

The purpose of the UP was to assemble a social alliance broad enough to support the planned transformations. It is hence important to note how the results of the government's economic policies influenced the political behavior of each group—and how, in the end, these policies frustrated the necessary social alliance.

The theoretical approach of the UP, as we have seen, emphasized structural factors. In this conception the political behavior of each social group was conditioned to a great extent by the nature of its insertion into the productive apparatus and by its immediate economic interests. According to the coalition's Program, the alliance was supposed to attract "workers' unions and social organizations, peasants, residents of urban squatter settlements, housewives, students, professionals, intellectuals, artisans, owners of small and medium-sized businesses. . . ." The workers would constitute the nucleus of the alliance; but this core would be supplemented by social sectors whose interests were not in conflict with those of the proletariat: salaried employees, smaller business owners and some groups of self-employed workers.[2]

The UP planned to cement its hold among workers, peasants and low-income salaried employees; and, in the worst of cases, it anticipated facing only a neutral attitude among owners of smaller businesses, who were not organically allied with big business. The smaller owners might perhaps vote for the opposition, but they would not throw their weight into open struggle with the government. The proletariat would play the leading role. It was pointed out that, as opposed to the Popular Front experience, where Center parties dominated their Left coalition partners, this time the latter would enjoy primacy.[3]

But how "natural" was this convergence of interests of the proletariat and the middle classes? Could a political accord between these two sectors be attained "spontaneously"? The dominant viewpoint within the UP underestimated the ideological and conjunctural factors. It was thought that the convergence of certain economic interests would by itself serve to draw the different social groups into an alliance. The importance of an already established ideological hegemony in everyday political conduct was not acknowledged. This hegemony, moreover, was very far from resting in the hands of the UP and its social bloc. The "vanguardist" emphasis on the proletariat led to an underestimation of the role of the middle classes, whose political presence was regarded as a temporary question, a mere tactical necessity. The role of the middle sectors, however, ought to have been understood strategically. This implied seeing that their interests were represented objectively rather than simply making transitory economic concessions to them.

Given its electoralist tradition, the UP was prone to confuse a social alliance with a winning block of voters. Its political actions, therefore, were marked by a bias for the short run. But the formation of a social alliance was a prolonged task, one which would have to be accompanied by the steady advance of the ideological and normal hegemony of the socialist project. In order to claim victory in this larger process, a simple majority would not suffice; much more popular support would be required than that necessary to control the organs of government democratically. Since an electoral majority could not initially be counted on, it would have to be pieced together through political alliances that would vary over the course of time. Meanwhile the hegemony of bourgeois and reformist politics heavily conditioned the electoral conduct of workers and employees—pillars of the Allende government.

Indicators such as those in Table 11-1 show that a substantial group of workers and employees voted for the CDP and the National Party, even though large numbers went over to the UP during the government period. But it was unrealistic to think that the central social conflict would develop workers' consciousness and by itself save the government, because the opposition was gathering strength at the same time. When it came to building the political alliances necessary for moving toward more favorable power conditions, the UP lacked a guiding conception capable of integrating ideological aspects and daily conduct on the one hand, with structural phenomena on the other.

Economic Outcomes and Political Behavior

In order to get at the causes of political behavior, it will not be enough to refer simply to bourgeoisie and proletariat. We must attempt a higher degree of precision. This means taking into account several criteria for distinguishing relevant social groups. As a first approximation we will use two criteria here: ownership of the means of production and income distribution. If we were seeking to explain the unfolding of the Chilean experience in simple, global terms, the analysis would center around two principal core groups: the owners of the large means of production (the big bourgeoisie), and the organized wage workers and salaried employees (the proletariat). Since, however, we want to explore the factors that altered the delicate balance of power, it becomes essential to observe the finer subdivisions within the two principal nuclei and, in particular, within the so-called middle sectors.

TABLE 11-1. Voting Behavior of Workers and Employees

| | Employees | | Workers | |
	August 1970	June 1972	August 1970	June 1972
Unidad Popular	24.1%	52.0%	48.9%	68.8%
Christian Democratic Party	37.1	36.0	26.6	25.6
National Party	38.8	12.0	24.5	5.6
Total	100.0	100.0	100.0	100.0

Source: Estimated on the basis of date from 1000 survey questionnaires administered by E. Hamuy in Greater Santiago.

Differentiation with respect to property ownership can be obtained through an inspection of occupational categories, as derived from the population census. The first important point is that the group of owners of the means of production represented only 3.1 percent of the employed labor force. Furthermore, given the high concentration of property ownership, the number of large owners directly affected by the UP program was far more restricted. It was reasonable, then, to imagine isolating such a quantitatively limited sector.

Let us now observe the size and distribution of the other bloc in the central conflict, the proletariat. If in a first approximation workers and employees are considered together, we can see that they totaled 71.3 percent of the employed population, a clear numerical majority (see Table 11-2). But these categories must be disaggregated in order to identify those components which in organization and political practice were consciously committed to the process of transformation. By themselves, workers employed in producing material goods came to 29 percent of the total labor force. Miners and industrial workers, the most organized of this group, accounted for only 10.6 percent of the total working population. To be more specific, it can be stated that a large number of industrial workers were employed in small or medium-sized firms. The organization and political activism of these workers, as well as their ideological cohesion, was significantly weaker than that of workers in the modern sector. As a result the most organized and coherent core of the proletariat made up less than 10 percent of the work force.

The two vanguard groups around which the alliance would be shaped, therefore, constituted a small percentage of the total population. As a result it was important to know how the other groups would align themselves politically and what factors were at work determining this alignment. It is clear that the antagonism between the bourgeoisie and proletariat is the point of departure for understanding the social and political dynamic of the period. The insertion of these two opposed groups into the productive structure was the determining factor in their class allegiance and political behavior.

As for the other groups, however, the relationship between location in the productive structure and their political and ideological characteristics was more diffuse. In the case of these groups, political and ideological factors acquired great significance, and here the ideological hegemony of the bourgeoisie was crucial. This was above all the situation with the so-called middle sectors.

The alliance assumed that the principal contradiction was between all of the large social groups on the one hand, and the big owners of the means of production on the other. It was assumed that secondary contradictions—those dividing workers, employees, smaller business owners and professionals—could be more easily managed; a certain cohesion could be maintained as long as the principal conflict persisted. Instead the secondary contradictions became more acute, ultimately wrecking the chances for the grand alliance. How can we explain this?

Part of the answer is evident once we observe the location of the different occupational categories in the income pyramid. Immediately noteworthy is the

TABLE 11-2. Employees and Workers by Economic Activity, 1970

	Employees	Workers
Agriculture	3.6%	28.8%
Mining	2.4	4.6
Industry	13.5	20.3
Construction	2.8	10.0
Other products (electricity, gas, water, transport, communications)	12.6	4.2
Commerce, services, financial, other	65.1	32.1
Total	100.0	100.0

Source: Instituto Nacional de Estadísticas, IV Censo Nacional de poblacíon y III de Vivienda, Santiago, 1971, Table 11-2.

considerable spread of incomes received within each occupational category. Once both criteria—ownership of the means of production and income distribution—are considered simultaneously, it can be seen that there existed groups of employers and self-employed workers (petty bourgeoisie) at the lowest income levels; while there were also significant groups of salaried employees and also some wage workers at the middle and upper levels of the income scale.

Certainly, the great majority of employers (82.9 percent) are to be found among the richest 20 percent and most workers (72.7 percent) among the poorest 50 percent, a fact which confirms the fundamental contradiction between these two classes. But salaried employees and self-employed workers, composing a high proportion of the labor force, cannot be pigeonholed so easily.

In conclusion, the dichotomistic proletariat-bourgeoisie analysis is inadequate, since it accounts for a relatively small percentage of the population. The relative complexity of the Chilean social structure is manifested in a continuous gradation which makes it difficult to impose marked separations between the different groups. The subtle gradations in the social structure prove essential in explaining behavior and in designing an effective transformational strategy.

The relative analytical importance granted to income distribution as opposed to ownership of the means of production has important political consequences. If the conflict is joined exclusively with the large property owners, the target is a very small percentage of the population, much less than 3 percent of whom all belong to the richest 20 percent. If, on the other hand, the struggle is directed against the richest people, then it affects a considerable portion of salaried employees and self-employed persons.

A majority of the salaried employees (62.4 percent) were to be counted among the richest 20 percent. While they would not feel threatened directly by state expropriation of the large firms, a far-reaching income redistribution would clearly disturb them. Since the UP strategy attacked on both fronts—property ownership and income distribution—simultaneously, it is not easy to decide which factor affected each social group more. Nevertheless, it is possible to attempt a summary account of what happened, in order to determine which factors were most disturbing for each one of the occupational groups.

The Owners

The owners of large firms, banks and rural estates reacted immediately in vehement opposition to the government—a fact which was predictable and inevitable. The small and medium-size business owners gradually joined forces with the big bourgeoisie, finally forming a single bloc. This latter development was not inevitable. The crucial question is whether it was possible to isolate the big owners from the smaller ones and what factors ultimately led to the success of the first group in drawing the second into an alliance.

It must not be forgotten that the big bourgeoisie in Chile moved with great adeptness from the beginning. They evaded attempts at isolation, diligently cultivating alliances with the smaller owners, attaching themselves to foreign capital, and seeking a political pact with the Christian Democrats.

There was certainly an initial predisposition on the part of the smaller owners to reject a government that was trying to alter the forms of property ownership and stimulate participation and workers' control. This predisposition derived from their class location, from the dominant ideology, and from the influences of the Center and Right parties. Nevertheless, there were also short-run economic factors that influenced their behavior and facilitated the strategy of the big owners.

In the first place, the government's failure to specify the limits of the expropriation process gave rise to all kinds of speculation. More than a year had passed before the government made public its final list of expropriable firms, and by that time even some small enterprises have already been intervened. The government's formal declarations granting guarantees to the owners of smaller firms were not translated into specific policies with a real impact. In the second place, the smaller owners were leery of workers' participation in the management of their enterprises. Even when formal ownership was not immediately threatened, the eventual control by workers over the direction of the firm was perceived as a first step toward a shift in ownership.

All private business owners regard two questions as unnegotiable: property ownership and control over internal decisions. During the phase of maximum tension, assurances by the government to the smaller owners on these two issues had to be nearly absolute; otherwise the ideological work of the largest owners would be much easier.

The UP's analysis of the middle sectors, particularly of the middle bourgeoisie, stressed the importance of economic considerations. It was thought that the increase in profits for small and medium firms (resulting from the expansion of demand and credits) would incline their owners toward the UP or at least help to maintain their neutrality. In practice, however, it turned out that even when this group was earning the highest profits in its history, their attitude toward the government remained extremely hostile. The fear of risks to their property obviously weighed much more in their thinking than the short-run benefits.

The big bourgeoisie also enjoyed success in gaining the overwhelming support of extranational interest groups, thus avoiding isolation on the foreign front. A well-publicized example was that of Agustín Edwards, owner of *El Mercurio* and head of a powerful business group, who turned to the United States to win political support.[4] This backing came not only from private corporations but also from the U.S. government itself, especially disturbed by the serious implications of the Chilean experience for Latin America and Europe. International political motives were the principal reason the U.S. government supported the big bourgeoisie in Chile. Local economic factors were of secondary importance in cementing the alliance of the Right with foreign interest. A successful UP strategy would have to isolate the large Chilean property owners both from their smaller cohorts in Chile and from foreign interests. A policy granting security and guarantees to the middle bourgeoisie might have yielded more maneuvering room and also would have helped in the confrontation with foreign interests during the initial phase.

In any event the important point is that the supremacy of the bourgeoisie in Chilean society did not depend on its economic power alone, but on its capacity to enforce ideological and cultural hegemony, involving the whole of the society in its project.

The Self-Employed Workers

Self-employed workers are a heterogeneous group, scattered, lacking in unity and organization. Free professionals, linked to the big and medium bourgeoisie, fell under this category, but so did an impoverished sub-proletariat. Of this group, 52.4 percent were to be found in the poorest half of the population, while only 17 percent fell in the richest 20 percent. In other words, most people in this category were low-income earners.

This heterogeneity makes a global analysis difficult. The most numerous and significant groups of self-employed workers were found in the cities. Here two sectors stood out: on the one hand there were the small storeowners, artisans, truck owners and liberal professionals; on the other hand there was a large sector of workers who had no access to tools or training, involved in dispensing small and temporary services. The first group shared the values of the big bourgeoisie; their hope was to become larger owners and employ wage labor. This tie made them especially susceptible to ideological domination by the interest-group organizations of the big bourgeoisie.

The fear of losing property was not such a decisive factor in the political alignment of this stratum, as it was for the large and medium owners. Instead, what threatened them was eventual dependence on the state and the emerging popular organizations. The economic factor that weighed most heavily in shaping their attitudes was the growing dislocation of the market, which injected much uncertainty and anxiety into their everyday dealings.

Two components of this group, store owners and vehicle owners, were in the forefront of the anti-government struggle. Their participation was crucial because of their capacity to paralyze critical economic activities. These smaller owners were attracted to an alliance with the big bourgeoisie by rightist propaganda which made them fear for their property. The catalyst that most incited the ire of truck owners was the difficulty in obtaining spare parts and new vehicles and the low fares and rates fixed by the government. The same concerns bothered shopkeepers, who resented the supply difficulties and the growing controls (real and imagined) of the state distribution apparatus. In sum it was not only the ideological activity of the Right that aroused their intransigent opposition, but also the existence of concrete economic problems.

The numerical and economic importance of the truck owners and storekeepers meant that the UP should have treated them diplomatically, avoiding polarization at all cost. Events in fact moved in the opposite direction, producing a reaction of unforeseen intensity among this group. It might have been possible, however, to limit this radicalization; the situation could at least have been handled at a lower level of conflict.

The largest group of self-employed workers were counted among the urban poor. They favored the transformational process, but they were prone to imprudent political behavior. The inflated expectations awakened in this group were exacerbated and used to advantage by the extreme Left. This group grew in importance as the process went on, and its support for the government was significant right up to the end. One fact that should be pointed out is that, contrary to other situations of high political mobilization, these groups were not manipulated by the Right and consistently developed their class consciousness.

Among independent workers, rich or poor, ideology had a large impact. Hence a more effective political approach by the Left could have neutralized the richer in this category and enlisted the poor sooner and more securely in the government's cause. If a politics of transformation is to succeed, the majority of independent workers must come to share the social and political values sustained by the proletariat.

The Salaried Employees

The political practice of salaried employees, both public and private, differed from that of the proletariat; and it was wrong to attribute to them a political attitude similar to that of the organized working class. There were two reasons for this discrepancy. In the first place was their insertion into the productive structure: most salaried employees worked in the services sector. More than 60 percent were occupied in commerce, financial services, or the state bureaucracy. These groups did not come into direct contact with the owners of the means of production. Their perception of the conflict between capital and labor was indirect and their aspirations were basically limited to higher pay and position.

In the second place their level of income was higher, on the average, than that of wage workers and the self-employed. While 72.7 percent of the workers and 52.4 percent of the self-employed were to be found among the poorest half of the population, only 11.1 percent of the salaried employees were included in this stratum. This meant that they were sensitive to any risk of losing their chance at upward social and economic mobility. The specter of "proletarianization" haunted them.

The UP was not anticipating such a violent reaction on the part of high-income, white-collar employees. This opposition was touched off as soon as people in this group felt that their positions of authority, both in private firms and in public administration, were threatened and that their social position was put in question by what they considered to be a frightening upsurge in workers' organizations.

The professional *gremio* most militant in its opposition to the government was the medical society. The violent hostility of this group and its subsequent political conduct demand more detailed study. Two causes can be pointed out here that seem to have determined their position. In the first place there was a high concentration of personnel on the job site. In Chile practically all doctors worked, even if only for a few hours, in the state-run National Health Service. As opposed to other professionals, who were involved with more varied tasks and were physically dispersed, doctors gathered together in a few hospitals, and hence could manage greater unity and organization. In the second place, the system of professional ranking and status was especially strong; stratification followed such well-defined criteria as technical capacity, specialty and age. The growing hostility of doctors to the government, then, is explained by threats to their status, the pressures and demands of the urban poor and organized workers for better health service, difficulties in maintaining their authority in hospitals, and deficiencies in supplies. Finally, the possibility that the government would extend the socialization of medicine, cutting down on free time devoted to private practice, was a specter threatening income, status and style of life.

Factors such as those mentioned above, however, were significant with only a small group of salaried employees, even though these occupied strategic positions. Most employees, both public and private, and particularly those with low incomes, continued to support the government.

The Wage Workers

Wage workers constituted the core of the UP's support. Together with peasants, residents of urban squatter settlements, low-income salaried employees and independent workers, they composed a vast social contingent that provided the coalition with enthusiastic and unselfish support. The workers' conduct derived from a class consciousness formed over a long period of struggle and fortified by the great parties of the Left.

Expansive and redistributive economic policies deepened popular mobilization, but in no way do they alone account for the degree of commitment exhibited by workers' organizations. Among less-organized sectors (peasants, workers in small factories, and low-paid workers in the service sector), income redistribution had a more direct effect on political mobilization, due to their lower degree of political consciousness. For the same reason it was peasants and the very poor residents of urban squatter settlements who were most prone to engage in spontaneous actions and were the most receptive to simplistic radical propaganda.

With all of this popular support achieved considerable maturity. Despite the intensity of the political struggle, the number of persons out on strike during the Allende government was actually less than the number registered in the last two years of the Frei administration. While the number of strikes grew—an indication of the gravity of the political conflict—the decline in the number of persons on strike confirms the fact that no popular movements against the government were involved.

The maturity and class consciousness of the workers also explains the distinctive nature of their political conduct. Unlike other social groups, their subordination to the professional leadership of the political parties was not as strong. For example, Christian Democratic workers acted in solidarity with their cohorts in the UP when the factories had to be defended against the threats posed by the October stoppage; they kept on working during the crisis. Thus, among workers belonging to the CDP, there prevailed a dualistic behavior: class solidarity in the fundamental conflicts, accompanied by electoral divergence at the polling place. The assumption that the UP could draw the CDP's base of support to its own camp proved most valid in the case of the workers.

The outright support or rejection of the Allende government was most evident in the case of the two core groups: the large and medium property owners on the one hand, and workers on the other. Both groups extended their base of support and improved their organization. Their relative influence over the middle sectors, however, developed differently than what had been assumed in the UP program. Here the hegemonic class ended up imposing its own views, demonstrating real dexterity in concocting alliances, seeking out new forms of organization, and managing the communications media. The *gremio* mode of organization adopted by the opposition was a clear example of this ideological and tactical effectiveness.

Gremio Organization and the Middle Strata

A considerable portion of the opposition action was channeled outside of political party organizations. In order to break out of its encirclement, the Right expanded *gremio* organization and seized the ideological initiative. Another central observation concerning the Chilean experience is that while the UP emphasized economic interests (changes in property ownership and redistribution), the Right attacked on the ideological front (stimulating fears of state control and loss of "liberty," proletarianization and chaos).

The advance of the *gremios* was spectacular. They were stimulated and encouraged by the associations of large property owners. These organizations dated back to the previous century and had always been distant from the smaller owners. Already during the Frei government and very rapidly during the Allende government, considerable numbers of the small and middle bourgeoisie were admitted to these groups. Thus, for example, the National Agricultural Society (founded in 1839) was traditionally an enclave of *latifundistas*, or large estate owners. Once the agrarian reform began in 1965, however, it was opened up to owners of medium-sized properties. The Society for the Promotion of Manufactures (funded in 1883) only admitted representatives of the largest firms: at the beginning of the 1960s its membership was barely

2200.[5] The National Mining Society, also founded in 1883, was composed of owners of middle-sized mines, since the largest mines were controlled by foreigners. The Central Chamber of Commerce (founded in 1858) grouped together wholesale traders and the owners of the largest stores in Santiago. All of these associations banded together in 1935 to form the Confederation of Production and Commerce. In 1953, the Chamber of Construction, representative as well of the largest interests in its field, affiliated with the Confederation.

Small owners were organized later. It was not until 1953 that the Association of Small and Medium Industry and Artisans was formed; the group had attracted 7500 members by the beginning of the 1960s. The Confederation of Truck Owners emerged in 1955, followed by the Retail Commerce Confederation in 1965. Both of these groups represented the classic petty bourgeoisie.

Until 1970 important conflicts of interests divided small and large property owners. These differences, however, faded during the Allende government: and at the end of 1971 the National Front of the Private Sector was formed, uniting all of the above-mentioned groups for the first time under a single umbrella organization.

On the professional front something similar occurred. Nine *colegios*, or professional associations, existed in 1970, their primary function being to regulate professional activity and to fix fees.[6] In May 1971, the opposition succeeded in organizing the Chilean Confederation of Professionals, and in July 1972, the Confederation of Professional Associations was founded. A few months later, during the October stoppage, the confederations of owners and professionals culminated this wave of organizing activity by setting up the Gremio Action Command.

The UP and the government responded in a confused and belated way to this advance. There were isolated attempts to organize small owners and professionals opposed to the Right, but these efforts were unsuccessful. The petty bourgeoisie was largely ignored and was also the victim of excessive ideological excoriation on the part of Left groups, gratuitous verbal displays which only increased their emotional resistance to the whole transitional process.

The Radicalization of the Middle Strata

Made up of heterogeneous groups which were differently linked to the productive structure, the so-called middle sectors had to be dealt with in a manner that attended to the specificity of each component. Specific economic policies had to discriminate between medium and small owners, small landlords, professionals, employees in the service sector, public or private employees and technicians.

The UP program, however, was dominated by global categories, which led to serious errors. The use of concepts like "class" and "class struggle" was simplistic and abusive. These concepts, it should be recognized, served two distinct purposes: they were slogans for political mobilization and they were also conceptual tools in a scientific analysis designed to orient decisions. For the first purpose, UP spokesmen reverted to a dichotomous language, asserting the existence of a fundamental conflict between the large property owners and everyone else, between rich and poor, exploiters and exploited. This only served a strategy of polarization. For the purpose of grasping reality and arriving at decisions, however, a finer analysis was required, one capable of recognizing intermediate positions between the two opposed classes.

According to the simplified version, all wage-earners were part of the proletariat. This category included over 70 percent of the population. On other occasions a strict structural definition of class was employed. This led to the conclusion that the middle class did not exist as such, that it was not a class, but rather a collection of ill-defined intermediate strata whose political alignment depended on the balance of power between the two basic poles: the big bourgeoisie and the proletariat. The inverse position, supported by the Center parties, stressed the existence of a coherent middle class with homogenous characteristics.

The structuralist emphasis was harmful, since in a process of rapid change it is essential to grasp the ideological and political aspects, which are decisive. Structural class position is one thing; actual class practice is another. The acceptance of "middle-class" self-identification by a large portion of the Chilean population in itself influenced their political attitudes. This self-classification encouraged them, in the first place, to hold themselves apart from the principal conflict. To people in this intermediate group it seemed that neither their conflicts nor their convergences of interest which the two other classes were fundamental. In the second place, they considered themselves to be one step up from the proletariat. The prevailing legal practice of transferring highly paid workers to the category of salaried employee reinforced this self-conception. This consciousness was an objective fact, difficult to alter over the short run.

The dealings with the Christian Democrats also suffered, as we have seen, from an economistic distortion. The UP analysis insisted on the multiclass composition of the CDP. Hence it was argued that a political and economic program benefiting workers and employees would, without further inducements, lead them to switch their allegiance to the UP. But the ideological cohesion within the CDP could not be so easily and so quickly undone by the economic actions of the government. The whole idea, therefore, of forming a social alliance without the corresponding agreements at the political level is open to question. It seems clear that the UP underestimated the role of the CDP in the political alignment of the middle strata and of some workers and peasants.[7]

Of all the diverse groups counted among the middle sectors, it was the petty bourgeoisie which played the crucial role. At the end of the UP period, their rejection of the government had become visceral and even more intransigent than the big bourgeoisie. Their animosity surpassed all expectations and constituted one of the most striking aspects of the Chilean experience. The potential for a fascist mobilization among these sectors recalled similar precedents in Europe, and it is one of the most serious risks undergone in a transformation process in complex societies.

DETERMINING FACTORS

The economic developments that had the most significant impact on the political behavior of the middle sectors were the following:

1. The dislocation of the market, which affected the relative position of these groups in income distribution and consumption. Subjectively, this disarticulation generated insecurity and fed their fears that a new form of property ownership and a new composition of production would cause them to lose ground. With respect to the control of the production process and authority in the administration of the economic system, professionals, technicians, and high-level employees also felt their relative positions threatened. Politically and ideologically, these changes offended against their notions of efficiency and order. Women in particular were more directly sensitive to the practical difficulties with supplies.
2. Deficiencies in economic policy. The second most important economic failing was in the design and application of policy (the increase in demand incompatible with internal supply) and in the manner in which the social area was created (imprecision, lack of guarantees for smaller owners, overwhelming of the government's administrative capacity).
3. Manipulation by the Right of these objective conditions. While economic development created favorable conditions for the Right, they were not determinant in fomenting this discontent. They were deliberately exacerbated by effective opposition ideological activity, in turn supported by the U.S. government. The UP could not forestall this development.
4. Absence of a clear alternative with which to refute the predictions of the opposition. It was often stated on the Left that the government was only one stage, to be followed by other, more advanced periods. In this first phase, therefore, the petty bourgeoisie were to be enlisted as allies in the struggle against the big bourgeoisie. Later the middle sectors would come under the influence of a new hegemony. This politically infantile notion hurt the whole project. The middle-class groups could not be treated as temporary, tactical allies; they had to be dealt with as a strategic element. This problem arose largely because the UP did not have a long range strategic vision in which Allende government's historical role was correctly situated in the construction of a democratic socialism.

The political polarization, while it reinforced both core groups, favored the big bourgeoisie more. The large owners and their allies were quicker to see what was at stake than most peasants, workers, and employees. Changes in political consciousness are slower than changes in the material base, particularly in such a short period. Organization among the workers took more time in spreading and consolidating than organization among these who felt immediately what they had to lose.[8]

The big bourgeoisie, and later the petty bourgeoisie were not dazzled by the high profits that they obtained initially; they threw themselves into the struggle over property ownership right from the start. Large groups of workers and employees, meanwhile, spent their social energies on pushing grievance claims, frequently attacking the government itself. This temporary lag between the intensity of the opposition's reaction and the emergence of a new support gave rise to a critical period in which the conditions of power deteriorate. The lag coincided, moreover, with the delay between the appearance of the disequilibria in the economic system and the creation of a new mechanism to regulate and control them.

The main problem in managing the transition period consisted, therefore, in reconciling the shifting balance of power with the magnitude of the maladjustments that were emerging. The process of transformation via the institutional route demanded the neutrality of the middle sectors and the ability of the government to channel the social forces supporting it through the established institutions so as to prevent polarization and the overwhelming of its capacities.

The economic program had to be implemented in such a way as to keep the alterations in the market place compatible with the limited powers of the government. The form in which the program was actually adopted, however, was not compatible with the basic assumption of a social alliance joining the proletariat to the petty bourgeoisie and other middle sectors.

The amplitude and cohesion of a social alliance are the result of the ideological and political leadership attained by the forces committed to the transformation. The more widespread the acceptance of the "national project" proposed by these forces, the deeper the changes that can be effected. Possessing a more mature political consciousness, workers are able to subordinate immediate aspirations to structural objectives. Social mobilization must not be attempted, therefore, by way of immediate economic concessions; reliance on such immediate material incentives always carries with it the risk of political collapse brought about by a setback in the economy.

The UP attained viability because its values had been widely propagated for many years and it shaped a political project that pulled together a significant social contingent. By the same token, its failure can be explained because it attempted a program of actions that exceeded the real political, ideological and moral force of the Left. Leadership derives from a prolonged evolution that precedes and conditions the exercise of power. The Right was able to recover and later extend its power thanks to its ideological hegemony. It was the inability to challenge this hegemony that proved the UP's downfall.

Notes

1. An example of this simplistic analysis is the deplorable statement of Rosenstein-Rodin: "Allende fell not because he was a socialist, but because he was incompetent; he died as an incompetent martyr." P. Rosenstein-Rodin, "Discussion on Chile: Diagnosis and Prognosis," Discussion Paper No. 7 (Boston: Center for Latin American Development Studies, Boston University, 1973).

2. The UP sought to carry out "a transfer of power from the old dominant groups to the workers, peasants, and progressive sectors of the middle classes. . . ." Basic Program of the UP. The President himself, in his first speech after assuming office, implicitly excluded small and middle property owners: "Workers, peasants, employees, technicians, professionals, and intellectuals will play the leading role in the country economically as well as politically." Speech of November 5, 1970 in the National Stadium, in S. Allende, *Salvador Allende: Su pensamiento político* (Santiago: Editorial Quimantu, 1972).

3. The Popular Front came to power in 1938 and lasted until 1941. The Radical Party, dominant in that coalition, represented chiefly middle-class sectors: the small and medium bourgeoisie and public employees.

4. After Allende's election, Edwards was installed in the United States as vice-president of Pepsi Cola. According to the U.S. Senate investigations, he was then put in contact with the CIA and President Nixon. "Director Helms also testified that the September 15th meeting with President Nixon may have been triggered by the presence of Agustin Edwards. . . . That morning, at the request of Donald Kendall, president of Pepsi Cola, Henry Kissinger and John Mitchell met for breakfast with Kendall and Edwards . . . the topic of conversation was the political situation in Chile and the plight of *El Mercurio* and other anti-Allende forces." United States Senate, *Alleged Assassination Plots Involving Foreign Leaders*, an Interim Report of the Select Committee to Study Governmental Operations with respect to Intelligence Activities (Washington, D.C.: U.S. Government Printing Office, 1975), p. 228.

5. See D. Cusack, *The Politics of Chilean Private Enterprise under Christian Democracy*, Ph.D. dissertation (University of Denver, 1970).

6. The main professional associations with their membership size were the following: the Medical Association (6000), the Lawyers' Association (6000), the Engineers' Association (7000), the Accountants' Association (19900), the Technicians' Association (4700), the Dentists' Association (3500), the Agronomists' Association (2700), the Architects' Association (2100), and the Journalists' Association (1900). See *Los gremios patronales* (Santiago: Editorial Quimantu, 1973).

7. The role of the CDP acquires more importance once we are aware that its vote had grown in the large cities and that it represented social groups tied to modern activities. Politically, the fate of the Chilean experience was determined among urban groups, and the middle strata played an especially important part there. With respect to these groups, Falletto and Ruiz, in a study on political parties and social structure, point out: "The rise of more dynamic political groups tied to the new forms of economic development alters the importance of those middle groups that came to power with the Popular Front . . . represented politically by the Radical Party. The new middle classes, the product of a higher level of economic concentration, emerge precisely where this concentration has its greatest impact—in Santiago." Comparing the CDP with the Radical Party, the authors observe: "The different significance which the large urban centers have for both these parties is well-known. While the Christian Democrats concentrate on the large cities, the Radicals are weakest in Santiago." E. Falletto and E. Ruiz, "Conflicto político y estructura social," *Chile Hoy* (Mexico: Siglo XXI, 1970), pp. 217–222.

8. Machiavelli, in *The Prince*, set out ideas that no revolutionary can afford to forget: "There is nothing more difficult to carry out nor more dangerous to manage than the initiation of a new order of things. This is because reform arouses enmity among all those who profit from the old order, but it inspires only a half-hearted defense among those who will be favored by the new order. This half-heartedness arises in part from fear of the enemy, who has the law in his favor, and in part from the inherent skepticism of men, who cannot truly believe in anything new until they have had some real experience of it."

CHAPTER 12

Political Leadership and Democratic Transition

In very broad terms the task of the political leadership was to implement the transformational strategy in a manner congruent with the shifting balance of power.[1] Once the strategy had been defined in rough outline, the leadership group has a double function: on the one hand, it had to disaggregate this strategy, spelling out the implications on each policy front and specifying the correct sequence of actions; on the other it had to carry out the proposed measures effectively. Both of these functions demanded a correct interpretation of the power conditions prevailing at any given instant and an accurate assessment of the resources necessary to undertake each of the various stages.

The Limiting Conditions of Power

As defined above, the task of the political leadership group amounted to managing the process of change by keeping it moving within viable limits. Events, however, led to a narrowing of these limits. The causes for this diminishing viability were analyzed in Chapters 10 and 11. In the economic area the emerging disequilibria surpassed control capacities, increasing the "inefficiency" of the process. In the political sphere the hostile groups responded more intensely and more rapidly than did the groups favored by the new policies, thus robbing the government of a measure of its "legitimacy."[2] Both factors—"inefficiency" and "loss of legitimacy"—had a direct impact on the decisive focus of power—the armed forces—and, as a result, on the government's capacity for coercion.

What were the power conditions implicit in the UP strategy? What factors determined these limits? First the commitment to an institutional, or political-legal, strategy was contingent on the possibility of coming to power through elections, by receiving a plurality vote, even if not an absolute majority. Under such conditions the UP had to seek out political accords in order to move its programs through Congress, and this meant some kind of understanding with the CDP. Access to the Executive granted what was called later only "a fraction of the power." It was implicit, therefore, that a parliamentary understanding would further limit the range of action within the political-legal framework.

In the second place this commitment implied the recognition that the institutional order enjoyed broad legitimacy and, consequently, it had to be respected. The institutional order was legitimate insofar as it was open to change from within. The use of existing mechanisms in order to attain the self-transformation of the system disallowed abrupt changes, permitting only a gradual advance, at least in the initial phase. Thus an essential dilemma of any transitional period—whether to make use of or replace the state apparatus—was obviated. In reality both courses must be pursued at once.

This restriction was reinforced by the ultimate and fundamental limiting condition: effective control of the armed forces. The government could count on the neutrality of the military, and could hence dispose of the corresponding coercive capacity in order to assure the integrity of the system in transformation, only so far as it operated within accepted institutional limits. While certain sectors with a higher political consciousness understood the significance of the total process and recognized the transitional character of the maladjustments, most people judged the process on the basis of its immediate effects. Thus the legitimacy attributed to the government was a function both of the perceived efficiency and of the level of political consciousness of the social groups pertaining to the UP alliance. Hence the lower the level of efficiency, the lower the level of legitimacy. But even given severe maladjustments, the deleterious effects on legitimacy would have been less damaging had an advanced political consciousness been more widespread.

Concerning the concept of legitimacy, some distinctions ought to be noted. Chilean society, seen in the 1970 vote, accepted the idea of change. In this sense the existing economic and social system had lost legitimacy, and consequently any government that promoted the desired changes could claim it. At the same time, however, the institutional order (the democratic political regime) retained high levels of legitimacy, a fact which made it essential to attempt its transformation only from within.

In sum, the legitimacy of the government (measured in part by its electoral support), the legitimacy of the democratic political regime, and the subordination of the armed forces to constitutional power were the elements defining the threshold of power, the boundaries of the zone of viability.

How did economic factors influence the correlation of forces? In the first place the efficiency of the process affected the availability of power resources. Efficiency in this context refers to the magnitude of the disequilibria, the extent of disarticulation in the market, the quality of macroeconomic management, and the administration of state-run enterprises. The balance of power would be affected in the short run by the intensity and breadth of the structural transformations. A process of rapid simultaneous changes on several fronts generated a series of immediate disturbances which caused efficiency to deteriorate. The magnitude of the dislocations could have been reduced with better technical management of the changes. The leadership ought to have adjusted the depth of the transformations in accordance with the balance of power and the capacity to create new mechanisms to regulate the system and carry out its new functions efficiently.

In a democratic regime efficiency is a factor that has a direct impact on the political attitudes of social groups.

In the case of Chile coercion was not independent of legitimacy. There could be no recourse to the first in the absence of the second. Thus legitimacy was a dominant restriction on the exercise of power. On its preservation depended the control of the armed forces. Given these limiting conditions, let us judge how well the political and economic leadership groups of the government performed—in particular, how successful they were in advancing the UP strategy within the limits of the power resources available to them in each phase of the process.

Economic Policy and Political Leadership

While the UP had put forward a global strategy, it failed to specify a trajectory or a sequence of changes, or their intensity. Certainly, it was difficult to define these factors in advance, given the complex and variable character of the process, but it was possible to establish certain guidelines in more detail.

The principal criterion consisted in utilizing institutional mechanisms as effectively as possible to change the forms of property ownership. Short-run economic policies, in turn, would help to gain electoral support. The changes in the economic base (the strategic objectives) would create new power conditions, allowing for substantive modifications in the institutional order. State power would increase, providing new instruments of control over the economy.

The actual trajectory, however, differed markedly from the course of events expected by the UP. The discrepancy can be explained in part by the manner in which the three main variables analyzed in Chapters 2 through 9 (income distribution, changes in property ownership, and popular support) interacted.

In order to provide a summary account of this interaction, two stages can be distinguished. In the first stage (1971), the policies of reactivation and redistribution had a generally positive effect and favored the lower-income strata. To the extent that this redistribution was brought about without affecting the real incomes of middle and upper strata, the reaction of these latter groups was weak. The resulting net increase in political support provided the impulse to initiate the deeper transformations.

Nevertheless, the intensity of the reactivation and redistribution policies produced a negative effect in the second stage (1972–73). The maladjustments in the marketplace persisted and expanded, affecting the whole population. Attempts to correct these disturbances through the extraction of resources from middle- and upper-income strata gave rise to fervent opposition. Later inflation eroded the initial gains in redistributions. It turned out that the more spectacular the initial success, the more negative the subsequent outcomes.

The changes in property ownership also influenced political support. In the first stage expropriation was confined to the large firms, banks and estates. The reaction of the owners was abrupt and immediate, while the small and medium proprietors exhibited a relatively passive attitude. Support among workers grew, but not as quickly and decisively as the reaction of the large owners. In the second stage conditions changed. The general dynamic caused the conflict to spread to the smaller firms. Small and medium business owners were subjected to the increasingly effective ideological campaign of the big bourgeoisie. Rejection of the government spread in these circles: but at the same time support for it continued to grow in other sectors. Polarization intensified steadily.

The superimposition of the effects of the programs of reactivation and redistribution and of changes in property ownership aggravated the disequilibria in the second stage. The new instruments of power in the hands of the government, while important, were insufficient to the task of controlling the economic disturbances. As a result, opposition grew among the middle strata. Once the mass of the middle sectors had turned against the government, while at the same time its base of support among the workers had been consolidated, the confrontation sharpened and could not be channeled through the political-legal system. The face-off and stalemate of the contending social forces fed the economic crisis and brought about the paralysis of the state apparatus. Thus the minimal power conditions necessary for the success of the process collapsed entirely. Both the efficacy and the legitimacy of the government had been decisively weakened.

The derailing of the process from the planned trajectory revealed the invalidity of certain assumptions concerning the functioning of a system in transformation. When we examine the economic policy of the UP in its entirety, an important inconsistency can be readily observed. While the analysis of the supply side of the economy was couched in thoroughly structuralist terms, policies directed at the demand side were inspired by Keynesian conceptions (wage and public spending policy). The change in the level and composition of supply (the "real" economy) would be produced once the new patterns of ownership in the means of production had been established. The state, with the participation of the workers, could capture a larger share of the economic surplus to expand investment and channel it toward the production of mass consumer commodities and capital goods. Existing productive capacity would also be redirected to the same end. This required, as well, greater autonomy in the technological sphere. All of these measures, however, would only come to fruition in the long run. Those policies tending to modify the composition and level of demand, in contrast, would have an immediate effect.

This inconsistency was the result not only of a deficient conduct of short-run policy; it also revealed the inadequate insertion of policies concerning wages, fiscal and monetary matters, and the balance of payments in the total socialist project. Economic policy ought to have responded not only to immediate aspirations, but also to the necessities arising from the structural change. The intensity and rhythm of short-run policy ought to have been adjusted to the strategic objectives in order to avoid perturbations with ungovernable consequences.

Many transformation programs are characterized by the proposal of sweeping long-range goals without corresponding attention to the phenomena of transition. Structural analyses explain the functioning of economic systems in terms of the operations of an invariant structure, but the same analyses are inadequate in explaining the functioning of a system whose fundamental structure is undergoing change.

The government's programs for property reform and the creation of the social area assumed that decisive changes in the legal forms of property ownership would quickly beget a new economic rationality, a new mode of economic functioning. The emphasis was placed on the expropriation of private firms, a step which was a necessary but not sufficient condition for the emergence of a new rationality. This latter change would not automatically follow upon the formal transfer of property. This was especially the case because the necessary efforts to improve the quality of management and reinforce planning were not carried out.

Another assumption central to the economic strategy was that there existed a close relationship between economic power and political power. It was thought that loss of ownership of the means of production on the part of the big bourgeoisie would result in a rapid decline of their total power. Similarly, the economic gains accruing to the middle sectors—small businessmen, salaried employees and professionals—would draw them to the government side. Both notions proved to be erroneous. While the first assumption was valid for the longer run, in the short run it was plainly mistaken. This emphasis emerged from an economistic conception which derived superstructural phenomena simplistically from the economic base, a conception which ignored the force of the dominant ideology and the political mediations between base and superstructure. The ideological hegemony of the groups the UP wanted to displace persisted and was capable of reversing the situation in their favor.

POOR COORDINATION BETWEEN THE ECONOMIC AND POLITICAL LEADERSHIP

Some of the discrepancies between plans and reality resulted from the weakness of the economic leadership in implementing its policies. In the first place there was an absence of liaison between the economic and political leadership groups. In the initial stage the political leaders acted in a gradualist manner, leaving room for a wider agreement with the CDP. The economic directorate, however, accelerated the redistributive process, with the idea of accumulating forces rapidly in order to bring about a more radical institutional change. In other words, the political assumptions underlying economic policy did not coincide with those guiding the activity of the political leadership.

This phenomenon had several causes. On the one hand, those responsible for economic policy failed to make explicit either the political requirements or the political consequences of the measures they advanced. The structuralist conception dominating their thinking favored recourse to administrative controls and disdained adequate attention to financial balances; it relied excessively on central controls.

This kind of approach had important implications. Extension of administrative controls assumed the existence of power conditions which the political leadership simply could not produce. Since the assumed political conditions did not exist, the economic leadership group was unable to control the maladjustments which emerged later. On the other hand the political leadership itself lacked an adequate understanding of economic phenomena. This inadequacy stemmed from the traditions of leftwing leadership. Leftist politicians came overwhelmingly from a parliamentary background. They had always been distant from Executive power, and hence lacked an adequate grasp of the administrative aspect of government. This unfamiliarity with the realities of government was aggravated by a populist inclination, nurtured in the practices of political struggle, typical of leftist parties in capitalist countries.

The insufficient understanding of the functioning of the economy was compounded by the uncertainties arising from the structural transformations. As a result the political leaders simply could not foresee the effects of a specific economic policies. Their reaction was always belated, occurring only after the economic outcomes had taken on political expression. Thus, for example, the persistent objections to a hyperexpansive policy (which came not only from the opposition, but also from members of the government's technical staff) were not heeded until the economic disequilibria had already spread and the criticisms, protests and marches had acquired alarming proportions.

The second important factor in explaining the inadequacies of the economic leadership was the lack of strategic definition that prevailed at the political level. As a result, important economic decisions were neutralized and paralyzed, or occasionally contradictory. Thus, in the case of the social area, an attempt to contain the pressures of the workers in order to reach an agreement with the CDP was frustrated by the simultaneous seizure of several firms. In the middle of 1972, both approaches were applied at once. The slogans advanced by the different parties of the UP also pointed in different and occasionally contradictory directions: the "battle for production" and "popular power" emphasized altogether different approaches to the dilemmas facing the government. The first advocated discipline and sustained effort, the second socialization of yet more private firms.

Anyone who observed the activity of the government from within can affirm the evident weakness of the leadership in confronting the complexity of the situation. The coordination among the ministers of the economy and finance, the Banco Central and CORFO was weak; no central command structure existed at all in the first phase. The Economic Committee, the group effecting liaison between the economic offices and the president, functioned precariously, and it was not until the middle of 1972 that a technical support staff for the Committee was organized. The torrent of everyday problems prevented the elaboration of a global analysis; decisions were implemented only partially; and there were no procedures for followup or evaluation. Since powers were shared and each group acted autonomously there existed no single focus of authority, no body or person responsible for the direction or economic policy as a whole. This was a major failure in the conduct of the economy.

The situation above can be explained to a great extent by the kind of relationship which existed between the government and the parties of the coalition. The influence of the different parties on the conduct of economic and political policy was exercised through party members who occupied high offices in the administration. The parties sought to maintain their relative importance at the ministerial level, at the level of decentralized government institutions, in the public enterprises, and at middle-level command positions. The result was a compartmentalization of the state apparatus, with decision-making parasystems structured along party lines—an arrangement which turned out to be paralyzing when policy differences among the parties emerged.

Each political group had considerable say in designating or replacing "its" officials. A dual system of authority was set up: officials had to respond both to the wishes of their superiors within the government and to the parties to whom they owed their appointments. At a time when the nature of the problems confronted demanded maximum unity, effectiveness, and rapidity of response, this dispersion of authority within the government was a serious matter indeed.

Furthermore, in the midst of each party another critical contradiction existed, one that was not correctly handled. The administrative and partisan-political functions of high-level executives in the public sector were seriously confused. The first was concerned with implementing the decisions of the government, while the second with the electoral interests of each party. These officials appointed as directors of the new state-run enterprises lived this contradiction most acutely, and the government was compelled to look on as its own officials occasionally refused to carry out actions ordered by their superiors.

MANAGEMENT OF THE ECONOMY IN A TRANSITIONAL PHASE

The conventional mechanisms of economic regulation were not suitable in confronting the contingencies of a stage of rapid changes. It was essential to deal with new problems that required different policy approaches. The Chilean experience allows us to identify several critical areas which must be subjected to control if potentially fatal disequilibria are to be regulated. These critical areas and the organization created to deal with them were the following:

1. *Wage policy:* The pressures of the unions and the extension of the state-run area forced the government to establish close coordination with the

labor organizations and to exert direct control over the agreements reached in each state-run enterprise. If this matter were left to direct negotiation between workers and the directors of the intervened enterprises, a "demonstration effect" would be created and the pressures on the government would increase considerably. With this in mind the National Commission on Wages and Salaries was set up, including both representatives of the workers and the state.

2. *The system of sales and distribution:* The redistributive goals were not attainable through wage increases alone. Hence, in order to assure access to essential goods for the poorest groups and circumvent speculation and the black market, it was essential to organize new state-run distribution channels and to coordinate this activity with the population in the poorer neighborhoods. In 1973, the government created the Executive Secretariat of Distribution, in order to plan and coordinate the activities of the state-run firms in this respect.

3. *Investment:* Private investment (both national and foreign) contracted abruptly almost as soon as the 1970 election returns were in. This reaction, to some extent inevitable, forced a rapid expansion of public investment. But this responsibility did not consist only in channeling more resources, but also in the design and execution of new projects. In 1972, the government set up the National Commission on Investments with this purpose in mind.

4. *Foreign trade:* The process of transformation in Chile had to come to grips with a cutoff in the flow of funds from the United States and the international agencies where American influence was strong. The balance of payments situation became critical in 1971. It was therefore essential to set up an administrative apparatus to allot the foreign currency funds available. In 1971, the government created the Executive Secretariat for Foreign Trade, which was charged with reconciling the origin of imports with the new sources of financing. This task, however, proved to be effective for only a restricted number of goods; it was impossible to plan for thousands of commodities, and the situation grew even worse when the rate of exchange lost its regulatory role.

5. *Transport:* Outright subversive activity was concentrated mainly in this area. The government had to set up a separate office charged with avoiding paralysis of the transport system, a function it placed in the hands of the military. It can be concluded from the Chilean experience that in the event of open conflict, there must exist a state-directed transport capacity in order to assure the carrying out of vital economic functions.

6. *Economic information:* In a process of accelerated change, those managing the economy must be supplied with almost immediate indicators concerning certain key variables. In Chile the existing indices were always several months behind the flow of real events, thus delaying the adoption of corrective measures. In the prevailing atmosphere of uncertainty, it was

essential to define certain limits for the most important economic variables. Once these threshold values were surpassed, immediate signals would be emitted to alert the policymaking staff. In this area the necessary measures were not adopted in time.

Our view of the areas above reveals the existence of inherent restrictions to all change processes. The magnitude of the transformations demanded the creation, from the beginning, of a decision-making system centered on the critical areas, in order to regulate and control those subsystems which were subject to the sharpest disturbances.

ECONOMIC DISTURBANCES IN COMPLEX SYSTEMS

The importance of economic phenomena for the success or failure of change processes is greater the higher the level of economic development of the society undergoing change. In this respect the Chilean experience suggests some conclusions applicable to those countries where structural change is attempted in complex economic systems.

The classic revolutionary experiences took place in countries whose level of development was below that of Chile. In 1970, per capita income in Chile was close to $700.[3] This figure was higher than in the case of all the countries of Eastern Europe and of the U.S.S.R. when they undertook the radical change in their socioeconomic system. In 1920, per capita income in Soviet Russia was $180. In 1938 in Poland, it was $104, and in 1947, $114; for the same years in Hungary, the figures were $112 and $113, respectively, and in Czechoslovakia, $176 and $165.[4]

In more developed economies, the density of national and international economic relations is higher. In such cases it is very difficult to isolate relatively independent subsystems. Oscillations occurring in one part of the system, therefore, are propagated rapidly throughout, hence changing the functioning of the totality.

In economies where a large proportion of the population is involved in agricultural activities and lives at a subsistence level, the economic impact of an abrupt change has limited effects. The rural population is relatively autonomous with respect to the rest of the economy. The situation is completely different in more advanced economies, which are industralized and exhibit high urban concentrations.

Consumption expectations are also higher in countries with higher income levels, and the pressures of low-income groups for immediate improvement of their situation are therefore likely to be more insistent. At the same time, because of their superior political organization and the acute awareness of their possibilities, middle and upper groups are less tolerant of any decline in their incomes: the higher the average income of a social group, the greater the political resistance to a decline in their earnings.

In complex systems it is more difficult to manage this kind of transition, since the consequences of the transformations are more generalized and the political importance of conjunctural economic stability is greater. Such changes require precise strategy and tactics which pay more attention to partial and gradual alterations in order to maintain control of the situation.

In the case of Chile and any other country highly dependent on international financing, these problems are aggravated. The weight of international political and economic ties, in the Chilean case to the United States, had a considerable effect, and hurt production and consumption levels in the final stages of the process. Just when the internal conflict had acquired maximum intensity, international pressure had decisive repercussions, amplifying all of the disequilibria. This dependence meant that the government had to more carefully, so as not to enter into maximum conflict with both domestic and international enemies at the same time. But this precaution calls for an analytical distinction between international and national factors in strategic and tactical design.

While the big national bourgeoisie is indeed tied to the interests of the multinational corporations, its interests are not identical to theirs. The holdings of the large multinational corporations in Chile, with the exception of copper, were marginal; they therefore had more flexibility to negotiate. The local big bourgeoisie did not enjoy this option; everything was at stake for them, and they were obliged to react violently. Had this distinction been attended to, the government might have avoided simultaneous confrontation on two fronts, a strategically perilous option.

Political Leadership and Popular Mobilization

Another central aspect of the transformation process was the popular mobilization necessary to attract more electoral support and the commitment of grassroots organizations. One condition of the institutional path to power consisted in channeling this popular mobilization so that the political-legal order was not overwhelmed. Hence a basic criterion for evaluating the viability of the UP experience consists in deciding whether or not the political leadership was sufficiently strong both to mobilize the popular base and control it so as to avert a massive social eruption and spontaneous acts exceeding the above mentioned limits of power.

The political leadership had to manage a delicate dialectic: popular support had to be enlisted through the mobilization of previously passive social groups, but it had to be channeled so as to avoid polarization. This would lead the middle strata to turn toward the Right and would effectively block any alliance with them against the wealthy few. But was this in fact possible? Was the political neutrality of the middle sectors compatible with a substantial popular mobilization involving the poorest urban sectors?

In fact the situation became impossible to control. Popular organization proved indeed to be massive and organic, but the government found it increasingly difficult to regulate the activities of this mass base. This in turn had strong repercussions among the petty bourgeoisie and other middle groups. The perceived threat to their status and the fear that expropriations would exceed the limits set by the government had already awakened stiff resistance among these groups. In addition the fact that grassroots organizations exercised control in industrial areas (in the form of the so-called "industrial cordons") and in small commerce (the JAPs, or Supply and Price Councils) was perceived by the middle strata as an additional risk to their position, power and style of life. The Right acted astutely to incite and capitalize on these reactions.

Both the spontaneous perception of a threat and the deliberate fostering of expectations are very important aspects of all transformation processes. The political leadership had to consider not only the "real" effects of its decisions, but also the "perceptions" or interpretations placed on an identical fact as viewed within distinct ideological contexts.

We can now see how important it was to understand both the manner in which certain changes were perceived by the different social groups and the effects of their reactions on the course of events, together with the manipulation of these reactions to obstruct the process. The fostering of expectations among the organized working class and the marginal urban strata was an essential factor in mobilizing the masses. But was the level of mobilization capable of being regulated? Could the UP parties control the process?

Studies of the behavior of workers in state-run enterprises during the 1971–73 period have thrown some light on this issue. One investigation of a textile mill which had been incorporated into the social area concluded that popular mobilization had its own dynamic, difficult to control by the government and by the UP parties.[5] According to this study the factors that sustained this mobilization developed before 1971: unions were strong and had for years been pressing for greater control; the ideology of the Left parties and their political practice previous to the UP government had encouraged the workers to believe that rapid gains in income were possible; the reform program of the Frei regime had stimulated these expectations even more; finally, the Allende campaign and the electoral victory seemed to vindicate the hope for an immediate improvement on all fronts. The actions undertaken by the government and the UP parties after 1970 in turn raised the level of expectations far beyond the limited capacity of the leadership to channel the consequent agitation at the base.

Another study of a larger number of enterprises in the social area arrived at similar conclusions.[6] Increased participation in the control of the enterprises and the wage increases created a "demonstration effect" in other factories. For the workers in private sector firms, the observed advances in state-run enterprises served as a catalyst more powerful than the government had counted on. Nevertheless, the same study indicated that once the moment of maximum conflict in each enterprise had passed, the newly created participatory organizations succeeded in imposing their own brand of labor discipline.

The period involved was too brief to allow firm conclusions to be drawn on this matter. Furthermore, an analysis based on the study of only a few firms is limited insofar as it tends to underestimate forces developing at the global level. From the larger viewpoint, considering the organizational resources and popular base of the UP parties, different conclusions can be sustained: the Left did in fact have the capacity to guide popular mobilization more effectively. More unified action and a clearer orientation on the part of the government and the parties in the coalition would have allowed for better regulation of the process, reducing the risk of polarization and uncontrollable crisis. These power resources, however, were not utilized. The failure to put these resources to work had two main causes: the mechanisms guiding the functioning of the parties and the coalition as a whole, and the distinct strategies that continued to compete for influence within the political leadership. The Chilean experience reveals the existence of a contradiction very difficult to overcome: in their opposition role, the parties of the Left mobilize the masses and encourage political awareness in order to win power; but once in the government, if they are not capable of channeling this energy, they soon lose control of the situation.

The task of initiating and realizing a process of profound changes in a society requires a political consciousness that is capable of viewing immediate aspirations from the longer-range perspective of structural transformation. Only this type of advanced consciousness can defeat the tendency toward populist errors and a mistaken emphasis on spontaneous actions. Political forces favoring the transformations project have to create a consciousness that includes a sense of strategy and tactics, an awareness of the problems of transition, of the necessity to reconcile immediate needs with the requirements of the advance toward strategic objectives. The emphasis on totalistic approaches and utopian schemes and the contempt for reality and the conjunctural situation inevitably result in frustration and harmful deviations.

ORGANIC WEAKNESS OF A COALITION

Analysts of the Chilean experience frequently find the paralysis of the political leadership in the final phases inexplicable. This risk was latent from the beginning and can be attributed both to factors inherent in the organization of a multiparty coalition and to specific differences in strategic thinking that existed within the highest circles of the UP. The parties constituting the coalition exhibited differences which had developed historically and were expressed in electoral rivalry and in the competition for primacy within the popular movement and in public administration.

A united focus of command was essential in order to allow for timely responses in this rapidly evolving process. The UP, however, lacked mechanisms to arbitrate differences expeditiously. Presidential authority was always exercised with great discretion, in order to maintain the unity of the coalition. Decisions were postponed whenever differences appeared irreconcilable, in the hope that they would diminish as time passed. The quest for unanimity in the most critical areas had serious repercussions on the speed of response in the face of new developments. The most critical situation occurred in the last few weeks of the government. The UP could not reach internal agreement on such fundamental issues as a decision to continue the dialogue with the CDP or to call for a plebiscite; meanwhile the imminence of a coup d'état grew from day to day. Such serious problems could have been overcome given the existence of a strong authority capable of mediating these disputes, although minor fissures in the coalition were inevitable. The myth of a total unity weakened the efforts of the president to impose binding decisions.

A second fundamental problem consisted in the interaction between the parties and the popular organizations. The parties had a considerable mass base, but the workers had their own organizations which functioned autonomously. This autonomy was an essential feature of the Chilean path to socialism; it assured the democratic and decentralized character of the emerging societal model. But at the same time this autonomy robbed the parties of some of their leadership capacity, forced as they were to alternate between their role in the government and their function of expressing the aspirations of the mass base. The less cohesive groups, like the Socialist Party, suffered especially from this tension, ending up by simple transmitting the positions of popular organizations, rather than acting as an apparatus capable of educating and leading.

The Left parties had always expressed mass grievances, and this tradition could not be altered abruptly. The electoral context, as well as the consequent competition within the UP and between the UP and CDP, accentuated these populist tendencies. The functions of the parties as elements of the government were thus seriously compromised. Compared with the case of a single ruling party, a coalition aggravates short-range pressures and is less capable of dealing with the resulting disturbances.

These problems could only be solved if the parties demonstrated sufficient consciousness, political maturity and organizational capacity to subordinate their immediate interests to strategic objectives. These qualities were more developed in Chile than in other countries of a similar economic level; they should have been utilized more.

Another factor which complicated the management of conflict was the polemical style of many in Left circles. The battle of declarations between groups gave rise to an escalating series of maximalist statements. The desire for notoriety and political distinctiveness was satisfied with the striking of ever more radical postures.

Some Left groups were prone to ideologizing, which led them to depict the actual situation in a simplistic form, to see "historical laws" at work in every situation, and to postulate strict historical parallels. This ideologistic tendency was also accompanied by the use of a vocabulary derived from other revolutionary experiences. The slogans used to mobilize public opinion themselves tended to amplify the conflicts.

Although prudence dictated that a specific policy should be presented in moderate language and then carried out swiftly and decisively, the opposite frequently occurred: measures were presented with great fanfare and then never carried out; worse still some policies were announced which were simply impossible to execute. The net effect was to increase the virulence of the anti-government reaction or to awaken expectations that were doomed to disappointment. Rhetorical power has its limits; once these are surpassed, it is converted into a liability.

THE INSTITUTIONAL STRATEGY AND ARMED STRUGGLE

One determining factor crippled the political leadership: the strategic differences in the midst of the UP. The institutional strategy was never quite liberated from the specter of armed struggle as a persisting alternative. This alternative possibility, although always a minority position, was consistently advocated by the MIR and by small groups within the UP. Partisans of this approach regarded a confrontation as imminent and inevitable.[7] According to this thinking it was essential to prepare for the coming conflict by stimulating mass-based organization and creating paramilitary defense groups.

Those in the majority within the UP did not deny that a drastic transformation could lead to a period of crisis and global confrontation. It was clearly understood that the powerful interest groups affected by the change program would resort to all possible means to avoid their displacement. But the analysis of the historical conjuncture led those in the majority to formulate a strategy aimed first at attaining significant advances in altering the economic base, thus leading to a transformation of the political-legal order, without producing a total polarization. This advance would be marked by a substantial expansion of the state apparatus and increased participation by the workers. In this manner new circumstances would be generated, allowing the final confrontation to be waged on more favorable ground. It was considered crucial that the UP, and not the bourgeoisie, should choose the moment and the conditions for global conflict.

In the first phase, that of the Allende government, the UP did not contemplate a global confrontation, but only partial conflicts, capable of resolution within the institutional order and providing the stimulus for its renovation. While the social dynamic inevitably led to polarization among the opposed forces, a conflict setting off the army against the government, the most likely outcome, would doom the UP project to failure. The state apparatus was an instrument to be used in transforming the socioeconomic base; it made no sense, therefore, to try to destroy it. The existing institutional system constituted the first line of defense of the government against an opposition determined to overthrow it.

Considering the period in its totality, it can be stated that the UP strategy was not sustained with the necessary fortitude. In this stage of the process, the institutional path was the only one possible; and it was plainly incompatible with a strategy of insurrection or armed struggle. There could be no wavering between the two: broad strategic approaches cannot be altered with the same ease as economic policy. The selection of a transformation path for a social system is a process of slow formation over a long period, and the choice remains valid for an entire historical period. It is not a tactical decision; hence it is not subject to abrupt changes over brief periods. The possibility for success depends on the creation of an historical project that surges forth and imposes itself against the ideological hegemony of the dominant social group. The ideas, the values, the essential impulse particular to this project must progressively gain legitimacy among wide sectors of the population. What is involved, then, is a long process of cementing alliances—a process which, as a matter of logic, precedes electoral triumph and the seizure of power and which must condition the conduct of the government.

The power resources available to undertake the transformation are relatively fixed in the short run, due to the prevailing structural and conjunctural conditions. The exercise of this power must be legitimated; it must be based ultimately on the widespread acceptance and the general mobilizing power of the basic values and ideas of the historical project. Consequently, it is absolutely inadmissible to attempt a change of strategy en route, replacing an institutional strategy with armed struggle.

This did not mean ignoring the possibility that a crisis insurmountable within the political-legal system might emerge. What this implies, in contrast, is that the institutional strategy itself had to include provisions for the accumulation of forces (electoral, grassroots, mass-based, ideological, institutional, and within the armed forces) sufficient to face this eventuality with success. This is not the same as pursuing both strategies at once.

The UP and its programs constituted one stage in the institutional transformation path, a process course which had been evolving in Chile over a long period of time. The Allende government was not the culmination of this process; hence, neither the problem of power nor the task of socialist construction would be resolved during the presidential period. Insofar as it was but one stage in a larger process, the UP government had to maintain its continuity with the institutional tradition, it was an error to hope for a sudden change once the elections were won. A commitment to armed struggle is not decided in a matter of months; instead it would have to have been the culminating of another process, of another strategic option—neither of which existed in Chile.

Nevertheless, elements of a noninstitutional strategy were always present in the midst of the UP. When there does not exist a political leadership to clear up lack of definition between two options, there is always the risk of ending up with an equivocal position that embraces the worst aspects of both. In the case of Chile, the UP period exhibited both the relative inefficiency of a democratic approach in the conduct of the process and the loss of credibility among the middle strata stemming from the perception of an eventual violent confrontation.

THE VALIDITY OF THE INSTITUTIONAL STRATEGY

It cannot fairly be stated that the collapse of the Chilean experiment proves that the institutional strategy lacked all validity. The events themselves—electoral victory and three years of profound transformations—demonstrate the real possibility of fostering significant changes using precisely this approach. Neither can the validity of the assumptions that underlay the UP strategy be judged in general terms. A correct analysis must specify the conditions and circumstances under which the fundamental hypotheses were valid and the actions undertaken efficacious.

The UP and the progressive sectors of the CDP had succeeded in breaking the hold of the dominant ideology, creating a consciousness of the necessity and validity of socioeconomic transformation. This accomplishment was in itself a significant force in favor of the institutional path. But there also existed a significant weakness in this area. The UP awakened consciousness as to the necessity of effecting economic transformations (nationalization of copper, expropriation of the large firms, redistribution of wealth and income), but it failed to create an awareness of the urgency of changes in the institutional structure (the armed forces, the judicial system, popular participation, and the communications media). This explains the higher degree of mobilization—and the less effective resistance—in the case of the first group of changes, and the dearth of concrete proposals by the UP in the second area. The UP also failed to put sufficient effort into the diffusion of the values of a new popular project; it never broke the hold of right-wing ideological hegemony in noneconomic matters.

In this respect the UP never overcame theoretically a central problem in modern socialist projects: the democratic character of the socialist process. Always persisting in the thinking of the UP, at least at the theoretical level, was the notion that at some unspecified moment the question of power would be resolved by a global confrontation as the result of which "total power" would have to be attained in order to install the dictatorship of the proletariat. While the political practice of the UP was indeed profoundly democratic (the only aspects which have been questioned are secondary matters: use of the legal provisions of 1932, "legal requisitions"), the theoretical debate on total power, widely broadcasted by the profusion of articles and public conferences, stirred up public opinion and led to rejection by the middle strata.

The concept of the dictatorship of the proletariat confused political conduct, since it was not clear to what extent the institutional strategy and the commitment to pluralism were compatible with this possibility. While at the abstract and simplistic level the dictatorship of the proletariat—understood as the exercise of power by this class—could be explained as the overcoming of the existing dictatorship of the bourgeoisie; at the level of everyday discourse, the idea was incompatible with democratic politics. In this area, therefore, the UP was vulnerable to ideological attack by the opposition, which argued that democracy in the hands of the Left was merely an expedient tactic which would be replaced in subsequent periods by "totalitarian" forms of government.

In a democratic socialist transition it is essential to drive home the point that structural changes in property ownership, the social relations of production, and the increase in participation serve to deepen and extend democracy. For the success of this historical project and ideological progress among the wide sectors that must be drawn into the political and social alliance that sustains it, it is essential to affirm and demonstrate that democracy is inherent to socialism.

The two central assumptions of the institutional strategy in Chile were first, the possibility of an alliance between the proletariat and the middle classes and, second, the constitutionalist character of the armed forces. Were these assumptions valid? Both were indeed valid for the specific stage represented by the UP and within strict limitations. In dealing with these problems, the political leadership fell into tactical errors; but, more fundamentally, its comprehension of the thinking of both the middle strata and the military and its appreciation of the limits implied in the central assumptions were both insufficient. This matter is today of central concern in many countries where the institutional path to socialism is being contemplated. Some final considerations drawn from the Chilean experience may therefore be of general interest.

Concerning the alliance with the middle strata, the UP always reasoned in strictly economistic terms. It was thought that the political behavior of these groups would be most strongly influenced by their immediate economic welfare. Easy credits, quick profits and firm declarations as to the nonexpropriability of their property would win the support, or at least the favorable opinion, of this group. This belief turned out to be mistaken, because it strongly underestimated the ideological domination of the big bourgeoisie over smaller property owners.

In addition the constitution of the alliance conferred a subsidiary role on the middle sectors. They were to be subject to worker's hegemony from the beginning, despite the fact that this kind of hegemony was a goal that could only be attained during along process. Thus the objective interests of the middle sectors were not represented by the UP; the coalition limited its commitment to these groups to general statements of good will.

As far as the partisan political expression of the alliance, the initial thesis of the Left, according to which the base of the CDP would automatically move towards the UP once they understood the progressive nature of the government's economic policies, proved to be erroneous. This thesis was upheld largely in order to put off an accord (partial or comprehensive) with the CDP. It underestimated the ideological factors that hold a political party together. An interparty alliance was necessary not only to attain more electoral strength and thus isolate the Right; it was also required if another essential assumption was to prove valid: that the political-legal system was sufficiently flexible to allow for progressive transformation from within. As a minority group in parliament, the UP had no other choice than to attain some kind of accord.[8]

The difficulty in arriving at some such understanding was caused, in addition to the factors mentioned above, by another typical feature of the Chilean Left: a strong bent towards ideology and a minimal sense of pragmatism. Exclusive ideologies and doctrines divided the CDP and the UP; both groups advocated totalist political projects which left little room for compromise between them. Individual political decisions had to be referred to these global schemes and be deduced from certain "fundamental principles." This led to the political practice of attributing concealed motives to all actions or statements of the opponent: behind the acts of the CDP, the defense of capitalism was always the dominant consideration; the deeds of the UP always concealed an attempt to impose its control and put an end to democracy. Personal barriers between the political directories of each group were set up, making the human relationships necessary to arrive at an agreement very difficult. This aspect is usually not discussed in global political analyses, but its importance was considerable.

The thesis as to the behavior of the armed forces is, without doubt, the most important and requires rigorous study. The political plans of the UP did not include an adequate analysis of the armed forces. In all of the ideological developments prior to 1970, there existed no coherent thinking as to the nature of the military, its ideology, the room for maneuver it might allow, and the best way to forestall intervention in favor of the Right once adherence to the institutional order no longer suited the latter group.

The UP's own thesis affirming the constitutionalist character of the armed forces became an unquestioned axiom which inhibited the concrete analysis of this reality. In future cases, it would be inexcusable to fall prey to similar delusions and hence ignore the subversive activities unleashed by the national bourgeoisie with the strong support of U.S. interests.

There existed certain limits with respect to the military which ought to have been recognized objectively. As a first analysis, two major sectors within the officer corps can be distinguished: the constitutionalists and those who interpreted social life essentially from a military point of view. The first group had elaborated a doctrine that took respect for democratic institutions as its first principle. The second group structured its thinking in terms of certain simple concepts: discipline, order, patriotism, a rejection of the "politicians," and a strong anticommunist sentiment.

Along with these two groups existed two quantitatively less important tendencies: one favorable to the changes, progressive, and to a certain extent pro-socialist; the other, fascist. The second group enjoyed some advantage over the first because they stressed the values of force and toughness, attitudes congenial to the military disposition; while the progressives favored more open, humanistic postures.

The UP and President Allende based their support on the constitutionalist officers, who, because of their superior rank, would preserve authority and cohesion within the whole of the armed forces. This was not an unreasonable hypothesis at this conjuncture. What turned out to be an error was the failure to specify the requirements which had to be fulfilled in order to preserve the primacy of the constitutionalist sector. At least two requirements were essential. In the first place, the UP had to win the support of a political majority in the country. Otherwise a political-legal impasse would ensue, as was the case with the proposed law governing the social property area. In the second place, firm authority had to be exercised; the government had to forestall an acute breakdown in public order and prevent spontaneous acts of violence from the far Right or the extreme Left.

When the government proved incapable of fulfilling these requirements, the constitutionalist sector within the military was weakened; and other factors, operating in the contrary direction, were set in motion. Chief among these, of course, was the existence of a powerful enemy, determined to frustrate the UP project: the political-economic Right and the U.S. government. These groups directed their maneuverings within the armed forces so as to appeal to ideological values within the military mentality potentially favorable to their position. The soldier's belief in order, discipline, and efficiency was played upon to foster the image of a country living in a presubversive situation, with its productive apparatus shattered. The concepts of nation and fatherland were stressed so as to arouse opposition to the class struggle directed by the UP, on the grounds that it was artificially dividing the people and weakening the nation. This campaign found fertile ground in an army immersed in Prussian military traditions and whose younger officers had been educated in the ideology of counterinsurgency. Both ideologies served as effective catalysts.

In summary, then, the success of the institutional strategy depended on the neutrality of the armed forces and the preservation of an alliance between the proletariat and the middle strata. But, in the delicate balance of power which existed in 1970, the government and the UP failed in such a way as to fulfill these conditions.

Conclusion

Those liberals who conclude that democracy and socialism are incompatible, and hence reject socialism, fail to comprehend the richness of the Chilean experience and the real possibilities which it opened up. Those students or followers of the classical revolutions who see insurrections as the only road to power ignore the viability of different paths of transition to socialism in complex social systems. As an overall synthesis of the present analysis, the following conclusions can be stated:

1. The Allende government was viable insofar as there existed a good probability of making substantial advances toward the democratization of Chilean society and the weakening and displacement of the dominant minority groups (the big bourgeoisie and the foreign interests). The viability of the UP project is not to be judged in terms of the transition to socialism, much less in terms of the immediate construction of a socialist society. The essential goal of this stage in Chilean history consisted in a radical change in the property ownership of the strategic means of production, the fortification of the state apparatus, the advance of the proletariat toward a position of greater strength, and the consequent isolation and later destruction of the dominant minority interests, both local and foreign.

2. The internal and external balance of power left room for significant advances, but only in the direction already indicated. The middle strata could be enlisted in the struggle to displace the big bourgeoisie and restore

national autonomy, but they would refuse to take part in a historical project designed to install proletarian hegemony, at least in the sense in which this term was traditionally understood. The nature of this balance of power, then, made any process leading to a global confrontation nonviable. Internationally, the Chilean process was unfolding within the sphere of influence of the United States, whose interests led it to oppose profound changes and to support the internal opposition. This fact meant one more restriction: head-on confrontation with the United States would also have to be avoided.

3. Since neither sharp polarization nor global confrontation was consistent with the actual balance of power, the project was viable only insofar as these possibilities were avoided. This in turn meant establishing a strategic alliance with the middle classes. Such an alliance might assure the viability of the program, creating new conditions for progress toward socialism later on.

4. Limited as it was within this framework of opposed forces, the UP program constituted in itself a significant advance. It ought not to have been understood as an end in itself, but rather as part of a longer-range process.

The radical revolutions of this century have occurred in relatively simple social, economic and political-legal systems. It is fair to say, therefore, that the Chilean experience has particular relevance for more developed economies, with complex social structures and stable political-legal systems, in countries which are inserted into an international framework dominated by transnational capitalism.

For Chileans, an adequate understanding of the experience they have undergone is a requirement for their historical advance. The basic contradictions of Chilean society continue in a latent form. Two options are possible in the future: the containment or repression of the popular movement with the consequent restriction or elimination of democracy, or the transformation of the economic structure and popular control over the economy and the political-legal order which will lead to the implementation of more advanced forms of democracy with a socialist basis.

The second option is the only one which can give rise to a new historical stage of stable progress. How this might come to pass is not subject to prediction, since events never repeat themselves. But the objective and detailed study of historical experience will allow for the more effective design of a viable path to socialism that preserves and develops human rights and democracy.

Notes

1. "Political leadership" here refers to the group of persons occupying the high positions in government and the heads of the political parties of the UP. Formally this group consisted of the President of the Republic and the secretaries general or presidents of the parties of the coalition. The economic leadership, analyzed sepa-

rately, was made up of the executive officers of the principal state agencies in this area: the Ministries of Finance and the Economy, the Banco Central and CORFO (the Corporation for the Promotion of Production).

2. In a polarized situation the legitimacy a government can claim varies from one social group to another. The UP government won high legitimacy among workers and salaried employees; however, its legitimacy was increasingly questioned among the middle strata. The same fate befell the legitimacy of the democratic political regime as a whole. To the extent that the latter proved incapable of containing and channeling the process of structural change, it also lost legitimacy among the middle strata, opening the way to the coup d'état.

3. According to Odeplán, the GNP per capita amounted to $700 in 1970. Odeplán, *El desarrollo economico y social de Chile en la decada 1970–1980*, Vol. 2 (Santiago, 1972), p. 11. According to CEPAL, the same index stood at $650 in 1969. CEPAL, "Tendencies y estructura de la economía latinoamericana," (Santiago, 1971), p. 68.

4. See A. Foxley, "Alternatives de descentralización en el proceso de transformación de la economía nacional," in *Chile: Busqueda de un nuevo socialismo* (Santiago: Ediciones Nueva Universidad, 1971). Numbers in 1938 dollars. When measured in 1970 dollars, per capita income in Eastern Europe fell below that of Chile.

5. A study carried out by P. Winn, an American historian, at Yarur, a textile firm.

6. See J. Espinoza and A. Zimbalist, *Economic Democracy* (New York: Academic Press, 1978).

7. For a discussion of the various positions present on the Left, see F. Castillo, et al., "Las masas, el Estado y el problema del poder en Chile," *Cuadernos de la Realidad Nacional*, No. 16 (April 1973), pp. 40–52.

8. One little discussed feature of the Chilean political system is that, as a general rule, the opposition is always in the majority in Congress. Government coalitions have on occasion won a majority in the Chamber of Deputies, but the general rule has been that the opposition controls a majority sufficient to block those initiatives of the Executive to which it has not given its previous consent, and that the government parties in turn control more than a third of the votes in each House, so that the opposition can not impose its own proposals. (The presidential veto, which can only be overridden by a two-thirds vote of Congress, would prevent such an eventuality.) This feature made the Chilean political system more stable, but it limited the possibilities for change. The UP was obligated to take account of this situation.

Index

political situation and, 82–84

1973 performance of, crisis in, 164–165

1973 perspective for

Cabinet Economic Committee meetings on, 148–149

essential goods distribution in, 145–146

final Allende program and. *See* Allende government, last economic program of.

maladjustments in, 146–148

March congressional elections and, 149–152

socialized industrial sector in, analysis of, 187–191

state apparatus in. *See* State, Chilean.

structural transformations and, analysis of, 181–182, 192–193

transformative program for. *See* Allende government, program of.

viability of, reflections on, 193–194

external debt of, 15

Christian Democrats

agrarian reform and, 68

Allende government and, June 1972 discussions with, 101–103

bank expropriation and, 68–69

economic program of (1970), 31–32

government overthrow and, 134

industrial expropriation opposed by, 73–77

MAPU split from, 12–13

National Party and, 47, 78, 83, 96, 101

October stoppage and, 112

populist line of, 90

reform package proposed to (1973), 169

social ownership disputes of 1972 and, 94–95

support base of, 11

Unidad Popular antagonism to, 20

worker support for, 208

Chuquicamata mine

exploitation of, 186

1971 production of, 63

post-coup production of, 187

Civilian-military Cabinet. *See* Cabinet, civilian-military.

Colegios. See Professional associations, Chilean.

Communist Party, Chilean

alliance policy of, 19

economic policy positions of, 147

founding of, 18

Lo Curro conclave and, 98

Prats initiative and, 141

Compañia de Acero del Pacifico, 72

Confederation of Production and Commerce, 209

Confederation of Professional Associations, 209

Confederation of Truck Owners, 209

Copper industry. *See also* Anaconda Copper Company; Kennecott Corporation.

nationalization of

analysis of, 185–187

compensation for, 69, 71–72

constitutional amendment for, 44, 69

factors affecting, 15

inadequacies of, 187

prices and, 63

production in (1971), 63

Corporación de Fomento (CORFO), 9, 14, 73, 102

Corporación de la Reforma Agraria (CORA), 14

Corporación del Cobre (CODELCO), 9, 14